From Parchment to Dust

ALSO BY LOUIS MICHAEL SEIDMAN

On Constitutional Disobedience

Silence and Freedom

Constitutional Law: Equal Protection of the Laws

Our Unsettled Constitution

Remnants of Belief (with Mark V. Tushnet)

From Parchment to Dust

The Case for Constitutional Skepticism

Louis Michael Seidman

THE
NEW
PRESS

NEW YORK
LONDON

Requests for permission to reproduce selections from this book should be made
through our website: https://thenewpress.com/contact.

Published in the United States by The New Press, New York, 2021
Distributed by Two Rivers Distribution

ISBN 978-1-62097-636-4 (hc)
ISBN 978-1-62097-693-7 (ebook)
CIP data is available

The New Press publishes books that promote and enrich public discussion and
understanding of the issues vital to our democracy and to a more equitable world.
These books are made possible by the enthusiasm of our readers; the support of a
committed group of donors, large and small; the collaboration of our many partners
in the independent media and the not-for-profit sector; booksellers, who often
hand-sell New Press books; librarians; and above all by our authors.

www.thenewpress.com

Composition by dix!
This book was set in Electra

Printed in the United States of America

2   4   6   8   10   9   7   5   3   1

To Lyra, in the hope that she grows up in a better world

CONTENTS

Introduction

Why should one be a constitutional skeptic? Consider the following facts:

In four out of the last eight presidential elections, a candidate became president even though a majority of voters chose someone else.[1] In two of these elections, the winner did not even receive a plurality of the vote.[2] Virtually all the money and attention in presidential elections is devoted to a tiny number of swing states that determine the outcome.

By 2040, 30 percent of the population of the United States will control seventy of the one hundred seats in the United States Senate.[3]

Nine individuals, appointed for life and responsible to no one, regularly make crucial and unreviewable decisions about matters such as the structure of healthcare in the United States, the nature of marriage, and the powers of the federal government and the states.

Former California governor Arnold Schwarzenegger and former Michigan governor Jennifer Granholm might have become serious presidential candidates but for a senseless, centuries-old constitutional provision requiring that the president be a "natural born" citizen.

All the justices on the Supreme Court insist that they are neutral and apolitical public servants who do no more than follow "the law" as it is written. Yet they are nominated by a process drenched in raw partisanship, and their votes regularly align with the partisan views of the people who appoint them.

Republican presidents have appointed thirteen of the last seventeen justices to the Supreme Court[4] even though they won the popular vote in only five of the last fifteen elections.[5] The last Democrat to serve as chief justice was Fred Vinson, whose brief and undistinguished career ended more than sixty years ago. Before that, one has to go back to Edward White, who fought on the Confederate side in the Civil War. (Even White was nominated for chief justice by a Republican, but his initial appointment to the Court was by a Democrat.)

The future of gun control in the United States turns on the Supreme Court's guess as to what people in the eighteenth century—who knew nothing of assault weapons, modern police forces, or mass shootings—meant by "the right to bear arms."

The Constitution protects the right of people who want to make movies catering to individuals who get sexual pleasure out of witnessing the sadistic crushing of innocent animals.[6] Yet it doesn't explicitly protect the rights of women, and it does nothing to protect the rights of all of us to a world that is not ravaged by global warming.

Huge popular majorities favor measures including more effective gun regulation, limitations on campaign spending, and rebuilding of our national infrastructure, yet because of the political structures that the Framers imposed on us, we are unable to enact measures accomplishing these objectives.

Customs of accommodation and constraint that keep our government functioning are rapidly eroding. For example, politicians now threaten a catastrophic default on the national debt to get their way, will not commit to respecting the results of elections, and refuse to compromise with their political opponents even when compromise is in the interests of both sides. But the Constitution does nothing to prevent this erosion, and all sides of political debate use constitutional rhetoric to bludgeon their political opponents.

These facts, and many more like them, should make any sensible person skeptical about our Constitution and about the role it plays in modern political culture. And yet, constitutional skeptics almost never get a fair hearing. Instead, our politics are saturated by reverence for an ancient and anachronistic document, written by people many of whom owned other human beings, and never endorsed by a majority of the inhabitants of our country. Liberals and conservatives, Democrats and Republicans, congresspeople and Supreme Court justices all insist on their own, partisan versions of constitutional obedience while our political culture collapses, crucial public needs go unmet, and the ties that bind us together as a country fray.

We need to understand that conventional constitutionalism is irrational and wrong. It attaches religious significance to a decidedly secular and deeply flawed document. It is standing in the way of saving our country. It has got to stop.

The first step is coming to a greater understanding of what constitutional skepticism is all about, especially since constitutional skeptics are skeptical about more than one thing.

At the specific level, they are skeptical about many individual provisions in the United States Constitution—provisions that entrench unjust, anachronistic, undemocratic, and unworkable requirements, practices, and limitations on our polity.

Also at the specific level, they are skeptical about many individual decisions made by the United States Supreme Court—decisions that purport to interpret the Constitution but that in fact impose contestable and sometimes downright evil, idiosyncratic judicial judgments on the rest of us.

On a more general level, they are skeptical of the proposition that our country's fate should be determined by a deeply entrenched, essentially unamendable document, written centuries ago in a very different country, by people who held views radically different from those of contemporary Americans and who had no notion of our modern circumstances.

Similarly, they are skeptical more generally about the role that a group of unelected, often partisan judges play in our polity. Contrary to conventional opinion, over its history the Supreme Court has been populated by lawyers who on average are of decidedly ordinary intelligence and ability, who have gained their seat through political or personal connections, and whose work product has been marked by arrogant misjudgments that have done serious harm to our country.

More generally still, constitutional skeptics worry about Constitution worship and Court worship—the uniquely American reverence for the Constitution and for the Supreme Court. This attitude denies our own responsibility to create the kind of country we want to live in.

On the broadest level, skeptics worry about the way that the Constitution encourages Americans to formulate ordinary political disputes in terms of "rights" that are absolute and nonnegotiable. The tendency exacerbates political tension and obstructs authentic dialogue that actually has the potential to persuade participants. It is driving the country toward irreparable fissure.

In this book, I elaborate on all these complaints, and I defend the proposition that, taken together, they form a coherent and unified skeptical stance toward conventional American constitutionalism. Of course, the reader might prefer to consider them individually. She might be persuaded as to some of my claims but not others. If that is so, I will claim a (partial) victory.

There is, however, one skeptical claim that I will not be making in this book. My argument should not be read as an attack on constitutions or constitutionalism in all times and places. At the beginning, constitutions may be necessary to get a polity off the ground. Constitutions may, at least for a time, resolve otherwise intractable disputes. The drafting of a constitution can be an act of national liberation and promote national solidarity. At one time, our Constitution may have served all these functions. But for us, that time was a long time ago. I am writing about how the American Constitution functions in our own time and place. I will leave to others who know more about it the debate about how other constitutions function in other societies.

Even with this caveat, I have no doubt that defending constitutional skepticism is an uphill fight. In our cultural and intellectual tradition, skeptics often get a bad rap. Skeptics are said to be doubters, cynics, and mindless destroyers. Pervasive skepticism can blind us to moral truths, block us from meaningful commitments, and paralyze us in the face of evil. And there is a well-known logical problem with skepticism: Don't pervasive skeptics have to be skeptical of their own skeptical stance?

These are important criticisms, but they oversimplify what the constitutional skeptic really thinks. Part of the problem is caused by confusing constitutional skepticism with global skepticism. A global skeptic, as I am using the term, is skeptical of all moral and political judgments. She believes that one moral claim (say, that the state should not interfere with acts of marital intimacy) is no stronger or weaker than another moral claim (say, that the state should not interfere with the release of pollutants into the atmosphere).

There is no necessary connection between global skepticism and the kind of constitutional skepticism that I defend in this book. In fact, many global skeptics have been conventional constitutionalists. They have defended American constitutionalism just because, they believe, the Constitution provides a way to resolve disputes without resort to problematic moral and political claims. Conversely, if one scratches the surface of a constitutional skeptic, one usually finds a disappointed idealist. Constitutional skepticism entails a doubt about whether things are working as they should. That doubt, in turn, must be generated by a comparison to an ideal of how things ought to work. In other words, constitutional skepticism is almost always rooted in some sort of normative judgment.

This normativity often takes the form of a vision of substantive social justice — a conception of what people deserve and what is necessary for human flourishing. Constitutional skepticism begins by noticing the gap between this view of how things ought to be and the reality of how they are.

Of course, the gap might simply represent the limits on what people acting in good faith can accomplish. Perhaps, for all our failures, we are doing the best that we can. But constitutional skeptics don't just notice that a gap exists; they are also angry about it. That anger, in turn, leads to another counterintuitive fact about constitutional skeptics: they tend toward optimism. Anger would have no target if one believed with the seventeenth-century philosopher Gottfried Leibniz (and Candide, the fictional character Voltaire used to satirize Leibniz's philosophy) that things are the best they could possibly be in this, the best of all possible worlds. Constitutional skeptics think that things could be different. Skeptics are doubters, all right, but what they doubt are the excuses and circumlocutions that obscure the possibilities for change.

Constitutional skeptics therefore insist on a clear-eyed view of the world. They are persistent puncturers of pretension. They are noticers of unchallenged received wisdom, cant, and hypocrisy. Constitutional skeptics try to look at the world afresh, to imagine other possibilities. They have little patience for defenses of the status quo that obscure what is really going on.

There is an obvious risk of contradiction in this stance. Why isn't a skeptical idealist skeptical of her own ideals? The constitutional skeptic's response is that there is indeed a contradiction, but it is a useful one. The contradiction means that a thoroughgoing skeptic will not be happy even if the reforms he favors are somehow put into place. Constitutional skeptics are perpetual malcontents, and skepticism is a continuing project without an endpoint.

This emotional predisposition can make constitutional skeptics really annoying. Dealing with a skeptic can drive you crazy. How can I satisfy this person? When will the ceaseless carping stop? Yet the skeptic's response is, in its own way, attractive. Skeptics are driven by millennial hopes that are always just out of reach. If the millennium is too far removed, it generates cynical resignation rather than hope. If the millennium has already arrived, it produces smug satisfaction rather than striving. Only a millennium in the middle distance provides the motivation for effective political action. It follows that the skeptic's twin enemies are pessimistic acceptance of inevitable evil, and smug embrace of an imagined utopia.

I'm ready to concede that we wouldn't want a world populated only by constitutional skeptics. I'm also ready to insist that our current world has too few of them. There is way too prevalent an assumption that our existing institutions are pretty good, or at least the best that anyone could expect. That assumption is enforced by willful blindness about how these institutions actually function and a lack of imagination about how they might function. Constitutional skepticism is an antidote to all that.

This defense of constitutional skepticism is part of my project, but it is not the whole project. This book is not just about constitutional skepticism; it is also about *the skeptic's constitution*. At least at first, that phrase seems to embody an oxymoron. How can a skeptic have a constitution? Constitutions are about commitment, faith, and obligation. Skeptics value flexibility, doubt, and freedom. Don't consistent skeptics have to be skeptical about constitutions?

The paradox might be resolved by focusing on different sorts of constitutions. A constitutional skeptic might be skeptical about some constitutions but not others. It turns out that even if one is not generally skeptical of constitutions, there are good reasons to be skeptical about the American Constitution.

According to the conventional account, more than two centuries ago wise and foresighted men gathered in Philadelphia to write a document that to this day constitutes us as a nation. The document that they produced guarantees liberty and equality for all. It is the glue that holds us together—a set of common commitments that transcend political disagreement.

The constitutional skeptic will have none of this. She knows that at the Constitution's very inception, many Americans saw the Constitution as embodying a counterrevolution, reestablishing the aristocratic government that the revolutionaries had over-thrown only a few years earlier. No women, no people of color, and few people who did not own property participated in its rati-fication. It is doubtful at best that a majority of those who were permitted to participate actually favored ratification. Proponents of the Constitution managed to force the country into a binary choice between the new Constitution and the failed Articles of Confederation. Many modern historians think that if the option of a new constitutional convention, called to write a very different document, had been on the table, a majority of Americans would have supported that option.[7]

In any event, the constitutional skeptic reminds us that no one alive today had any role in the ratification process. Even as amended, the Constitution to this day mandates a system of gov-ernment that is wildly out of touch with what the country has be-come. We are stuck with a document that is both the oldest extant constitution in the world and perhaps the most difficult to amend. Written for a different time and place, it is out of sync with the country that it supposedly constitutes.

And it is not what it seems to be. Instead of creating a govern-ment that speaks for "we the people," as its preamble promises, it entrenches a system that is undemocratic. Instead of provid-ing "for the common defence and general welfare," it divides us by class and systematically privileges some citizens over others. Instead of leading us toward "a more perfect union," it promotes hypocrisy and dishonesty and encourages zero-sum and explosive disputes that threaten to drive us apart.

A fair answer to all this criticism is the response that skeptics face always and everywhere: OK, I get it. But tearing down isn't the same thing as building up. If you are going to tear down, then don't you have an obligation to provide some positive alternative to replace what you have destroyed?

I take this criticism seriously. Taking it seriously means not ignoring the oxymoron problem mentioned earlier: What kind of substantive constitution could a skeptic possibly endorse? To resolve the dilemma, we need to address fundamental questions about what constitutes a just and stable political community.

For the constitutional skeptic, a written text is unnecessary to preserve such a community. Indeed, a written text can (and has) gotten in the way. A skeptic's constitution is like the British constitution in the sense that it is not reducible to a single, integrated document. One will not find it in the National Archives or reproduced in constitutional law casebooks. Its commands don't take the form of fixed, technical rules. Instead, the skeptic's constitution requires citizens to keep an open mind; an economy that produces a reasonable level of material well-being and at least rough equality of wealth and opportunity; habits of thought and action that encourage compromise in the pursuit of political goals; the patience to listen to others and respond flexibly to changed conditions; and a minimal sense of common purpose and respect for fellow citizens. Put more succinctly, the skeptic's constitution is a set of customs, attitudes, practices, and mutually observed constraints that we share without much thinking about them, and that are necessary to unify a country where people disagree about many foundational questions.

There are documents that embrace or reflect bits and pieces of the skeptic's constitution—for example, the opening paragraphs of the Declaration of Independence, some of the vague but powerful aspirations expressed in the Preamble to the standard Constitution, Martin Luther King Jr.'s "I Have a Dream" speech, and writings by people including Henry David Thoreau, Frederick Douglass, and Franklin Delano Roosevelt. But the skeptic's constitution itself is nowhere codified, and its exact content is subject to reasonable disagreement. It is both implemented and amended daily in the way that ordinary Americans and their leaders engage with each other.

Once one understands the skeptic's constitution, it becomes clear that it is actually conventional constitutionalists who are the skeptics. They are the ones who doubt the ability of citizens to engage in untrammeled and mature deliberation and debate, who believe in "situational ethics," and who want us to subordinate our sense of right and wrong to a piece of parchment. It is constitutionalists who are frightened of reasonable disagreement. By committing themselves to blind obedience to decisions made by others years ago, they reveal their deep skepticism about the capacity of contemporary Americans for self-rule.

Readers will no doubt notice an obvious problem with the skeptic's constitution. It does not answer some pretty important questions. For example, it does not tell us when a bill becomes a law, whether the District of Columbia is a state, or when the president's term ends. Because matters like this are important, written constitutions may be crucial to get new polities up and running.

But our government has been functioning for several centuries by now. We have established understandings and ways of doing things. If the skeptic's constitution is in place—if we have the habits of thought and mutual understandings (some of which, concededly, were formed by the original Constitution)—then most people will not want to induce chaos and anarchy by lightly challenging established institutions. Of course, institutional redesign will be on the table in the way that it currently is not. If someone challenges the composition of the United States Senate, it will not be a sufficient response to say "Article I of the Constitution says it has to be this way." But it may be a sufficient answer to say "Changing things at this late date is not worth the disruption that it would produce." That answer, in turn, invites rather than shuts down dialogue.

Paradoxically, and in some tension with what I have just written, we might find a guide to the skeptic's constitution in the text of our written Constitution—but only if we look in the right place. Our focus should not be on specific, technical commands—for example, the prohibitions in section 9 of Article II against a state "lay[ing] any Duty of Tonnage" or against "Capitation or other direct, Tax[es]" being imposed unless "in Proportion to the Census or Enumeration." Our focus instead should be on the open-textured but nonetheless powerful rhetoric in the Constitution's Preamble:

> We the People of the United States, in Order to form a more perfect Union, establish Justice, insure domestic Tranquility, provide for the common defence, promote the general Welfare, and secure the Blessings of Liberty to ourselves and our Posterity, do ordain and establish this Constitution for the United States of America.

A skeptic's constitution should provide a guide for how to achieve these great ends not in the tiny, rural, slave-dependent republic that we were in the late eighteenth century, but in the sprawling, complicated, disorderly country that we have become. Accordingly, I have organized this book around some of the goals contained in the Preamble. How might a constitutional skeptic go about achieving those goals in today's environment?

Chapters 1 and 2 take seriously the Framers' claim to speak for "We the People." Whatever the truth of that claim in the beginning (and there are plenty of reasons to doubt it), the conventional Constitution today stands in opposition to true democracy. It entrenches indefensible hierarchies of power, both between different groups of people alive today and between the living and the dead. The beginning of realizing the Framers' promise is to imagine a constitutional system that in fact creates a government authorized to speak for "We the People."

Chapter 3 addresses the problem of "establish[ing] Justice," with particular focus on the United States Supreme Court. Instead of uniting us around a common set of ideals, the modern Supreme Court regularly divides us into warring factions. Instead of a palladium of justice, it has become a site of incompetence, arrogance, and unaccountability. This chapter addresses the kinds of reforms that would be necessary to create a Court that actually established justice.

Chapter 4 casts a skeptical gaze on whether the Constitution actually "promote[s] the general Welfare." I argue that liberal and conservative constitutionalists alike regularly assume that existing and unfair distributions of wealth should serve as the baseline for constitutional analysis. This assumption, in turn, means that— far from promoting the general welfare—constitutional law entrenches privilege and inequality.

Of course, the Constitution is not only about economics. It also affects cultural and social power. In Chapters 5 and 6, I address the ways in which the constitutional goal of "securing the blessings of liberty" has been perverted to entrench the cultural power of elites.

Chapter 7 turns to the issue of creating a "more perfect union." I argue that the rhetoric of rights that constitutional law promotes fails to unite us. Instead, it unnecessarily drives us apart.

Chapter 8 addresses the problem of securing "domestic tranquility." The United States is among the most violent countries on the face of the earth, with higher crime rates, more guns, and more police violence than any other developed country. The Constitution is not responsible for all of these problems, but it is responsible for some of them. This chapter addresses how the conventional Constitution might be reimagined so as to make our country more peaceful.

Chapters 9, 10, and 11 explore the history of constitutional skepticism. If only we look in the right places, we can find in our history a vibrant tradition of skeptical constitutionalism that we might build upon to "ordain and establish" a skeptic's constitution that makes our country a more just, humane, and decent place.

The concluding chapter explores the potential for a skeptic's constitution to embody a way of life and habit of thought, instead of forcing upon us a set of prefabricated rules. We live in an era when that way of life and habit of thought are threatened as they have been only a few times in our nation's history. Our sense of common purpose is unraveling, customary constraints rooted in mutual respect are eroding, and our hopes for equality and material well-being are fading. Things are coming apart, and conventional constitutionalism is contributing to, rather than solving, the problem.

There is no more urgent task than thinking in a sustained and serious way about what will put things back together. Undertaking that work is the ultimate project of this book.

ONE

We the People, Part 1

The Problem of Democracy and Representation

If not quite on life support, American democracy is in critical condition. The origins of the malady go very deep and can be traced to decisions made by the Framers more than two hundred years ago. Fortunately, there are available treatments, but they require strong medicine—medicine that the patient has, so far, been unwilling to take. For the constitutional skeptic, there is no more urgent task than convincing Americans that our democracy is indeed sick and that there is something that can be done about the disease.

One need not be a great diagnostician to find symptoms of our illness. According to Gallup polling data from 2020, only 13 percent of Americans have a "great deal" or "quite a lot" of confidence in Congress, compared to 42 percent in 1973. (Today, 45 percent characterize their level of confidence as "very little" or "none.")[1] Confidence levels in the presidency are not much higher. Thirty-seven percent of Americans have little or no confidence in the chief executive, compared to 16 percent in 1975, when memories of the Watergate experience were still fresh.[2]

Other polls, asking broader questions, confirm that our political system is in serious trouble. For example, a Pew poll found that 58 percent of Americans are dissatisfied with how democracy is working.[3] Fifty-nine percent of Americans have "not very much trust" or "no trust at all" in the wisdom of the American people in making decisions.[4] Asked whether the statement "elected officials care what ordinary people think" describes current realities, 58 percent responded "not too well" or "not well at all."[5] Shockingly, a YouGov poll found that almost a third of all Americans and 43 percent of Republicans can conceive of a situation where they would support a military coup in the United States.[6]

Pollsters collected this data before the onset of the coronavirus pandemic and the controversy about the 2020 presidential election, at a time when the country was more or less at peace, when there was low unemployment, and while we were in the midst of the longest run of economic expansion in our history. They reflect a secular and more general decline in faith in democratic institutions—a decline that is apparently unrelated to specific, external events.

Unsurprisingly, these attitudes produce related pathologies that should also concern us. Perhaps the most disturbing is the delusive belief that our disagreements might be settled without the hard work required to engage our fellow Americans in authentic political dialogue. It is instructive, for example, to compare approval levels for Congress and the president with approval levels for the Supreme Court. The confidence level in the Court is also nothing to brag about, but unlike the other two branches of government, it retains the trust of a plurality of Americans. Thirty-eight percent of Americans express a great deal or quite a lot of confidence in the justices, as compared with only 28 percent who express little or no confidence in them.[7]

It's debatable whether the Court deserves the support that it receives, but it's revealing that, of the three branches of government, people have the least faith in the branch that is the most democratic (Congress) and the most faith in the branch that is the least democratic (the judiciary).

More disturbing still is the unrivaled popularity of another government institution that easily wins the confidence sweepstakes: An astonishing 72 percent of Americans have a great deal or quite a lot of confidence in the military, with only 8 percent telling poll-sters that they have little confidence and 1 percent saying that they have no confidence.[8] Whatever else can be said about the military, no one would mistake it for a democratic or representative insti-tution. Only a tiny percentage of Americans serve, and they are hardly a cross section of the country. The military's internal struc-ture is hierarchical and authoritarian. Its whole external purpose is to use force or the threat of force, rather than dialogue, to settle disputes. Yet instead of making Americans suspicious of the armed services, these attributes are, apparently, a source of comfort.

It is not as if confidence in the courts and the military has gone untested. There is powerful evidence of a culture of sexual as-sault in the military, sometimes tolerated by senior officers. And although most troops perform admirably in wartime conditions, there are also disturbing reports of atrocities. Similarly, Americans have retained their faith in the Court despite its divisive and, by some lights, blatantly political decisions settling the 2000 elec-tion[9] and establishing a right to gay marriage.[10] The faith has weathered repeated 5–4 decisions in important cases, where the votes of the justices line up with the party affiliation of the presi-dent who appointed them. Confidence has remained unshaken even by Senate majority leader Mitch McConnell's successful and unashamedly political effort to remake the Court, and by the rancorous and disastrous Brett Kavanaugh confirmation hearing.

One wonders whether the respect for these institutions is grounded in their undemocratic character. Do they reflect a long-ing for something that will save us from democracy? Too many Americans hope that they will not have to deal with their fellow citizens, and that some apolitical institution—the Supreme Court or the rule of law itself—will impose the solution they favor with-out the messy bother of elections and compromise. They admire an institution like the military because it is a place where people serve selflessly and for the common good without partisan bicker-ing. It is a place where there is no backtalk, no argument, and, they suppose, no politics.

We see the same impulse in the way that Americans approach issues that, in a healthy democracy, would be subjects for political disputation. On the left, consider the misguided trust that opponents of President Donald Trump placed in the Mueller investigation. For many, Robert Mueller's monkish self-restraint and integrity symbolized the apolitical and neutral majesty of the law itself. People actually believed that if only Mueller were allowed to complete his job, his work product would force their fellow citizens to share their negative views about the president. Similarly, they imagine that objective and neutral interpretation of the Constitution can avoid disagreeable and disorderly disputes about questions like gay marriage and reproductive freedom.

On the right, many conservatives are apparently terrified by changes in the electorate. Rather than trying to build a coalition that includes newly prominent groups, conservatives seem intent on limiting access to the ballot and, indeed, access to the country. Moreover, conservatives share with liberals an infatuation with solutions to national problems imposed from above. Unable to convince their fellow Americans of the evils of the Affordable Care Act, of gun control legislation, and of the administrative state, they imagine that they can get their way through the supposedly unbiased and apolitical application of constitutional text.

What produces these views? Perhaps modern Americans believe that they hold too little in common with their fellow citizens to make real dialogue attractive or even possible. Perhaps they think that even if others could be persuaded, structural barriers would prevent turning political success into actual public policy. Whatever the reason for these beliefs, though, there can be no doubt that they are dangerous. Americans need to grow up. We are not going to be saved by some benign father-like institution that will impose order and justice. For better or worse, we are stuck in a country where people have diverse lifestyles and cultures and radically disagree about fundamentals. There can be no refuge from the enervating, aggravating, never completed, and often futile task of trying to convince fellow citizens of the rightness of our views. And, of course, part of that task involves holding ourselves open to the views of others. If our politics cannot foster the minimal level of trust and common commitment necessary to engage in this dialogue—in other words, if the skeptic's constitution does not hold—then there is little hope that we will be able to meet the challenges that surely lie ahead.

It would be a mistake to suppose that the conventional Constitution is the source of all these difficulties. The decline of liberal democracy is a worldwide phenomenon, and there are doubtless multiple causes. In the rest of this chapter, I make a more modest claim: that the problems in the United States are made worse by what the Framers thought and did, and that our modern worship of their work gets in the way of clear thinking about possible solutions.

We can begin with the original assumptions and misguided aspirations that gave birth to the American Constitution—what might be called Madison's mistakes. True, some of the "mistakes" were not necessarily tied to those assumptions and aspirations. Instead, they were more or less reluctant compromises necessitated by political exigencies. In particular, without the coddling of slavery (embodied, for example, in the clauses counting slaves as three-fifths of a person and obligating free states to return escaped slaves)[11] and the gross malapportionment of the Senate, it is doubtful that the Framers could have come to agreement.[12] The compromise with slavery set us on the course toward civil war. Although partially undone by the Reconstruction Amendments enacted after the Union victory, the tragic legacy of that compromise affects our politics to this day. The Seventeenth Amendment, enacted in 1913, provided for the popular election of senators, but there has been no effort to undo the initial compromise giving each state two senators. It, too, shapes our politics two and a half centuries later.

Given the balance of political power in late eighteenth-century America, these compromises might have been necessary then, although I am sympathetic to the view that no set of circumstances can justify the decision to protect and tolerate slavery. Whether or not such compromises were justified then, it is puzzling why we should feel ourselves bound by them now.

As troubling are sources of our current political difficulties that were not compromises at all, but fully intended consequences of the system the Framers created. It turns out that distrust of democracy and the desire to establish institutions that avoided democratic engagement were the whole point of the enterprise. Thanks to the Framers' efforts, these stances are built into our constitutional DNA.

For evidence, we need look no further than the iconic defense of those efforts—the Federalist Papers. Written pseudonymously principally by James Madison and Alexander Hamilton and addressed to the people of New York, the essays were intended to influence the state conventions organized to consider ratification of the Constitution. It is a mistake to suppose that they reflected the uniform views of all the Framers, but they are nonetheless the most sophisticated and influential statement of their aims and ambitions.

If there is a single theme that runs throughout the papers, it is a desire to limit and channel the kind of direct democracy that flourished at the state level under the Articles of Confederation. State governments with weak executives and courts, where legislatures served for short terms and where popular pressure was sufficient to force enactment of redistributive and debtor relief legislation, badly frightened the Framers. Their ambition to curb what they called "democratic licentiousness"[13] is most clearly expressed in two of the most famous essays, Federalist 10 and Federalist 51, both authored by James Madison.

In Federalist 10, Madison explicitly warned against "pure Democrac[ies]," which, he claimed, "have ever been spectacles of turbulence and contention; have ever been found incompatible with personal security or the rights of property; and have in general been as short in their lives as they have been violent in their deaths."[14] Democracies produce these misfortunes, Madison insisted, because they give rise to the "dangerous vice" of "faction," which he defined as "a number of citizens . . . who are united and actuated by some common impulse of passion, or of interest, adverse to the rights of other citizens, or to the permanent and aggregate interests of the community."[15] Faction cannot be completely avoided, but its effects can be limited by placing wise people—statesmen—in control.[16]

The central aim of the Constitution, on Madison's account, is to provide this buffer between the people and public policy. We can do so, Madison thought, by creating large political units over an extended geographical area, so as to hinder ordinary people from organizing and unifying around common passions. He praised the new Constitution for establishing a system where "men who possess the most attractive merit and the most diffusive and established characters" are shielded from "the vicious arts by which elections are too often carried."[17]

To be clear, Madison did not favor dictatorship or monarchy. Ordinary people—at least if they were male, white, and property owners—had a role to play. But the role was indirect. They would choose "fit characters"[18] to represent them, but, having done so, their job was over. The actual task of governing would be left to the kind of people capable of understanding and acting upon "the permanent and aggregate interests of the community."[19]

To his credit, Madison did not completely trust these "fit characters" always and everywhere to transcend their self-interest. He specifically warned that "[e]nlightened statesmen will not always be at the helm."[20] Put differently, he recognized the risk that the governing class might itself become a "faction." In Federalist 51, Madison argued that the Constitution provided "auxiliary precautions" to avoid this possibility.[21] His basic strategy was to divide and conquer. As he put the point, society "will be broken into so many parts, interests and classes of citizens, that the rights of individuals, or of the minority, will be in little danger from interested combinations of the majority."[22]

The Framers accomplished this objective by creating a dizzying array of obstacles to concerted action—what modern political scientists call "veto gates." The House of Representatives can assert its will, but only if it has the acquiescence of the Senate. Even if the two houses unite, a presidential veto can negate their decision. If the president and both houses of Congress agree, the Supreme Court can invalidate the resulting statute. And even if the entire federal government coalesces around a program, its freedom of action is limited by the commitment of broad powers to the state governments.

Each of these branches of government is responsible to different constituencies elected at different times and under different circumstances. The chances that they would unite around a common "passion" are therefore remote. The chances were further reduced, Madison thought, because the quest for power among the members of the various branches would provide a motive for resisting the power of other branches. In that way "[a]mbition [is] made to counteract ambition," and "the private interest of every individual may be a sentinel over the public rights."[23]

Before exploring the modern consequences of this scheme, it is worth exposing the unarticulated presuppositions that lie behind it. Madison's starting point requires two problematic assumptions. First, he believed that political mobilization and the "passions" that produce mobilization are presumptively dangerous and evil. He ignored the possibility that popular organization and unity around common aims might instead be an exhilarating manifestation of self-governance.

Second, he assumed that the evil of faction would be mitigated by empowering "fit characters" who could be relied upon to transcend their self-interest and act in the public interest. He ignored the possibility that there might be good-faith disagreement between these elites and ordinary people about what exactly was in the public interest and that ordinary people might sometimes have the better of the argument.

True, Madison also suggests "auxiliary precautions" against

misbehavior by the "fit characters," but the precautions are based on other problematic assumptions. Madison was so preoccupied with the risk that popular majorities would suppress the rights of minorities that he overlooked the possibility that minorities might suppress majorities. He wrote that minority faction was not a problem because of "the republican principle, which enables the majority to defeat its sinister views by regular vote."[24] Much of modern political theory is devoted to demonstrating that this faith is badly misplaced. The regular ability of well-organized and concentrated interest groups—that is, minority factions—to overwhelm diffuse and relatively powerless majorities provides ample empirical refutation of the argument that "regular vote" controls minority factions. Madison simply ignored this possibility.

Madisonian theory also rested on an implicit commitment to status quo distributions of power and resources. The underlying concern that motivated the entire scheme was that government might upset this status quo. Madison and his colleagues assumed that the multiple veto gates obstructing the formations of the political coalitions would protect "the aggregate interests of the community." But what if vigorous government intervention, rather than government paralysis, served these aggregate community interests? Madison ignored the possibility that factions hostile to these aggregate interests (for example, large corporations or tech giants like Facebook and Google) might flourish in an environment where they need not fear a political check. He was obsessed with checking the power *of* government and oblivious to the danger posed by private power left unchecked *by* government.

Eighteenth-century political theory would be of little significance if it did not have twenty-first-century consequences. In fact, though, there is a link between some of our modern difficulties and the commitments that the Framers made centuries ago.

In obvious ways, the Framers' preference for elite deliberation over popular mobilization is reflected in the undemocratic character of the institutions they established. For example, it is not a coincidence that presidential elections are sometimes won by the candidate who fails to achieve a popular majority. The Framers were unwilling to leave the choice of president to the people. Instead, the Constitution established the Electoral College, with its members to be chosen as state legislatures directed and with no guarantee that the electors reflected the popular will. The original purpose of the Electoral College system was to establish a mechanism whereby popular preferences were filtered through elite deliberation. Today, of course, the electors no longer play this role, but it does not follow that the problem has gone away. We are left with a hybrid system that no one intended and that gives us the worst of both worlds. On the one hand, there is no longer any actual deliberation by the electors. On the other, we regularly elect presidents who lose the popular vote.

The problem with the Electoral College extends beyond how presidents are elected. It also infects the way that presidents govern. Ideally, a newly elected president would reach out to his opponents and form a broad coalition that included a majority of the country. Instead, the Electoral College encourages presidents to pursue a "base" strategy. So long as they retain the loyalty of a minority—sometimes an extreme minority—strategically situated in "swing states," presidents can win reelection. The result is the kind of divisive politics that have become all too familiar.

Similarly, it is not a coincidence that large popular majorities— favoring, for example, the rebuilding of infrastructure, gun regulation, and lower prescription drug costs—are unable to secure passage of legislation accomplishing their goals. Multiple veto gates and the shielding of private factions from government control are just what Madison and his colleagues intended. Changed circumstances that they did not anticipate again leave us with the worst of both worlds. The Framers accepted the risk of government paralysis in part because they thought that rivalry between the branches would protect liberty. Their hope was that with ambition constrained, leaders would deliberate over the public good. Unfortunately, though, they failed to anticipate the development of the party system. Today, House Speaker Nancy Pelosi's ambitions are more likely to be satisfied by alliance with fellow Democrat Joe Biden than by alliance with Republican minority leader Kevin McCarthy. We have therefore ended up with both government gridlock *and* domination by the factions that control the Democratic and Republican Parties.

These institutional realities, in turn, have systemic and more general cultural consequences. Is it any wonder that the percentage of Americans who vote is far below the level found in most other developed countries[25] and that most Americans are distrustful of politicians and feel alienated from the institutions of government? The system is working the way its creators wanted it to work. They have succeeded in turning politics into a spectator sport with the spectators relegated to angry jeering from bleachers located far from the field.

The barriers to meaningful political action might conceivably be overcome if people were willing to devote the huge effort necessary to surmount those barriers. At this point, though, another feature of Madisonian republicanism kicks in: it is not worth the effort. Even if ordinary people could somehow get the attention and approval of a majority of their representatives, the veto gates that the Framers deliberately created make it virtually impossible for the majority to enact legislation.

And there are still broader consequences. Even before the COVID-19 crisis, our country was in the grip of overlapping epidemics of drug abuse, suicide, loneliness, and social breakdown. It would be going too far to blame all this on Madison's mistakes. James Madison is not responsible for and could not have anticipated the status and cultural anxiety, racial and class tensions, and economic insecurity that plague late-stage liberal capitalism. Still, one wonders, might the situation be improved if, contra Madison, we actually had a few more factions?

In early nineteenth-century America, Alexis de Tocqueville was astonished by the number of civic organizations Americans joined.[26] (A "faction" might be defined as a civic organization that one disapproves of.) Since he was writing within a half century of the Constitution's ratification, it is hard to make the case that the Constitution is responsible for our current social isolation years later.

Still, the diffuse and atomistic political system that the Framers established makes it harder to fight the disintegration that we currently face. Today, too many Americans not only "bowl alone," as the distinguished social scientist Robert Putnam has told us. His careful study demonstrates that citizens no longer participate in the range of communal activities that Tocqueville observed.[27] Instead, they sit alone in their bedrooms stewing over the state of the country as they read siloed political websites and send out enraged tweets. If these people actually felt some agency about their political fates—if they saw any point in joining civic organizations and participating in actual political engagement with others—they might be less angry, less isolated, less powerless, and less despairing about the future of the country.

These pathologies are associated with specific decisions made by the Constitution's Framers centuries ago. But the tension between democracy and constitutionalism runs deeper than this. It turns out that the very act of writing a constitution—any constitution—and entrenching it against change is inconsistent with democratic engagement.

This claim is paradoxical because constitution writing can also be a powerful source of community self-definition and engagement. In fact, the history of our own Constitution supports this more optimistic view. True, the original drafting occurred in secret and without meaningful participation by the mass of citizens. But the ratification process was quite different. We should never lose sight of the fact that large numbers of Americans were excluded from this process, but the white men who did get to participate engaged in a relatively open, rambunctious, and disorderly argument about the country's future. As John Adams wrote:

How few of the human race have ever enjoyed an opportunity of making an election of government, more than of air, soil, or climate, for themselves or their children! When, before the present epocha, had three millions of people full power and a fair opportunity to form and establish the wisest and happiest government that human wisdom can contrive.[28]

We can share in Adams's enthusiasm, but only if we ignore three words in his first sentence: "or their children." The problem is that there is a zero-sum conflict between the democratic engagement enjoyed by the constitution-writing generation and the democratic deficit imposed on later generations bound by their ancestors. The whole purpose of an entrenched constitution is to limit the range of choices available to future generations. Entrenched constitutions discourage politics by taking important political questions off the table. John Marshall unintentionally captured the contradiction when he wrote in *Marbury v. Madison* that

> the people have an original right to establish, for their future government, such principles as, in their opinion, shall most conduce to their own happiness. . . . The exercise of this original right is a very great exertion; nor can it, nor ought it, to be frequently repeated. The principles, therefore, so established, are deemed fundamental. And, as the authority from which they proceed is supreme, and can seldom act, they are designed to be permanent.[29]

The problem with Marshall's formulation is that it privileges the right of some people over the right of other people. When the decisions of some people are "designed to be permanent," other people are deprived of their right to establish "such principles as, in their own opinion, shall most conduce to their happiness." Why should the rights of "we the [dead] people" trump the rights of "we the [living] people"?

It was for just this reason that Marshall's contemporary Thomas Jefferson believed that constitutions should not be permanent at all, but should last for only one generation. As he expressed the point:

> [B]y the law of nature, one generation is to another as one in-dependent nation to another. . . . [N]o society can make a perpetual constitution. . . . The earth belongs always to the living generation. . . . Every constitution, then, and every law, naturally expires at the end of 19 years. If it be enforced longer, it is an act of force and not of right.[30]

Unfortunately, though, Jefferson's contemporaries mostly ignored his concern about binding future generations. Instead, Article V of the Constitution makes the document virtually impossible to amend, at least under modern circumstances.

None of this would be a problem if we, the living, agreed with them, the dead. But suppose that we don't? What should we do then?

TWO

We the People, Part 2

Some Modest Proposals

Finding remedies for Madison's mistakes poses a daunting problem. It is not just that constitutional obstacles to democracy are deeply entrenched by the steep hurdles the Framers erected to constitutional amendment. That difficulty is serious enough, but it is made worse by a chicken-and-egg problem that makes almost any reform seem utopian. As currently constituted, the system benefits the people who control it. Their power depends upon the fragmentation, disempowerment, and demoralization of the electorate outlined earlier. Obviously, those in control are not eager to give up their power and will therefore vigorously resist reforms, and the system in place will greatly aid them in this effort. The very problem we want to solve—the malfunctioning of our democracy—blocks the possibility of implementing solutions.

Given these discouraging facts, we might as well think big. Remember, constitutional skeptics are optimists by nature. Skepticism wouldn't be worth it if one didn't believe in the possibility of real change. Oddly, the more seemingly utopian the proposal, the better the chance of enactment. The built-in constraints on popular mobilization argue for proposals that grab people's attention and motivate them to engage in collective action. The slim possibility of change at the margin doesn't do that. We need instead to open our minds to truly bold transformation.

Here, then, are some modest proposals that, if enacted, might actually make a difference. I start with ideas that are a political stretch but are at least on the table and then extend the discussion into the realm of the truly utopian.

For starters, Congress might encourage political participation by making voting and other forms of political engagement easier. As many others have proposed, we could provide for automatic registration to vote and make election day a national holiday.[1] We might make voting by mail a universally available option.[2] We might adopt one of the many proposals that would provide citizens with vouchers that they could use to contribute to the candidate of their choice.[3] Perhaps we should even consider making voting mandatory.

More ambitiously, we should end the practice of partisan gerrymandering. As things stand today, legislators routinely create grossly misshapen voting districts deliberately designed to produce a predetermined outcome. The doleful effects of this practice are obvious. Like the malapportioned Senate, political gerrymandering can both disempower popular majorities and understate the strength of minorities. It leads to the cynical but often accurate view that "the fix is in." Moreover, legislators frequently use their power to create "safe districts" for incumbents. That practice has the twin effects of ceding control to the extreme poles of each party and of effectively disfranchising the minority trapped in an unfavorable district. Is it any wonder that in a system like this, much of the electorate is disengaged and disillusioned with democratic processes?

The Supreme Court has repeatedly declined to address the partisan gerrymandering issue, claiming that there were no "judicially manageable standards" that could remedy the problem.[4] It is hard to see how that makes this issue different from countless other issues where the Court uses vague and amorphous tests to adjudicate constitutional claims. Abortion regulation is constitutional if it does not "unduly burden" the abortion right.[5] Racial classifications are unconstitutional unless they serve a "compelling state interest."[6] Even in the gerrymandering context, the Court has been satisfied with a test that is hardly self-applying. When the gerrymandering is racial rather than political, it is unconstitutional if race is the "predominant factor" and leads to the "subordina[tion of] traditional race-neutral districting principles."[7] If it were so inclined, the Court could use a similar test in the political gerrymandering context.

That said, the Court is on to something when it insists that determining the "fairness" of various systems of representation is bound to be complex and controversial. Suppose, for example, that the problem was turned over to a "nonpartisan" commission. What guarantees do we have that the commission would remain truly nonpartisan? Given how high the stakes are, both parties would have a large incentive to infiltrate the commission with their supporters. The result might be the same amount of partisan gerrymandering with less visibility.[8]

Suppose, alternatively, that the commission remains truly nonpartisan and tries to draw district lines that avoid the evils of gerrymandering. Unfortunately, two of the evils—noncompetitive districts and unfair representation—sometimes cut against each other. In order to create fair representation, the commission is likely to create a large number of noncompetitive districts so as to ensure victory for the "right" party in the "right" number of districts. But these "safe" districts produce representatives who worry only about being "primaried" by the most motivated factions of their own party and who are therefore more extreme than the average voter.

Nonpartisan districters might instead strive to create more competitive districts. But if one favors "fair" statewide representation, this approach also creates problems. If every district in the state is competitive, then a small change in the statewide balance of power between Republicans and Democrats might allow one party or the other to win in every district.

It does not follow, though, that nothing can be done. One sure way to eliminate partisan districting is to eliminate districts.

Congress might substantially improve things by providing for the at-large, statewide election of all representatives.

Taken by itself, at-large representation has its own problem. It unfairly overstates the power of the majority. Suppose that Democrats win 51 percent of the votes in a state. At-large representation could lead to their electing 100 percent of the representatives. The solution to this problem is a cumulative voting system. If a state were allotted, say, ten representatives, all voters within the state would cast ten votes. Voters could divide their votes among candidates in any way they chose, perhaps concentrating them on a small number of candidates, or spreading them among ten different candidates.[9]

This system would allow statewide minorities to concentrate their ballots and so be assured of some representation. That possibility in turn, combats the demoralization that currently poisons our politics. If people understood that they had a real chance to have their voices heard, they might opt for authentic political engagement.

Statewide cumulative voting would likely also break up the two-party duopoly that has a stranglehold on our politics. Many Americans believe that both parties are corrupt and out of touch, and therefore they choose to sit on the sidelines. Cumulative voting would make it easier for new, smaller parties to gain some seats, whereas a "first-past-the-post" system, where the person receiving the most votes in each district wins, makes it difficult or impossible for a third party to gain traction. Instead of enforcing rigid party discipline, legislators would have to put together coalitions among diverse groups. Dominant parties would be forced to give in on issues that they care less about so as to achieve a governing majority. And minorities would have some say on issues that matter the most to them. Politicians would be forced to engage in bargaining and dialogue with groups that are currently excluded. That is what healthy politics is supposed to be about.

Many other countries have cumulative voting or some other form of proportional representation and do not seem to have suffered for it. Even in the United States there has been experimentation with cumulative voting, and scholars who have studied the experiments have found that they have, for the most part, been successful.[10] These new formations might attract the allegiance of Americans who have given up on finding a political home.

Direct elections for president and abolition or substantial reform of the Senate are other obvious measures that would undo some of Madison's mistakes. There is no good reason why a majority of the country should not be permitted to choose its own president and its own Senate.

From the very beginning, Americans have been dissatisfied with the Electoral College. The Framers adopted it as a last-minute compromise, but no one in Philadelphia expressed real enthusiasm for it. Since then, there have been repeated efforts to abolish the College, some of which nearly succeeded, but all of which ultimately foundered because of short-term political considerations and the high barriers posed by the amendment process.[11]

Defenders of the Electoral College claim that without it, candidates would focus exclusively on heavily populated urban and suburban areas and pay too little attention to minorities living in rural parts of the country. One might begin by wondering whether this is a problem at all. Why shouldn't candidates devote most of their attention to places where most people live?

Of course, there are reasons to protect minorities, but the Electoral College system does nothing to protect regularly abused minority groups like people of color, the poor, or people with unorthodox religions, sexual preferences, or lifestyles. Of all the minorities that we might protect, why should we choose people who happen to live in Wyoming and Vermont?

Moreover, even if we should be protecting these minorities, the argument fails on its own terms. In fact, candidates for president spend relatively little time worrying about either Wyoming or Vermont. Instead, they devote their attention to a tiny number of swing states where campaigning might actually make a difference. I know of no theoretical justification for the overrepresentation of these voters at the expense of the rest of us.

The best argument for retaining the Electoral College is that in a close election, it avoids the necessity of an unwieldy recount. As messy as the Florida recount was in 2000, it was at least confined to one state and to a limited number of voters. Recounting all the votes cast throughout the nation would be a nightmare, or at least so defenders of the Electoral College claim.[12]

These defenders have a point, but the problem may be less serious than they imagine. In fact, the national popular vote has not been all that close in recent presidential elections. It is far more likely that our present system will require recounts in one or more crucial swing states. Moreover, if an election is extremely close, then the outcome is more or less arbitrary even if all votes are counted accurately. A recount producing a different arbitrary winner makes a big difference politically, but little difference in terms of the fairness of the outcome. What we really have to worry about is not random mistakes, but systematic bias in the counting. One might combat this evil, while also keeping recounts in check, by requiring some sort of showing of fraud or bias within a jurisdiction before permitting challenge to the outcome. If our experience in the 2020 presidential election is any guide, establishing this kind of fraud or bias is likely to be difficult.

Suppose, alternatively, that we had to completely abandon recounts in presidential elections. What we would be trading off would be an occasional mistake in extremely close elections for a system that regularly, predictably, and nonrandomly allows the loser of the popular vote to assume the presidency. Surely the trade is worth it.

The case for the radically malapportioned Senate is even weaker. Even in the beginning, few made a principled argument for the overrepresentation of small states. Instead, as noted earlier, creation of the Senate was a compromise necessary to secure ratification. The compromise might have made sense when it was made, but that provides no explanation for why we should be forced to live with it several centuries later. And matters are getting worse. The population is moving toward concentrated urban and suburban areas, and the disproportionate power of rural America is growing. As noted earlier, by 2040, a scant 30 percent of the population will control a majority of the Senate.[13]

To avoid this unacceptable outcome, we need to apportion Senate seats according to population. Beyond that, and whether or not apportionment is changed, it makes sense to eliminate the Senate as a veto gate. Instead, the Senate might serve the function currently served by the House of Lords in the United Kingdom. It could delay legislation for a reasonable period and suggest amendments, but ultimately it could not block proposals enacted by the House.

Suppose we opt to think even more boldly. One might imagine legislation requiring that one-quarter of the House of Representatives be chosen by lot, similar to the mechanism currently used to choose juries in criminal and civil cases.

Political theorists have a name for such a system—sortition—and it goes back to ancient Athens.[14] The Athenians did not use sortition to choose members of the Assembly; that body consisted of any citizens who happened to show up—a selection method that would obviously be impractical in modern America. Instead, sortition was the method by which the committees that actually ran the government were chosen.[15] Transplanting this system to modern America also has a large downside. Expertise and experience are arguably more important attributes for people in administrative positions.

However, other political entities—notably the Renaissance city-states of Lombardi, Venice, and Florence—delegated some or all legislative authority to citizens chosen by lot.[16] In 2010, Iceland experimented with a randomly selected constitutional assembly to recommend revisions of its constitution.[17] There are many modern political theorists who have advanced proposals to utilize sortition for various purposes, including one favored by famed political scientist Robert Dahl.[18]

How would such a system work? The details would have to be carefully worked out, but we can imagine the broad outlines of the system. Representatives might be chosen by lot from a pool of citizens who agreed to volunteer two years of their time to service. They would be provided with an adequate salary and reimbursement for travel and living expenses and would be guaranteed the right to return to their jobs after their service ended. Each representative would be assigned experienced staff to help them with their work.

There are obvious objections to this proposal. In the ancient world, many writers complained that the Athenian system led to poor decision-making by credulous and inexperienced citizens. In a modern context, one might worry that randomly selected legislators would be manipulated by lobbyists or by their staff. They might lack the incentives, experience, or ability to master the details necessary to formulate sound public policy. There is no guarantee that the people volunteering their services would be representative of the population as a whole or that random choice from this pool would produce "fair" representation. The system might even be thought antidemocratic, in the sense that it would deprive voters of the right to select candidates of their choice.

Some of these problems would be mitigated by the fact that only a quarter of the members of Congress would be selected in this fashion. The hope is that randomly chosen legislators would provide fresh ideas and different perspectives, but they would have to persuade some of their elected colleagues in order to succeed in passing legislation that they favored.

Other objections rest at least in part on an exaggerated view of the competency and public-spiritedness of current members of Congress. After all, there is a reason why so many Americans hold Congress in such low regard. Elected representatives are also manipulated by lobbyists and their staff. They, too, are often chosen for reasons that have little to do with their intelligence or diligence, and they, too, often vote on measures that they do not fully understand.

It is true that sortition is undemocratic if one automatically equates democracy with electoral choice. But sortition is radically democratic in the same sense that unelected, randomly chosen juries are democratic. Citizens chosen at random for two years would not be dependent on rich donors for their reelection. Providing them with a generous salary and a guarantee that they could return to their old jobs when they finished their service would provide some assurance that they would not be wealthier, better educated, whiter, and maler than their fellow citizens. Because they would not be professional politicians eager for reelection, they would be less tempted to engage in demagoguery and deception. Paradoxically, because they would not have been chosen by "the vicious arts by which elections are too often carried," they would also be less susceptible to the very factional control that Madison feared.

Most significantly, though, if the system worked, it would provide a real-world demonstration that Madison was wrong when he asserted that ordinary Americans cannot participate meaningfully and effectively in the task of self-government. That demonstration, in turn, might be the first step in restoring faith in the system. It might motivate the people who do not serve to identify more with those who do.

No doubt these proposals will strike many readers as completely unrealistic. And no doubt they are unrealistic — at least under current conditions. That fact alone suggests just how sick our democracy is. Trying to think about a system that actually engaged its citizens in the task of self-government necessarily entails overturning institutions and ways of thinking that are deeply entrenched. We cannot even begin that task without heroic imagination and optimism.

Worse yet, even if we were to summon the imagination and optimism necessary to enact such a program, much of it would be blocked by the Supreme Court's interpretation of constitutional text. For example, the Electoral College is constitutionally entrenched by Article II, section 1. Sortition might be barred by Article I, section 2, which provides that representatives be chosen "by the People of the several States, and the Electors in each state shall have the Qualifications requisite for Electors of the more numerous Branch of the State Legislature." Correcting the malapportionment of the Senate is blocked by the Seventeenth Amendment, which provides that "[t]he Senate of the United States shall be composed of two Senators from each state." That requirement is even further entrenched by Article V, which provides that "no State, without its Consent, shall be deprived of its equal Suffrage in the Senate."

There are constitutional workarounds that might solve some of these problems. For example, Nebraska and Maine currently depart from the winner-take-all system for awarding electors and choose them, instead, by congressional district. Some problems would be solved if all states adopted this model, but only at the cost of introducing the gerrymandering problem. Fifteen states and the District of Columbia have opted for a more radical reform. They have joined an "Electoral College compact" that would commit each state to casting its electoral votes in favor of the nationwide popular majority winner. The compact would go into effect only when enough states joined to guarantee the election of the winner of a popular majority.[19]

Perhaps with tongue in cheek, a student note in the *Harvard Law Review* suggested that Congress could resolve the Senate problem by making each neighborhood in the District of Columbia a separate state. This greatly enlarged Senate together with the House and state legislatures might then first repeal the Article V language that blocks amendments regarding the Senate and go on to rewrite the Seventeenth Amendment. Its work done, the various District of Columbia states would then be consolidated into one state.[20]

A less creative solution is also at least marginally less fanciful:

the Senate's malapportionment would be alleviated if the District of Columbia and Puerto Rico were made states, thereby increasing representation for urban voters currently underrepresented in the Senate. Alternatively, or in addition to this reform, with the approval of the affected states, Congress could divide large-population states into smaller states that would each be entitled to two senators.

No doubt these measures would be attacked for what they are—transparent efforts to evade constitutional requirements. It is not hard to imagine the Supreme Court invalidating at least some of them on just those grounds. Moreover, before we even get to that point, the ideas would somehow have to be enacted—hardly a likely prospect under current political conditions. These facts, in turn, suggest what we should already know: that making a real break with the past requires more than technical tinkering with institutions, however ingenious the effort. What is required instead is a dramatic change in attitude. We need a clean break with our unthinking worship of the Constitution and the structures that it created. That sort of break, in turn, requires demystifying constitutional law. Perhaps the first step in that process is demystifying the institution that thinks of itself as embodying constitutional law—the Supreme Court of the United States. Chapter 3 turns to that work.

THREE

Establishing Justice

The Problem of the Supreme Court

Perhaps the most inviting target for constitutional skepticism is the United States Supreme Court. There is no necessary association between the Supreme Court and American constitutionalism. All federal officeholders take an oath to support and defend the Constitution, and one could imagine a system where the Constitution was enforced by Congress, the president, and state officials. Still, in American constitutional culture, the Supreme Court has assumed such a central role that it is often taken to be the embodiment of constitutionalism.

The justices themselves do everything they can to promote this image. They protect their reputation by working in secret. According to hallowed tradition, no one other than the justices attends the sessions where cases are actually decided. The justices rarely hold press conferences or make public statements. They virtually never defend their actions and opinions in the public sphere. Moreover, the quasi-religious claptrap that surrounds the Court—the robes the justices wear, the marble temple in which they are housed, the solemnity and formality of the oral arguments that they conduct—are meant to symbolize the grandeur, neutrality, impersonality, and majesty of The Law, and of the Constitution whence it derives.

An interlocking web of myths buttress this imagery. The justices are thought to be brilliant jurists who work extraordinarily hard. They are wise women and men who take the long view and are above the petty squabbling that engulfs the rest of government. They are apolitical public servants who lead monastic existences devoted solely to the rule of law. Their independence guarantees that they are answerable to no political party or faction, but solely to their conscience and to the United States Constitution.

A constitutional skeptic takes delight in demonstrating that all of this is arrant nonsense. Historically, the Supreme Court of the United States has been populated mostly by people of decidedly ordinary intellect and ability who have gotten pretty cushy jobs through their political connections. The notion that independence—insulation from political accountability—guarantees that justices will be motivated by devotion to law rests on a logical fallacy and has little empirical support. In fact, unaccountability produces just what one would expect—a freedom to indulge personal quirks, obsessions, foibles, and ideological projects without having to account to others for one's actions.

These are pretty serious charges. What is the evidence that supports them? Let's start with the myth that being a Supreme Court justice is hard work. Sixty years ago, the renowned legal scholar Henry Hart attributed the sloppy reasoning in the Court's opinions to the fact that the justices were overworked.[1] If this was ever true, it certainly is not true now. Unlike most Americans and virtually all other government officials, Supreme Court justices enjoy annual, three-month-long summer vacations. Many of the justices use their free time to travel, lecture, teach, write, or relax.

What occupies the justices during the other nine months when they are actually doing their job? The justices have virtually complete control over their docket, and in recent years they have used this freedom to cut the number of cases they decide by more than half. During the 2019 term, the most recent term for which data is available, the Court issued full opinions in only fifty-nine cases,[2] down from the seventy-two that it decided in the prior term[3] and from the hundreds of cases the Court regularly decided a generation ago.[4] That means that each justice is responsible for an average of six and a half majority opinions per year.

The justices also write dissenting and concurring opinions, which tend to be shorter and presumably require less work. Some justices frequently write to express their own views, while others are more often content to acquiesce silently in the work of their colleagues. For example, during the 2019 term, Justice Clarence Thomas wrote separately in twenty-six cases, while Justice Elena Kagan wrote dissents or concurrences in only four cases.[5]

Suppose we focus on total production, including majority, dissenting, concurring, and unsigned (*per curiam*) opinions. During the 2019 term, the justices produced 1991.2 pages, for an average of 221.2 pages per justice. There was, again, considerable variance, with Justice Samuel Alito producing 376.7 pages, while Justice Ruth Bader Ginsburg was responsible for only 129.3 pages.[6]

Of course, the justices have other responsibilities. The chief one is to decide which cases to hear from among the thousands of petitions filed with the Court every year. The justices also write occasional opinions dissenting from or concurring in the decision not to hear a case (denials of certiorari), and they spend time deciding whether to grant temporary stays of lower court decisions, reading briefs, attending oral arguments, discussing cases with their colleagues (although much less often than one might suppose), and, one hopes, thinking about what they are doing.

The important point, though, is that the justices do not face these tasks alone. They have the benefit of legal briefs, submitted by both sides and by many other interested parties, that do much of the research for them and lay out the principal arguments on each side. They are also assisted by clerical staff and numerous librarians. In addition to all this, each justice is provided with four law clerks who are smart, ambitious, and top graduates from the nation's leading law schools.

Decisions about whether to grant or deny petitions to hear cases have been almost entirely delegated to the clerks, who write recommendations that the justices typically follow. More disturbingly, the dirty little secret is that, with varying levels of supervision from their bosses, the law clerks ghostwrite many opinions. The practice is not uniform. Some justices allow their clerks to write first drafts, which the justices heavily edit. Others on at least some occasions rely on their clerks for research help but do their own writing. Still, in many cases, the work product is at best a collaboration between justice and clerk and at worst essentially the clerk's.

There is no way to measure with precision the contribution that clerks make. We do know, however, that there are four of them per justice, that they are bright and industrious, and that they work very long hours. It's hard to believe that they are wasting their time. Suppose, then, that the clerks in effect halve the opinion-writing labor that an individual justice would otherwise have to perform. Then the total annual output per justice is reduced to something like 110.6 pages, which translates into under a third of a page per day.

That kind of workload would be the envy of, say, a young associate in a law firm, an academic trying to secure tenure at a major law school, or, for that matter, a busy doctor attending to scores of patients. It is harder to measure how this level of effort stacks up against other sorts of work, but I'm confident that many manual laborers and office support workers would gladly trade their burdens for those of a Supreme Court justice.

The role of clerks also creates a disturbing gap between the jobs of deciding and justifying. In theory, the custom of opinion writing disciplines the justices. The practice of providing reasons supposedly provides a check on arbitrary decision-making.

Even under the best of circumstances, it is unclear that opinions actually accomplish this objective. The justices answer to no one, and no one has the authority to edit their work. No one other than fellow justices, whose votes they may need to secure a majority, can insist that they rewrite an unclear passage, clean up sloppy reasoning, or provide decent support for statements of fact and law. There is no enforceable requirement that their opinions make any sense at all.

Still, to the extent that the justices care about their reputations and have pride in their work, they have an incentive to write opinions that demonstrate professional competence. One might think, therefore, that the justification requirement would discipline the range of outcomes that a justice can reach. No doubt it does to some extent. But this effect assumes that the person doing the deciding is also doing the justifying. In an ideal world, the justices would read the briefs, attend oral argument, and allow the justifications to lead them to an outcome. But clerks are, in effect, justification machines that permit the justices to reverse this process. Justices can put a very wide range of predetermined outcomes into the machine and count on brilliant young lawyers to make sense of them. That fact, in turn, leaves the justices free to decide many cases based on untested intuition or even bias.

Over the years, justices have used their considerable freedom to indulge and, often, hide from public view a wide variety of quirks, failings, obsessions, and foibles. Here are only a few examples.

- In the early nineteenth century, John Marshall saw no problem with serving as secretary of state and chief justice of the United States at the same time. In perhaps the most famous case in American legal history, *Marbury v. Madison*, Marshall as chief justice ruled on the legal implications of actions taken by Marshall as secretary of state.[7]
- Also during the nineteenth century, Justice Henry Baldwin was hospitalized for "incurable lunacy" and missed an entire term of Court. He nonetheless returned to the bench and remained on the court for years. Richard Peters Jr., the Supreme Court's reporter of decisions, stated that "most courtroom observers of Baldwin agreed that 'his mind is out of order. I have heard in one day not less than five persons . . . say 'he is crazy.'"[8]

- According to Justice Stephen Field's biographer, during his last years on the bench, Field's "questions in the court room at times indicated that he had no conception of the arguments that were being made" and that "he voted on cases and then forgot how he had voted."[9]
- Justice Robert Grier, who had suffered a disabling stroke, cast the deciding vote in one of the most crucial decisions in American history, holding that Congress lacked the power to make paper money legal tender. Unfortunately, it appears that he acted without having any clear idea of what case he was voting on. His behavior caused all of the other justices to plead with him to resign. To make matters worse, Chief Justice Salmon Chase participated in the decision and voted to invalidate the paper currency even though a few years earlier, while secretary of the treasury, he had enthusiastically urged passage of the legislation he now found unconstitutional.[10] Catastrophe was averted only because President Grant was able to fill two seats on the Court immediately after the decision — one produced by Grier's resignation, the other because Congress increased the size of the Supreme Court — and the Court promptly reversed itself.[11]
- In the twentieth century, Justice James McReynolds was a notorious and vicious racist and anti-Semite.[12] He was unremittingly hostile to his colleague Louis Brandeis because Brandeis was a Jew. When asked to accompany Brandeis and other justices to a ceremony in Philadelphia, he wrote Chief Justice Taft, "As you know I am not always to be found when a Hebrew is abroad."[13] When Charles Hamilton Houston, the renowned African American civil rights attorney, argued a civil rights case before the Court in 1938, McReynolds turned his back on him. He referred to Howard University, where Houston was dean of the law school, as "[n— —] university."[14]
- Justice Willis Van Devanter was regularly haunted by the

fear that he would find something more in the record if he just did a little more research. As a result, he was routinely unable to finish writing the opinions assigned to him, which then had to be reassigned to other justices.[15]

- Similarly, Justice Charles Whittaker was often unable to decide how to vote or to keep up with his work. Once, when assigned to write a majority opinion, he ended up turning the task over to Justice William O. Douglas, who, out of pity, ghostwrote it for him even though Douglas had also written the dissenting opinion.[16] Ultimately, Whittaker was forced to resign after he suffered a complete mental breakdown.[17]

- Justice Frank Murphy spent his last years on the Court so hopelessly addicted to drugs that he could not carry out his duties. Instead of casting votes himself, he often delegated the responsibility to his colleague Justice Wiley Rutledge.[18]

- While running successfully for the United States Senate, future Justice Hugo Black joined the Ku Klux Klan and gave anti-Catholic speeches at Klan rallies. At a statewide Klan rally, he thanked the Klan and acknowledged that without its support, he would not have won the Senate primary. When he was nominated to the Supreme Court, rumors circulated about his prior Klan membership, but Black remained silent and allowed one of his Senate supporters to state publicly that Black had denied ever belonging to the Klan. Shortly after he was confirmed, the *Pittsburgh Post-Gazette* uncovered irrefutable evidence of Black's Klan membership. A huge scandal ensued, but Black managed to contain it by delivering a radio address in which he admitted his prior Klan membership but provided misleading information about the extent of his alliance with the Klan.[19]

- After becoming an associate justice, Abe Fortas regularly provided advice to his former client, President Lyndon

Johnson, despite the fact that the Johnson administration was often a party before the Court. Fortas was forced to resign when it became known that he had accepted payments from various interests with potential business before the Court, including from financier Louis Wolfson, who was under investigation for securities fraud at the time. There is persuasive evidence that Fortas lobbied Johnson to provide a pardon for Wolfson.[20]

- While serving as a law clerk for Justice Robert Jackson, William Rehnquist prepared a memorandum arguing that the Court should reaffirm the "separate but equal" doctrine announced in *Plessy v. Ferguson*. When confronted with the memo at his confirmation hearing, he swore under oath that, contrary to what the memo in fact said and despite persuasive evidence from contemporaries, it did not reflect his personal views.[21]

- Throughout his long career on the bench, Justice Thurgood Marshall never voted to uphold a patent.[22]

- For reasons that remain mysterious, Justice Douglas harbored a deep hatred for the Internal Revenue Service and regularly sided with taxpayers with unexplained votes that thoughtful commentators have called "extreme" and "puzzling."[23]

- During oral argument in an employment discrimination case, Chief Justice Warren Burger announced that women were better at secretarial work than men were.[24] He reportedly told his law clerks that Blacks made talented gardeners because they had a great sense of color, but that they could not get mortgages the way Jews did because Jews were generally more able, successful, and trustworthy. Women should not be allowed to serve as judges in rape trials, he added, because they were too emotional and incapable of fair judgment.[25]

- Justice Antonin Scalia routinely insulted his colleagues in vitriolic separate opinions. For example, in one of his last opinions, he accused his colleagues of engaging in a "Judicial Putsch."[26] The majority opinion, he claimed, was "egotistic,"[27] reflected "astound[ing] . . . hubris,"[28] lacked "even a thin veneer of law,"[29] was "profoundly incoherent," and relied on "the mystical aphorisms of the fortune cookie."[30] Scalia stated that he would "hide my head in a bag" if "even as the price to be paid for a fifth vote" he joined an opinion containing the Court's rhetoric.[31] In another case, he favorably referred to legal opposition to homosexuality as a "Kulturkampf"—an apparently positive reference to nineteenth-century attacks by the German imperial government on the Roman Catholic Church.[32]

- Justice Thomas barely won Senate confirmation of his nomination after he was credibly accused of sexually harassing a subordinate while serving as the chair of the Equal Employment Opportunity Commission, a charge he denied under oath despite considerable supporting evidence.[33] Another statement he made under oath was less consequential but even more improbable. He swore that even though he was a student at Yale Law School when *Roe v. Wade* was decided and had served as a chair of the EEOC and as a federal judge, he could not remember a single instance when he had personally engaged in a discussion of *Roe* and had not once commented on whether the case was correctly decided.[34]

- While Brett Kavanaugh's nomination to the Supreme Court was pending before the Senate Judiciary Committee, Christine Blasey Ford accused him of a vicious sexual assault years earlier.[35] Ford's account was corroborated by earlier statements she had made to her therapist, by a lie detector test that indicated she was speaking truthfully, and by other accounts of Kavanaugh's misbehavior when intoxicated.[36] In sworn testimony, Kavanaugh responded with fury. He called the hearings a "national disgrace"

and attacked Democrats for trying to destroy his life.
When questioned by Democratic senator Amy Klobu-
char about his drinking habits, he responded by asking
her whether she had a drinking problem. Ultimately, the
Senate confirmed Kavanaugh's nomination by a near
party-line vote.[37]

There are enough examples of this sort of behavior to be troubling. Moreover, the secrecy that surrounds the Court means that
we have no way to know how many other instances of incompetence, misconduct, and florid eccentricity have influenced the
Court's work. Still, I do not mean to claim that these examples
are representative. No doubt most justices have done their best at
what is concededly a difficult job.

In some ways, the more serious problem is not flagrant incompetence or mendacity but plain vanilla mediocrity. For every
Louis Brandeis, there are many Sherman Mintons.[38] For every
William Brennan, there are many Gabriel Duvalls.[39] The truth is
that most of the justices have gained their seats because of inside
connections, political deals, and ideological commitments. Their
performance on the bench is consistent with what one would expect from individuals selected on this basis.

If one looks at paper credentials, the modern Court scores
higher than the historical average. All of today's justices have
distinguished academic records, and there is no reason to doubt
their intelligence. That said, their range of experience is quite
limited. None of the justices has had to meet a payroll or make decisions outside of a huge bureaucracy. None has run for or served
in elective office. Although criminal cases are overrepresented on
the Court's docket, no sitting justice has ever served as a criminal
defense attorney. The Court regularly decides technical and complex cases about specialized matters like patent law and employee
benefits law, but no sitting justice has devoted significant time
to studying these matters. The Court's opinions routinely rely on
empirical assumptions, but the justices appear woefully ignorant

of statistical method. Most of them have little or no background in the social sciences, much less in philosophy, literature, or the hard sciences.

Perhaps more significantly, no one should confuse the justices with apolitical and neutral students of jurisprudence. Many of them got their jobs because they were connected to politically powerful figures. Consider in this respect Justice Antonin Scalia's unintentionally damning defense of his failure to recuse himself from a case in which Vice President Dick Cheney was a named a party after Scalia had gone duck hunting with the vice president:

> Many Justices have reached this Court precisely because they were friends of the incumbent President or other senior officials—and from the earliest days down to modern times Justices have had close personal relationships with the President and other officers of the Executive. John Quincy Adams hosted dinner parties featuring such luminaries as Chief Justice Marshall, Justices Johnson, Story, and Todd, Attorney General Wirt, and Daniel Webster. . . . Justice Harlan and his wife often "stopped in" at the White House to see the Hayes family and pass a Sunday evening in a small group, visiting and singing hymns. . . . Justice Stone tossed around a medicine ball with members of the Hoover administration mornings outside the White House. . . . Justice Douglas was a regular at President Franklin Roosevelt's poker parties; Chief Justice Vinson played poker with President Truman. . . . [40]

Not only have modern justices been cozy with political figures, but their prior service has also established deep ties of personal and political loyalty. Here are some examples:[41]

- Before his appointment to the Supreme Court, Chief Justice John Roberts served as associate White House counsel for Ronald Reagan and as the political deputy in the Solicitor General's Office for George H.W. Bush.

- Justice Samuel Alito worked as assistant solicitor general and at the Office of Legal Counsel under Reagan.
- Justice Stephen Breyer worked in the Johnson Justice Department and was the special counsel to the Senate Judiciary Committee while it was under Democratic control.
- Justice Elena Kagan befriended Barack Obama while they were both teaching at the University of Chicago Law School. She went on to serve as special counsel to the Senate Judiciary Committee under Joe Biden, as associate White House counsel and deputy assistant to the president for domestic policy under Bill Clinton, and as solicitor general under Obama.
- Justice Brett Kavanaugh drafted the Starr Report claiming that Bill Clinton had committed potentially impeachable offenses, worked for the Bush campaign on the Florida recount in 2000, and served as Bush's staff secretary in the White House.

There is nothing dishonorable about service in any of these positions. Still, it strains credulity to believe that the justices suddenly shed their political predispositions upon assuming the bench. The justices take office as fully formed human beings. They have had a lifetime of experiences, habits of thought, and associations. There are occasional instances in American history where justices have been dramatically transformed by their appointments, but the much more usual story—the story that can be told about all the contemporary justices—is that they have performed pretty much as their patrons hoped that they would.

It should therefore come as no surprise that in case after case with political implications, the justices vote as their patrons would like. Of course, the practice is not universal. Even Trump-appointed justices resisted the baseless claims that the 2020 election had been stolen.[42] More generally, Chief Justice Roberts has shown occasional willingness to break with his conservative colleagues, perhaps out of a desire to shield the Court from the charge of raw partisanship.[43] But occasional deviations should not distract our attention from the broad trend: in many, many cases, the votes of the justices can be predicted by examining the positions endorsed by their political patrons.

In response to a provocation from President Trump complaining about a politically biased judiciary, Chief Justice Roberts issued an unusual public statement asserting that "[w]e do not have Obama judges or Trump judges, Bush judges or Clinton judges. What we have is an extraordinary group of dedicated judges doing their level best to do equal right to those appearing before them."[44] For the constitutional skeptic, it is obvious that Trump is right and Roberts is wrong. Of course there are "Obama judges" and "Trump judges." To believe otherwise is to believe that the media is reporting irrelevant information when it regularly identifies the president who appointed judges hearing important cases. It is to believe that it is mere coincidence when judges interpreting the same legal materials regularly divide along party lines. In short, it is to accept uncritically a legal ideology that has no contact with the real world.

None of this would matter much but for the fact that the justices exercise extraordinary power. The power is not unlimited. The Supreme Court could not completely remake the country over the opposition of a coalition of elites and popular majorities. (For that matter, neither could Congress or the president.) But the Supreme Court can nonetheless make important social policy, render decisions affecting the legal rights of millions of citizens, and substantially influence political events.

The problem comes into sharp relief when, as in recent years, the Court has been evenly divided, so the real power devolves to a single justice. Until his retirement, many constitutional questions came down to what Justice Anthony Kennedy thought about the matter. Without in any way disparaging Justice Kennedy's intellect or seriousness of purpose, we must ask whether granting this authority to one individual, never elected by anyone and who gained his seat more or less through historical accident, is a sensible way to run a country.

If Justice Kennedy and his colleagues were simply and mechanically following "the law," then they would have no power at all. But no serious person believes that the meaning of "equal protection," "due process," "executive power," or "unreasonable searches and seizures" can be read directly off the constitutional text. Translating these words into legal outcomes inevitably requires the justices to supplement the text with appropriately contestable value judgments. By what warrant did Justice Kennedy bind 320 million people to the personal, occasionally quite eccentric value judgments that he happened to make?

Moreover, even if the decisions the Supreme Court regularly renders could and should be determined algorithmically from uncontroversial first premises, we have no guarantee at all that the justices will follow the rules. The bottom line is that because they are accountable to no one, within a very wide range they can do whatever they want.

All institutions are imperfect. It would be easy to find abuses of power, incompetence, and a wide variety of other failings in other branches of government. So why pick on the Supreme Court? One answer is that a good constitutional skeptic is a nondiscriminatory iconoclast. Other institutions also deserve and should receive the skeptic's withering gaze.

Still, there are things that make the Supreme Court an especially inviting target. Congress, the president, and state governments gain their acceptance from the notion that they are responsible to the public. People know that these public officials often fail us, and there is a good deal of cynicism about their performance. They nonetheless manage to retain some legitimacy because there is a potential democratic remedy for poor performance.

The existence of that remedy is itself something of a myth, but it is a different kind of myth from the one that protects the justices. The justices' perceived legitimacy rests on the opposite hypothesis—that they are shielded from a democratic check and that this protection allows them to act with rectitude and strict adherence to the requirements of law. People will put up with the mendacity of other public officials because they can always be voted out. Because the justices cannot be voted out, the Court's reputation for saint-like probity, wisdom, and restraint is all the protection that it has.

Constitutional skeptics believe that this reputation is undeserved. If the Court's actual processes and performance were presented candidly and clearly to the American people, we would never put up with them. And so they are not presented candidly and clearly. Instead, the Supreme Court is protected by an ideology, promoted by conservative and liberal justices alike, that makes the Court appear to be something that it is not and cannot be. Journalists and academics, who should and usually do know better, reinforce the ideology because they are caught in a corrupting web produced by the power and influence the justices possess.

Not surprisingly, this ideology, together with the hubris that it encourages, has done considerable harm to the country. Over its history, the Court has rendered many, many truly terrible decisions. This is not the place for a comprehensive history of the Supreme Court, but some highlights from that history convey a sense of the role that the Court has played in our political and legal culture.

In the earliest days of the Republic, Federalist judges, including Supreme Court justices, vigorously enforced the Alien and Sedition Acts, which criminalized criticism of the president and resulted in the jailing of opposition leaders throughout the country.[45]

In the run-up to the Civil War, the Court consistently sided with slave owners. For example, in *Prigg v. Pennsylvania*,[46] Justice Joseph Story, writing for the Court, held that a Pennsylvania law that prohibited the extradition of African Americans for the purpose of enslaving them was unconstitutional. In one of the most notorious decisions in the Court's history, Chief Justice Roger Taney wrote for the Court to hold that even free African Americans could not be citizens of the United States and that Congress's efforts to outlaw slavery in the territories were unconstitutional.[47]

After the Civil War, Congress enacted a comprehensive program to eradicate the badges and incidents of slavery and to protect the newly freed slaves from violence and discrimination. Fearful of judicial interference, the Reconstruction Congress enacted the Fourteenth Amendment to insulate its program from constitutional attack. Unfortunately, this effort was mostly unsuccessful. The Court read the amendment in an indefensibly narrow fashion and proceeded to invalidate much of the Reconstruction program.

An especially notorious case involved the Colfax massacre. After the Republican candidate for governor of Louisiana won a narrow victory, white terrorists attacked a group of African Americans who had occupied a local courthouse. The African Americans surrendered, but the terrorists murdered them anyway. No one knows exactly how many people died because bodies were thrown into a local river. Historians estimate that there were between 60 and 150 murders.[48] Some of the terrorists were subsequently indicted and convicted under a Reconstruction statute, but the Supreme Court reversed the convictions on the ground that federal efforts to control private violence were unconstitutional.[49] The Court used similar reasoning to strike down statutes that prohibited racial discrimination in public accommodations[50] and that protected the right of African Americans to vote.[51]

When political pressure on the South eased, southern states enacted a comprehensive system of racial apartheid. African Americans were consigned by law to separate schools, separate sections of trains, separate eating establishments, separate bathrooms, and separate water fountains. In *Plessy v. Ferguson,*[52] the Court, in an infamous opinion by Justice Henry Billings Brown, found that this "separate but equal" regime was constitutionally permissible. It was "in the nature of things," Brown wrote, that the Fourteenth

Amendment "could not have been intended to abolish distinctions based upon color, or to enforce social, as distinguished from political, equality or a commingling of the two races upon terms unsatisfactory to either."[53] If the statute "stamps the colored race with a badge of inferiority," then that was "solely because the colored race chooses to put that construction upon it."[54]

The statute in *Plessy* supposedly mandated equal facilities for Black and white patrons, but in a later case, where the opinion was authored by Justice John Marshall Harlan, who had dissented in *Plessy*, the Court held that it was constitutionally permissible for a community to operate an all-white high school even though there was no high school of any kind for African American students. Bizarrely, the Court held that victory for the plaintiffs would result only in the closing of the white school, which would not benefit African Americans.[55]

Utilizing similarly tortured reasoning, Justice Oliver Wendell Holmes, writing for the Court, rejected a lawsuit brought by an African American claiming that the voting registration system in Alabama was a "fraud on the Constitution" that systematically permitted the registration of white voters but prevented African Americans from voting.[56] Holmes did not quarrel with the factual basis for the suit. Instead, he reasoned, if the system was indeed a fraud, then it would be the duty of the Court to invalidate it. But that would mean that the Black plaintiff could not be registered under the system. "How" he asked, "can we make the court a party to the unlawful scheme by accepting it and adding another voter to its fraudulent lists?"[57]

The Court did no better at enforcing civil liberties during this period. Throughout the nineteenth century, it regularly ignored infringements on speech and free exercise rights.[58] In an especially shameful decision, the Court gave its approval to a massive eugenics program that resulted in the forced sterilization of thousands of women.[59] "It would be better for all the world," Holmes wrote in his opinion, "if instead of waiting to execute degenerate offspring for crime, or to let them starve for their imbecility, society can prevent those who are manifestly unfit from continuing their kind. The principle that sustains compulsory vaccination is broad enough to cover cutting the Fallopian tubes. . . . Three generations of imbeciles are enough."[60]

With American entry into World War I, the Wilson administration embarked on a vigorous program to suppress dissent, utilizing the newly enacted Espionage Act of 1917 and Sedition Act of 1918 to jail many opponents of the war. The Court upheld these convictions in every case that came before it,[61] including the conviction of the Socialist Party leader, Eugene Debs, who received millions of votes for president while sitting in a jail cell.[62]

In the late nineteenth and early twentieth centuries, populism and progressivism emerged as an important political force, and state governments began to enact various forms of economic regulation. For example, state statutes mandated minimum wages and maximum hours, prohibited "yellow dog contracts" that prevented workers from forming unions, and provided for price regulation of public utilities. During the same period, the federal government enacted the first, modest tax on income.

The Supreme Court's response to these reforms was uncertain and inconsistent but, in general, hostile. In *Pollock v. Farmers Loan & Trust Co.*,[63] decided in 1895, Chief Justice Melville Fuller wrote for the Court to hold that the federal income tax was unconstitutional. The decision stood for almost twenty years, until Congress and the states were able to enact the Sixteenth Amendment, which permitted the tax.

Ten years after *Pollock*, the Supreme Court decided *Lochner v. New York*,[64] a decision that came to symbolize judicial overreaching. According to the Court, a New York statute protecting employees of bakery shops from having to work more than ten hours per day and sixty hours per week violated the "freedom of contract" protected by the Fourteenth Amendment's due process clause.

Writing for the majority, Justice Rufus Peckham found it "impossible for us to shut our eyes to the fact that many of the laws of this character, while passed under what is claimed to be the police power for the purpose of protecting the public health or welfare, are, in reality, passed from other motives."[65] He believed that "the real object and purpose were simply to regulate the hours of labor between the master and his employees . . . in a private business, not dangerous in any degree to morals or in any real and substantial degree, to the health of the employees."[66] It apparently went without saying that this motive made the law unconstitutional.

The Court also upheld some economic legislation during this period, but *Lochner* was hardly an outlier. In all, between 1905 and 1930, the Court invalidated some two hundred statutes imposing economic regulation.

Some scholars have suggested that the Court was applying "neutral principles" during this period and not merely protecting the economic interests of the rich and powerful. Perhaps so, but some contradictions are difficult to overlook. For example, in *United States v. E.C. Knight Co.*,[67] the Court held that application of a federal antitrust act to prevent the monopolization of the sugar industry was unconstitutional because Congress was attempting to regulate purely local activity. Yet in *Coronado Coal Co. v. United Mine Workers*,[68] the Court upheld application of the same statute to prevent a union from striking against a mining company on the theory that the strike affected interstate commerce. Similarly, the Court invalidated a federal statute prohibiting the interstate shipment of goods made through child labor,[69] but it upheld a federal statute prohibiting the interstate shipment of lottery tickets.[70]

Concern about the Court's ideological motivations came to a head during the New Deal period, when the Court blocked some important New Deal programs and threatened to invalidate many more. After his overwhelming victory in the 1936 election, President Franklin Roosevelt moved to discipline the Court by increasing its size from nine to fifteen justices. (Roosevelt had not been able to appoint a single justice during his first term.) Congress ultimately rejected the proposal, but the Court more or less simultaneously backed off from confrontation with a popular president. Roosevelt remained in office long enough to appoint all nine justices, and these appointments inaugurated a period during which the Court abstained from interfering with economic regulation.[71]

Some justices on the newly liberal court (for example, Felix Frankfurter) understood the lesson of the *Lochner* era to be that the Court should not interfere with political judgments even when they did not involve economic policy. As a result, the Roosevelt Court's defense of civil liberties was, at best, spotty. The Court occasionally defended the rights of unpopular speakers, but in moments when civil liberties were at greatest risk, it refused to intervene.[72]

For example, after the Japanese attack on Pearl Harbor the Roosevelt administration ordered the exclusion of thousands of loyal Japanese American citizens from their homes. The Supreme Court held that the action was constitutionally permissible even though the exclusion was based solely on ethnicity and the excluded individuals were given no opportunity to demonstrate their loyalty.[73] For Justice Hugo Black, Roosevelt's first appointee to the Court, who wrote for the majority, it was enough that "Congress, reposing its confidence in this time of war in our military leaders—as inevitably it must—determined that they should have the power to do just this."[74]

Similarly, when German saboteurs were captured on American soil, the Court approved a hastily constituted military tribunal that sentenced them to death. Even on the assumption that the defendants were American citizens, the Court held that they had no right to a jury trial or ordinary criminal procedure protection.[75]

When the McCarthy panic hit the country in the postwar period, the liberal justices again caved to public pressure. They acceded to criminal convictions and firings of scores of people because of their political affiliations.[76] Writing for a plurality of the Court in a case upholding the conviction of leaders of the American Communist Party, Chief Justice Fred Vinson conceded that there was little or no possibility that the defendants might actually succeed in overthrowing the government. Nor was there any indication that the defendants were currently attempting to do so. Instead, he wrote, it was enough that there was a "clear and present danger" that the defendants might mount an unsuccessful attempt to overthrow the government sometime in the indefinite future.[77]

Due to a series of historical accidents, by the mid- to late 1950s power on the Court had shifted to justices who viewed themselves as legal reformers. During the brief heyday of the Warren Court, the justices acted vigorously to dismantle racial apartheid in the South,[78] reform the criminal justice system,[79] require equality of population in voting districts,[80] and provide some constitutional protection for poverty-stricken Americans.[81] Even after Chief Justice Earl Warren had retired and a conservative president had somewhat changed the complexion of the Court, it rendered pathbreaking decisions protecting reproductive autonomy[82] and attacking gender discrimination.[83]

Although the Warren Court experience ended almost a half century ago, its hold on the American imagination remains strong. For many conservatives, the Warren Court remains an exemplar of arrogant and lawless judicial overreaching. Its more important impact, though, has been on the attitude of many progressives. Anyone looking at the entire sweep of the Court's history would understand that the Court has pretty consistently stood with the most shortsighted and venal impulses in American society. Still, the Warren Court interregnum supports the hope that if only the right justices could somehow be appointed, the Supreme Court might yet be an engine driving us toward the Preamble's promise that we "establish justice." That hope, in turn, softens the criticism that many progressives might otherwise direct toward the Court.

In light of this effect, it is important to emphasize three points about the Warren Court experience. First, this judicial Camelot did not last very long. Activists on the Court gained a reliable working majority when Justice Arthur Goldberg replaced Justice Felix Frankfurter in 1962. By 1972, Richard Nixon had added four justices to the Court, leaving conservatives again in control.

Second, for all of its ambition, the Warren Court's actual accomplishments were limited and fragile. Dismantling the Jim Crow system was an important achievement, but, as many scholars have pointed out, the Court's orders were widely ignored. Real change did not come until Lyndon Johnson's huge victory in the 1964 election and the breaking of the southern stranglehold on Congress.[84] Even then, the Court failed to move much beyond the formal eradication of separate but equal. As a practical matter, so-called de facto segregation replaced explicit or de jure segregation. Perhaps paradoxically, *Brown v. Board of Education* was seized upon by racial conservatives to justify a deeply racist status quo. Now that schools were formally no longer separate, the argument went, they were definitionally equal. Therefore, government was no longer responsible for the starkly unequal outcomes faced by people of color.

Many other Warren Court reforms were similarly ineffective. The Court addressed some of the worst manifestations of police violence and lawlessness, but it also invented the concept of "qualified immunity" for government officials who violated civil rights, thereby shielding them from meaningful legal accountability.[85] It was Chief Justice Warren himself who wrote for the Court in *Terry v. Ohio*[86] to endorse "stop and frisk" tactics that resulted in the systematic harassment of millions of Black men living in the inner city. None of the Warren Court reforms prevented the disastrous trend toward hyperincarceration that eventually led us to the imprisonment of a greater percentage of our population than any other nation on earth.

At first, the Court's insistence on the one-person-one-vote principle resulted in a significant shift in the balance of political power, but politicians quickly figured out how to undermine the reform through political gerrymandering, which the Court has refused to control.

The final fate of *Roe v. Wade* is yet to be determined. It unquestionably produced short-term gains for women, but at this writing it, too, is being systematically undermined by bad-faith regulation that has made abortion all but inaccessible in some states, especially for poor women.

These developments, in turn, lead to the third point about the Warren Court. The Supreme Court's history is important and often misunderstood, but the crucial question to answer is how the Court operates *now* and how it is likely to operate in the immediate future. Unfortunately, though, instead of disowning its sordid history, modern justices revel in it. As law professor Richard Lazarus reports, the chairs the justices use in their private dining room date from 1795. The mugs used by each justice in the courtroom contain the names of all the justices who previously occupied their seat. Similarly, in the justices' dining room, they sit in seats based on where their predecessors sat.[87] As my colleague Lisa Heinzerling observes:

> One might wonder what it is like for a female justice to be assigned a pewter mug etched with the names of only men. Or for a justice of color to receive a mug etched with the names of only white justices, some number of whom were slave owners. Remarkably, there appears to be no official reckoning of the number of Supreme Court justices in our history who owned other humans, but we can say that today's justices have, on their pewter mugs, the names of more former justices who owned other humans than of men of color or women of any background. And the portraits of Chief Justices Jay and Marshall that Chief Justice Roberts has chosen to keep in the justices' conference room commemorate slave-owning justices. "Tradition" in the U.S. legal system has a complicated meaning for women and for people of color. . . . It is important to remember that "the space in which justice is done shapes what we think it means."[88]

Given the atmosphere in which they work and the mindset that it reveals, it should come as no surprise that, whatever our experience during the Warren Court era, the modern Supreme Court has returned to its historical role as the defender of class privilege, racial hierarchy, and reaction.

Any evaluation of the modern Court must begin with the obvious political bias that infects many of its decisions. The most famous example is its blatantly political interference in the 2000 presidential election that ensured the victory of George W. Bush.[89] With stunning hypocrisy, the Court utilized a federal statute specifically designed to keep the justices out of the election process to assert judicial dominance over it. It condemned the Florida Supreme Court for allowing local jurisdictions to utilize different standards in recounting ballots even as it required recognition of the initial results that were riddled with at least as many inconsistencies. And lest someone suppose that its decision was about anything other than determining the outcome of this election, the Court warned that its "consideration is limited to the present circumstances, for the problem of equal protection in election processes generally presents many complexities."[90] So much for apolitical neutral principles.

Bush v. Gore is the Court's most prominent case skewing political outcomes in favor of Republicans, but it is far from the only one. The Court has invalidated as "racial gerrymandering" state and congressional districting decisions designed to *fairly* reflect African American voting strength.[91] Yet it has also reversed lower courts that have attempted to control political gerrymandering designed to *unfairly* dilute the strength of one or the other political party.[92] It is no secret, of course, that African Americans disproportionately favor Democratic candidates. Although both parties use political gerrymandering, it is clear that, overall, the practice substantially benefits Republicans.

The Court has also upheld voter suppression techniques such as demanding photo identification at polling places.[93] The practice has an obvious discriminatory impact on poor voters who, again, skew Democratic. At the same time, it has gutted legislation designed to limit the ability of very wealthy Americans to dominate elections by making huge campaign contributions.[94] Most egregiously, the Court struck down key provisions of the 1965 Voting Rights Act, which for half a century provided federal oversight against changes in voting procedures that had the purpose or effect of impeding the right of African Americans to vote.[95]

Not satisfied with distorting the processes through which public policy is made, the Court has also invalidated a raft of progressive, substantive legislation that has emerged from that process. True, the Affordable Care Act barely survived a Supreme Court challenge. The four most conservative justices would have struck down the entire statute. Chief Justice Roberts was apparently unwilling to endure the political blowback that would have accompanied the first judicial decision in eighty years to invalidate a president's most important legislative initiative. He cast a crucial vote to uphold the statute as a whole. He did so, however, only after striking down sections of the law relating to Medicaid expansion on patently frivolous grounds and announcing commerce clause and spending clause tests that threaten a wide variety of other federal statutes.[96]

In other cases, with Chief Justice Roberts's support, the Court has bolstered the conservative political agenda with regard to race. It has turned the original purpose of the equal protection clause on its head so as to protect the white majority supposedly disadvantaged by measures aimed at remedying the harms imposed by slavery and Jim Crow.[97] It even struck down voluntary school desegregation measures of the sort that the Warren Court once found constitutionally compelled.[98]

Finally, in one of its most controversial decisions, the Court for the first time read the Second Amendment as guaranteeing the right of an individual to own a firearm for purposes of self-defense.[99] At this writing, it remains unclear how far the Court will extend this new right, but at the very least its decision complicates the already difficult task of assembling a political majority to control gun violence.

It is worth emphasizing that the Court handed down virtually all these decisions before Trump appointees reinforced the Court's conservative majority. It is anyone's guess what the conservatives will do with their newly won power, but we can be reasonably certain that a return of Warren Court liberalism is nowhere on the horizon. Instead, the Court seems poised to cut back still further on the few Warren Court reforms that remain viable, to invalidate already anemic legislative measures designed to combat racism, to protect religious conservatives from civil rights legislation, and to reinvigorate long-abandoned doctrines that limit government regulation of economic markets.

It remains unclear whether the Court will be satisfied with symbolic and marginal efforts along these lines or whether it will attempt to assert real political muscle. The Court is a complex institution, and both generalizations about its past and predictions about its future are hazardous. Even in its darkest hours, there are scattered decisions throughout its history that deserve our praise. Perhaps there will be such decisions in the future. Still, the preceding discussion should be sufficient to demonstrate that the Supreme Court hardly deserves the reputation that it enjoys, and there is no good reason to think that it will earn that reputation anytime soon.

So what is to be done? In the wake of the Senate's unprecedented refusal to consider President Obama's nomination of Merrick Garland to the Court and the debacle surrounding the nomination of Brett Kavanaugh, academics and political figures have proposed a variety of reforms. The simplest to implement would be an expansion of the Court's size. The Constitution does not require that there be only nine justices, and the Court's size has varied throughout our history. A variant on this proposal would allow the Court's size to fluctuate so as to allow each administration a set number of appointments.

Other, more complex proposals would change the Court's functioning in dramatic ways. For example, political analyst Norman Ornstein has proposed eighteen-year term limits for Supreme Court justices, with a justice relegated to service on the lower courts after eighteen years so as not to run afoul of the constitutional guarantee of life tenure.[100] Former presidential candidate Pete Buttigieg[101] has borrowed from a far-reaching proposal advanced by law professors Daniel Epps and Ganesh Sitaraman.[102] Under this scheme, there would be fifteen justices, with ten equally divided between the two parties and those ten choosing the remaining five. Epps and Sitaraman have also suggested that all lower federal court judges be named to the Supreme Court, with rotating panels of nine chosen by lot deciding cases.

Many of these proposals are designed to restore the Court's political balance. Liberals are rightly furious about the Senate's refusal to act on President Obama's last Supreme Court nomination while rushing to confirm President Trump's last nominee. They claim that their reforms would return the Court to its previous role as a fair and apolitical enforcer of our constitutional values.

Conservatives respond by turning the table on liberals. Far from making the Court apolitical, the reforms would turn the Court into a political football. After all, the reforms are premised on the assumption that the current justices are acting in a partisan fashion—something that conservatives deny. And two can play the same game. Conservatives believe that it is liberal justices who are distorting the Constitution. If Democrats add liberals to the Court in the name of constitutional fidelity, Republicans will have no compunction about adding conservatives under the same banner once they gain control. The result, they claim, will be an endless game of tit-for-tat that will destroy the Court.

For the constitutional skeptic, much of this argument is beside the point. Liberals, conservatives, and centrists alike assume that the exercise of judicial power is just fine so long as the power is exercised the "right" way. All sides assume that they are enforcing neutral constitutional principles, while the other sides are engaged in a nakedly ideological and political campaign. But no one has clean hands in this struggle. Yes, the Republican judges are on an ideological mission, but constitutional liberalism and "mainstream" centrist positions are also ideological. Both advocates and opponents of reform remain in the thrall of the very conception of constitutional law that has gotten us into the mess in the first place: as a magical resolution to our disagreements without the necessity of resorting to the dirty business of assembling political majorities.

Consider in this regard the Court's decision in *Obergefell v. Hodges*,[103] upholding the constitutional right of gay Americans to marry. For liberals, the decision is one of the Court's very few acts of decency in recent memory. There can be no doubt that the case removed one source of pain and discrimination directed against the LBGTQ community. Still, that outcome should not obscure the ways in which the decision reflects constitutional sickness rather than health.

The Court was divided 5–4, and the outcome depended on Justice Kennedy, who wrote the majority opinion. Apparently because of his personal experiences, Justice Kennedy seems to have a special awareness of the plight of gay Americans, an awareness that does not extend with anything like the same force to other disempowered groups. The case again illustrates the oddity of resolving important policy questions based on the quirks of a single justice.

Beyond that, even defenders of gay rights cannot miss the opinion's tendentiousness. At least superficially, the Constitution has nothing to say about homosexuality or, for that matter, about marriage. True, under a certain conception of equal protection and due process, one might argue that the right to marriage is constitutionally protected and that the right extends to same-sex marriage. But under a different conception, "marriage" does not include "gay marriage," and a requirement that all marriages be between men and women does not deny equality. Which conception one adopts precisely tracks the ongoing political struggle over gay rights.

The pity is that before the Court acted, that struggle was being won by supporters of gay rights. The bravery and persistence of these advocates forced open the closet door. The upshot was that most Americans came to see the irrationality and cruelty of homophobia. Ironically, Justice Kennedy's opinion transformed a movement marked by organizing and an emerging collective consciousness into a claim of individual, isolated rights. The opinion celebrates marriage as a refuge from politics, rather than as the outcome of a political struggle. By doing so, Kennedy fueled the contradictory individualist claims by religious conservatives, who argue that gay rights protections threaten their own "right to be let alone." With some justification, these conservatives feel aggrieved by the Court's insistence that our foundational document rejects their deepest religious convictions, and, of course, they are acting on their grievances.

All that said, *Obergefell* still marks a victory for inclusion and tolerance. But at what price? In exchange for a result that within a few years would have been achieved politically anyway, liberals endorsed the exercise of institutional power that, over the range of cases, promises much more reaction and injustice. Was the trade really worth it?

For these reasons, reform measures meant to return the Court to a mythical past when it acted apolitically are misguided. Still, in an unintended way, the proposed reforms might help move us in the right direction. Oddly, they might do so for exactly the reasons that conservatives marshal to oppose the reforms.

The conservative complaint is that radical change in the Court's composition and functioning would politicize the body. But perhaps this is a feature rather than a bug. There is no doubt that, just as conservatives say, if Democrats succeeded in "packing" the Court to make up for the lost Garland seat, Republicans would retaliate when they got control. The resulting game of tit-for-tat would do much to destroy the Court's credibility. But that is a good outcome, not a bad one. For far too long, the Court has benefited from its undeserved reputation. Tarnishing that reputation is the first step toward preventing the Court from further damaging the country.

Are there other reforms that might advance this goal more directly? Here are some proposals that the Supreme Court itself could adopt in the unlikely event that it were so inclined.

- *Ditch the robes and the "Your Honors."* Supreme Court justices are not gods or priests. They are ordinary human beings. In a country without an aristocracy, respect is never based on station. Instead, it must be earned and is always held provisionally. The justices should act, and should be treated, like every other citizen.
- *Require a seven-justice majority to invalidate a statute.* Nothing in the Constitution mandates majority voting by the justices; indeed, by internal rule, the Court has deviated from majority voting in deciding whether to grant review over cases. Over a hundred years ago, the famed Harvard Law School professor James Bradley Thayer wrote that a statute should be invalidated only when its unconstitutionality was "so clear that it is not open to rational question."[104] The logic of that proposal flows naturally from skepticism about the special wisdom and probity of the justices. If the justices are more or less ordinary people, then there is no reason to prefer their contestable judgments to those of legislators. A way to institutionalize Thayer's insight is to require at least a seven-justice majority to invalidate a statute. If three justices think that the statute is constitutional, it is hard to say that their judgment is "irrational" and hard, therefore, to see why the judgment of six justices should prevail over the judgment of the political branches.
- *Media coverage.* For years, there has been argument about whether Supreme Court oral arguments should be

broadcast on live television. The Court seems to be moving haltingly in this direction, but this change does not go nearly far enough. The Supreme Court's conferences should be offered for live broadcast. I know, I know—how are the justices supposed to be candid with each other if every word they speak is made public? But, for goodness's sake, these folks have life tenure. What is this protection for, if not to allow the justices to say what they think without worrying about retribution? Members of Congress seem to do just fine with public markup sessions on bills even though they risk electoral defeat if they offend the wrong people. If the justices in fact feel a little pressure to think more carefully about what they say at conference, this would be a good result, rather than a bad result. And if they decide to avoid the public conference by holding more informal, behind-the-scenes meetings (the apparent result of many "open meetings" laws), this outcome, too, might improve the deliberative process.

- *Draft opinions.* The Court should release draft opinions for public comment before they are finalized. Why not? Administrative agencies have functioned this way for years. Congress does not usually keep important legislation secret until it becomes law, and when it tries to do so, it is subject to harsh criticism. It is terrifying that the Court produces major legal documents in final form without giving interested parties the opportunity to point out errors and suggest revisions.

- *Reverse oral arguments.* After the draft is made public, the Court should conduct reverse oral argument, where lawyers for each side can question the justices about the opinion. Why is it only the justices who get to ask the questions? A reverse oral argument, with the advocates posing the hypotheticals and testing limits, might uncover unintended consequences of an opinion or flabby argumentation. Moreover, forcing the justices to defend their opinions is bound to provide more incentive to think carefully about what they are doing.

- *Stop hiring law clerks.* Stripped of protective staff, the justices might be compelled to interact directly with one another and to think in a serious way about the problems they are addressing. The dismantling of the Court's administrative apparatus might also produce a more subtle but nonetheless significant effect. A large and obsequious staff is part of what makes a Supreme Court justice an Important Person. Forcing the Justices to do their own work is a useful corrective to the arrogance and self-importance that is an occupational hazard.

Will the Supreme Court adopt these reforms on its own? Don't bet on it. We again face the chicken-and-egg problem: the justices have power, and their power rests on mystification. We can hardly expect the beneficiaries of this system to dismantle it voluntarily.

It does not follow, though, that debate about these proposals is pointless. The necessary first step toward forcing the Court to give up its power is to delegitimize the Court in the eyes of the public. And the first step in accomplishing that objective is asking why, exactly, the justices are so terrified of reforms that would end the pervasive mystification that encases the Court's work. Even considering proposals like these punctures the pomp, pretension, and grandiosity that supports the Court's power.

More than that, thinking about these proposals reveals the sheer ridiculousness of the Court. Yes, we need to advance reasoned arguments for why this institution is harming the country. But for the constitutional skeptic, more than just argument is required. The Court should be the object of derision, mockery, and contempt. We need to start making fun of the pomposity and pretensions of the justices.

Remember, skeptics are optimists. They believe that attitudes can change and that changed attitudes result in changed institutions. If only we can bring ourselves to see through its pomposity and pretensions, the Court will lose its power over us. Once it does, the American people can begin the serious work of debating among themselves what it would take to establish justice— work that cannot and should not be delegated to an arrogant elite in robes.

FOUR

Promoting the General Welfare

The Problem of Economic Distribution

What kind of economic distribution serves the general welfare that the Constitution's Preamble promises to promote? The Supreme Court has too often assumed that the promise requires promoting the welfare of some over the welfare of others. Constitutional skeptics insist that we must reject this warped and outdated view of the general welfare and start again from a framework that truly values the welfare of *everyone*.

It turns out, though, that questions about what policies achieve this end are complicated and controversial— way too complicated and controversial to be resolved for all time by the Constitution's spare text. Constitutional skepticism requires that we resolve these questions in a political realm where we can all be part of the conversation, rather than in a legal realm where elite judges and constitutional Framers who have been dead for centuries have the final say.

Why are the questions complicated? At least at first, it may seem that we are in agreement about the starting point: All people are of equal worth. They are "created equal," in the words of the Declaration of Independence. Therefore, it is wrong for government to prefer the welfare of some of its citizens over the welfare of other citizens. As the legal philosopher Ronald Dworkin put the point years ago, everyone is entitled to "equal concern and respect."[1] That is why the Constitution's Preamble requires the government to promote the *general* welfare, and not one person's particular welfare at the expense of another. It is why Article I of the Constitution limits Congress's spending power to measures that "provide for the common Defense and the general Welfare of the United States." It is why the Fourteenth Amendment contains a clause guaranteeing all persons "equal protection of the law."

But even this starting point is more controversial than one might think.

For example, the modern Supreme Court has held that for constitutional purposes, "the people" do not include foreigners living on foreign soil.[2] Even if that holding is wrong, few would suppose that the American government has a duty to extend precisely the same concern and respect to Belgian citizens living in Belgium that it extends to American citizens living in America.

What about the obligation to care equally for all American citizens? At the federal level, only the president and the vice president are chosen by a national electorate. No one seems to think that there is a problem when senators and representatives care particularly about their own constituents, and sometimes about only some of their constituents (their "base").

The law is less clear about the extent to which one American state must take account of the welfare of residents of other states when it makes government policy. No one would say that New Jersey has to open its public schools to residents of New York or that it has the same duty to aid New Yorkers suffering from a natural disaster that it has to its own residents.

On the other hand, the Constitution guarantees to "the Citizens of each State" all "Privileges and Immunities of Citizens in the several States." The Supreme Court has held that the clause means that "a citizen of State A who ventures into State B [has] the same privileges which the citizens of State B enjoy."[3] In a set of complex and confusing decisions, the Court has also held that a state violates the commerce clause or the equal protection clause if it engages in certain forms of discrimination against out-of-staters, even if they have not "ventured into" the discriminating state. (For example, a state may not discriminate against the importation of goods from another state.)[4] It has also held that a state may not favor new residents over old.[5]

For reasons that are mysterious, neither a legal nor a moral mandate of equal concern and respect extends to the private sphere. On the contrary, at the individual level, almost everyone thinks that we have a moral obligation to maintain "particularist" preferences. It would be bizarre to claim that I should give primacy to the "general welfare" if that meant caring as much about strangers as I care about my immediate family. Someone who was incapable of extending special love and care to particular individuals is the appropriate object of pity and moral opprobrium, not praise. Legal doctrine reflects this intuition. The law requires people to provide support for their own children, not the children of others. Indeed, the Supreme Court has held that extending to nonparents the rights that parents have with regard to their children is unconstitutional.[6]

Yet even on the individual level, our intuitions are confused and unstable. Years ago, the writer and political activist Clare Boothe Luce wrote that she cared more about the broken leg of her pet bird than she did about starving children in Africa.[7] Luce's comment was widely condemned, but the issue she raised turns out to be complex. On the one hand, everyone who spends money on food for their dog that they could contribute to international food relief organizations demonstrates by their actions that they agree with her views. On the other, it is hard not to cringe when the views are stated with Luce's brutal candor.

For these reasons, a commitment to the "general welfare" is complicated and contested. As these examples demonstrate, whatever our official pronouncements, most of us have contradictory intuitions about duties of universal concern and respect to all people (never mind all living creatures) on the one hand and particular commitments to those closest to us on the other. It is one thing for the Constitution to say that the United States is committed to advancing the general welfare. It is a very different thing to read the document as setting out rules for how our ambiguous and conflicting intuitions on the subject should be cashed out in terms of public policy.

Things become still more complicated and uncertain if we ask what conclusions the "general welfare" clause has for actual distributions of wealth. One set of problems relates to the permissibility of trade-offs between citizens. Suppose that a particular set of institutions (say, free markets) raises the overall standard of living but leaves some citizens less well off than they would have been under a different system (say, a socialist pattern of distribution). In one sense, the sacrifice of the few for the many undervalues the welfare of the victims. But in another sense, depriving the many of the benefits they would otherwise achieve for the benefit of the few undervalues the majority's welfare.

A related set of problems deals with the fact that citizens may be differently situated with regard to their needs. Some people in our country suffer from sickle cell anemia, a disease that causes debilitating and lifelong pain. Does allocating more resources to deal with this problem than we allocate to, say, finding housing for people displaced by hurricanes overvalue the welfare of those suffering from sickle cell anemia? Or is the state treating everyone with equal concern and respect, because if any other citizen had the same disease, she would receive the same resources? And what if differences in need stem not from "natural" misfortune, but from past wrongdoing? Suppose, for example, differences in need are rooted in the fact that some of us have ancestors who were enslaved, while others do not.

Issues about general welfare become even more complicated when we talk about what people deserve. Suppose that two brothers begin with equal resources. One works hard and gets rich. The other refuses to work at all and becomes poor. Would it undervalue the rich person's welfare to take money from him to give to the poor brother? Suppose the poor brother is starving to death. Or suppose work is easier for the rich brother because he is born with superior intelligence or great physical strength. Or suppose the poor brother's refusal to work can be traced to his genetic predisposition, to alcoholism, or to his mistreatment by his parents. What then?

These are authentically hard questions, and one could fill libraries with the efforts by philosophers and political theorists to answer them. Yet throughout our history, extending to the present day, liberals and conservatives alike have insisted that economic distributions are governed by the text of the Constitution and therefore should not be resolved by ordinary citizens engaged in ordinary politics.

This is a mistake. The Framers' hope that the Constitution would promote the general welfare forces us to think about distributional questions, but it does not answer them. How could it? These are questions about moral and political theory that all of us must wrestle with. Our conclusions are bound to be conflicted, inconsistent, contextual, and tentatively held. They are not, in other words, the appropriate subject of a legal document that is supposed to bind everyone for centuries.

The big mistake, then, is assuming that because the problem of the "general welfare" is mentioned in the Constitution, and because it is pervasive and important, it therefore must have a constitutional solution.

A second mistake makes the first one worse: many people have wrongly thought that we have learned our lesson and that courts have given up on a constitutional solution to distributional problems. Most mainstream accounts treat modern constitutional law as leaving issues of economic distribution to the political process. As we shall see, however, it is not actually possible to divorce questions of economic distribution from questions about civil liberties that mainstream constitutionalists think the Constitution *is* equipped to answer. The result is that economic distribution issues come in through the back door. Those who look to the Constitution's text for guidance on everything from flag burning to press freedom ultimately must depend on a constitutional view of the proper distribution of wealth to promote the general welfare—whether they realize and admit it or not.

The mistaken idea that the modern Supreme Court properly abstains from rulings on the distribution of wealth, stems from a titanic battle the Court fought with Franklin Roosevelt in the mid-1930s. Many of Roosevelt's New Deal measures required economic redistribution and regulation of private markets. The Supreme Court invalidated some of the New Deal—for example, Roosevelt's National Industrial Recovery Act[8] and the first Agricultural Adjustment Act[9]—on the theory that the Constitution required a particular conception of the general welfare that mandated respect for supposedly free markets. And the Court threatened to invalidate the rest.

An angry president responded by threatening to "pack" the Court by expanding it with six new justices who would see the Constitution his way. Congress eventually rejected Roosevelt's court-packing plan, but the conventional story claims that he lost the battle but won the war. The Court ended up backing down, allowing Roosevelt free rein to implement the New Deal (in part perhaps in reaction to the political firestorm it had caused, in part because Roosevelt stuck around long enough to appoint new justices to all nine of the existing slots).[10] Many justices and commentators, conservative and liberal alike, have insisted that ever since these traumatic events, the Court has left "social economic questions"—questions about who gets what—to the political sphere.

But they are wrong. The debate about distribution is baked into the fabric of conventional constitutional law, and conservatives and liberals alike participate in that debate even as they claim to abstain from it. In often unnoticed ways, most of ordinary constitutional doctrine assumes answers to distributional questions that should be left unanswered. If we were, in fact, to leave questions of distribution unanswered, we would have to abandon many of our conventional constitutional rulings and precedents across a whole range of issues, not just economic policy (a good thing, in the view of the constitutional skeptic).

For the constitutional skeptic, our views about "the general welfare" should embrace rather than try to resolve contradiction. We should not pretend that we can give meaning to these words for all time even on the individual level, much less by interpreting a foundational document meant to bind everyone for "ages to come." The skeptic's constitution contains no fixed rules for resolving these contradictions, but encourages all of us to engage in good-faith debate about them.

The persistent disagreement about just distributions—about what counts as "the general welfare"—goes back all the way to the founding. Both sides of the ratification debate claimed that the government should promote the general welfare, and both sides favored strong government action necessary to do so, albeit at different levels of government where different people exercised power. The problem was that the founding generation, like our own, disagreed about what the general welfare amounted to, and therefore disagreed about *which* government should be strong.

Many Federalists were angered and frightened by the bold actions of state governments, which were experimenting with debt forgiveness, paper money, and inflationary policies. They believed that these governments had been taken over by "factions"— special interest groups that were not promoting the general welfare, but were instead acting out of narrow class interest. On their view, governments should act for public-regarding reasons, and when they simply took from debtors and gave to creditors, their edicts were illegitimate. The Federalists' aim was to provide for a stronger federal government that, they thought, would control state government power, and that was less likely to be dominated by faction.

Antifederalists shared the Federalists' worry about government capture, but reversed its valence. Because they favored strong *state* governments, they opposed a strong *federal* government. For them, the new Constitution amounted to an aristocratic coup. It put the wealthy in charge of a central government that, instead of promoting the general welfare, would redistribute wealth from ordinary farmers and mechanics to the emerging commercial classes.

A second dispute about distribution intersected in complex ways with the first dispute. In a large part of the country, wealth took the form of ownership of human beings. The Constitution's Framers were confronted with questions about whether this distribution should be entrenched or whether the promise of redistribution in favor of enslaved persons should be on the table. Even southerners who otherwise favored a strong national government wanted to restrict national power to prevent this sort of redistribution.

What is striking about both disputes is not so much the disagreement, but the overlap of views. Both sides worried that government might be "corrupted" by private interests, and both sides thought that constitutional barriers were necessary to prevent the corruption. But both sides also thought that a vigorous and uncorrupted government—one that in fact promoted the "general welfare"—was essential. The real issue was how to conceptualize the general welfare. What economic distributions promoted the public good and not just private interests?

In the end, the Federalists won the battle over ratification, and slaveholders secured important protections for their "property." In doing so, they succeeded in entrenching provisions that affect distributive questions to this day. The structure of Congress provides an especially striking example. As discussed earlier, no one expects senators and congresspeople to cast their votes based on a disinterested evaluation of the general welfare. Instead, they regularly vote based on the preferences of their constituents, or the subset of their constituents that they depend upon for reelection.

If everyone had equal electoral power and all congresspeople and senators behaved in this fashion, the end result might be public policy that reflected the general welfare. But, as we all know, electoral power is not distributed equally. The compromise the Framers made to secure support for the new Constitution means that the Senate remains permanently and grossly malapportioned. Widespread political gerrymandering in the House leaves it unrepresentative as well. And even if these problems were somehow solved, the impact of money on elections and the well-known defects of interest group politics means that public policy often reflects the particular preferences of those with the most economic power rather than preferences that vindicate the general welfare.

For now at least, we are more or less stuck with these structural obstacles to a polity devoted to the general welfare. But although the structure is biased in a certain direction, that has not squelched continuing political and legal arguments about distribution. Indeed, these arguments dominate modern politics.

The beginnings of the modern version of the dispute are rooted in the late nineteenth and early twentieth centuries, when populists and progressives used their growing political power to enact regulatory legislation intended to shift distribution toward workers and consumers. The newly energized reformers thought that this redistribution served the general welfare, but the United States Supreme Court often disagreed. It invalidated many regulatory statutes that the justices viewed as "class legislation"—that is, laws the Court felt were enacted because a particular private group had secured government power, rather than for the general welfare.[11] For many of the justices, interference with private markets amounted to taking what rightly belonged to one person and giving it to another.

Populists and progressives responded by claiming it was the Court itself that was dominated by private interests. On their view, it was the justices who were in the hip pocket of the wealthy, and by invalidating democratically enacted regulatory legislation, *the Court* was frustrating the general welfare.

According to conventional accounts, after things came to a

head with the fight between Franklin Roosevelt and the so-called Old Court that was obstructing the New Deal, the battleground shifted away from constitutional terrain. For both conservative and liberal justices, the Old Court's loss to FDR stood as a warning of what happens when the justices overreach. There was general agreement that matters of economic and social policy should be left to the political sphere. As Justice Black, Roosevelt's first appointee to the Court, summarized the point in 1963:

> The doctrine . . . that due process authorizes courts to hold laws unconstitutional when they believe the legislature has acted unwisely—has long since been discarded. We have returned to the original constitutional proposition that courts do not substitute their social and economic beliefs for the judgment of legislative bodies, who are elected to pass laws. . . . It is now settled that States "have power to legislate against what are found to be injurious practices in their internal commercial and business affairs, so long as their laws do not run afoul of some specific federal constitutional prohibition, or of some valid federal law." [12]

And superficially, it seemed that the Court adhered to this new principle of restraint in the economic realm. It refused to invalidate a whole series of regulatory measures, even when it was reasonably clear that the measures were enacted at the behest of special interests and not in pursuit of the "general welfare." This abstinence was reinforced by the writings of political scientists at the time, who rejected the very idea of the "general welfare" and saw all of public policy as amounting to no more than deals between interest groups. [13]

But there is much less here than meets the eye. At the very moment when the Court was moving away from activism in cases involving economic regulation, it was embracing a new civil liberties orthodoxy that required judicial activism when certain rights that the Court viewed as fundamental were at stake.[14] The very Court that was unwilling to restrain the political branches from regulating markets was quite willing to strike down laws that, in its view, invaded free speech rights, harmed minority groups, or, in later years, threatened interests like reproductive freedom. The post–New Deal Court drew a sharp distinction between "general welfare" regarding property rights and distribution on the one hand and "general welfare" regarding civil liberties and human rights on the other, with the former subject to political adjustment and the latter fixed by constitutional law.

The problem, though, is that constitutional rulings about civil liberty and human rights issues inevitably require constitutional rulings about economic distribution. It is impossible for the Court to rule in one area while abstaining from the other.

Cases about the right to burn the American flag offer a clear example. The Supreme Court has held that the free speech clause of the First Amendment guarantees the right of a person to burn an American flag as a symbol of protest.[15] Importantly, though, individuals have the right to burn only *their own* flag. They have no right to tear down the flag of a neighbor or one hanging over the United States Capitol and burn it.[16] Those flags do not belong to them, and in the second case, there is the added fact that there is no right to destroy government property.

This limitation on the right seems uncontroversial, but it produces a big problem. In the post-1937 world, the Court has held that the political branches are free to redistribute property interests. It follows that Congress could pass a statute providing that, henceforth, all American flags belong to the United States. If it did so, then there would no longer be a free speech right to burn flags.

This example is hypothetical. The Court has not faced a case like this, although after the Court's flag-burning decision, Congress actually considered a measure that would give the government an ownership interest in American flags.[17] The point is that the Court's ruling on a free speech issue *implicates* a question of property ownership and distribution, whether or not the Court actually intends to make a ruling on economics.

Another example is not hypothetical at all. A federal statute prohibits individuals from placing matter in mail slots unless the matter is distributed by the United States Postal Service. But the Supreme Court has held that the First Amendment guarantees the right of people to send and receive information, including information sent to and received in private homes.[18] These decisions mean that the statute is constitutionally problematic because people have to buy postage stamps from the government in order to exercise their First Amendment right.

The Supreme Court nonetheless refused to invalidate the statute.[19] That fact alone is not terribly surprising. There were many grounds on which the statute could be upheld. But the ground that the Court actually chose is surprising. It turns out that (who knew?) another federal law proclaims that all postboxes and mail slots are government property. A person is entitled to use her own property to speak, the Court held, but has no right to use government property. Therefore, the limitation on the use of mail slots was constitutionally unobjectionable.[20] In this case, the government's ruling about who owns the mailbox has a direct bearing on the home owner's First Amendment right.

These examples demonstrate that the post-1937 compromise, which would have the Court protect civil liberties while abstaining from matters involving wealth and property, is untenable. The exercise of civil liberties almost always requires access to some sort of property. Moreover, the flip side of this argument is that if the Court can't control the government's ability to redistribute wealth, it likely can't control the government's ability to quash civil liberties.

There are two possible ways to resolve the tension between fluid property rights and fixed civil liberties. If the Court wants to protect civil liberties, it can implicitly protect the property rights associated with them. If, instead, the Court is hostile to or indifferent to particular civil liberties, it can effectively permit a redistribution of the property rights. Either way, though, it cannot eat its cake and have it, too, by protecting civil liberties but not status quo economic distributions.

In fact, in different cases the modern court has resorted to both alternatives, protecting current property distributions when that favors the particular civil liberty the Court is defending, and de facto permitting property redistributions when that undermines a particular liberty that the Court is attacking.

Free speech provides the primary example of cases where the Court has used the first option. In case after case, the Court has upheld free speech by effectively protecting free market outcomes. The Court has upheld the "free speech" rights of the well-off by striking down political expenditure limits on wealthy individuals and corporations, thereby stymieing congressional efforts to regulate the effects of large accumulations of wealth on political campaigns.[21] It has held that private organizations have a First Amendment right to exclude gay applicants. It has protected the "free speech" of tobacco companies by sharply limiting the ability of government to control cigarette advertising.[22] It has dealt a serious blow to the union movement by finding that a key component of unionization—compelled contributions to unions by government employees to finance collective bargaining that benefits all workers—violates freedom of speech.[23] And it has ruled that a utility has a free speech right not to include a statement encouraging conservation in its bills to customers.[24]

For many liberals, these decisions amount to a distortion of, rather than a vindication of, free speech rights. What liberals ignore, however, is that all free speech law ultimately rests on a constitutionally fixed distribution of wealth. The great press critic A.J. Liebling had it about right when he said years ago that "[f]reedom of the press is guaranteed only to those who own one."[25] After all, speech must occur somewhere and, under modern conditions, must use some things for purposes of amplification. In any capitalist economy, most of these places and things are privately owned, and in our capitalist economy, they are distributed in dramatically inegalitarian fashion. Protecting speech in contemporary America means protecting the current distribution.

Consider, for example, *Citizens United v. Federal Election Commission*,[26] where, relying upon the First Amendment, the Court afforded corporations unlimited "campaign speech" in the form of "independent expenditures." That ruling, along with several others effectively eradicating limits on what the wealthy can spend to advance the interests of candidates of their choice, has resulted in the election of politicians chosen to protect the economic status quo, making it difficult to enact redistributive legislation that would harm the interests of the wealthy.

Many liberals criticize *Citizens United* while praising freedom of the press. They ignore the fact that media companies are also corporations and that their endorsements of candidates also amount to expenditures in support of candidates. Owners of American media companies, like owners of other large corporations, tend to be very wealthy people. They, too, are responsible to their stockholders, rather than to the "general welfare." No one elected Jeff Bezos to run the *Washington Post*, Rupert Murdoch to create Fox News, or the Sulzberger family to publish the *New York Times*. Protecting their speech rights means protecting the economic distribution that allows them to publish. It also protects their right to suppress speech that they don't like by refusing to publish it.

It bears emphasis that this outcome is not the result of conservative distortion of free speech theory that might easily be remedied if progressives controlled the Supreme Court. The immunity of newspapers and book publishers from government control is a bedrock free speech principle. But that immunity, like the immunity the Court granted to Citizens United, favors people who are wealthy enough to acquire these assets.

Because all property has the potential to fund speech, any property redistribution affects speech opportunities, and therefore, in some sense, gives government control over speech. The logical endpoint for a Court intent on protecting free speech would be an interpretation of the Constitution that outlawed the other branches of government from enacting any redistribution — an interpretation supposedly discredited when Franklin Roosevelt won his battle with the Old Court.

The Court has yet to embrace this extreme position, and probably never will. Still, for a constitutional skeptic, the many cases where the Court has rejected redistribution so as to protect its version of civil liberties are troubling. They suggest that the Court's post-1937 settlement—protection for civil liberties but not property rights—cannot work, and that questions about what kinds of distribution promote the general welfare cannot be settled for all time by a Court purporting to interpret constitutional text.

By contrast, in cases where the Court is hostile to the civil liberty being invoked, it has effectively permitted redistribution of property entitlements so as to undermine the civil liberty. The Court's rulings on the right to procedural due process provide a fairly damning example. Once again, the Court pretends that its rulings have nothing to do with economic distribution. In fact, though, distributional issues are at the center of who gets due process protection and who doesn't.

The modern Court has held that the Constitution requires some sort of hearing before the government deprives a person of life, liberty, or property. For example, the Court has held that a welfare recipient is entitled to a hearing before welfare benefits are terminated,[27] and that, at least under some circumstances, a government worker is entitled to a hearing before being fired.[28] The difficulty, though, is that one is entitled to be heard only about questions that are relevant to the government's decision, and the government can usually determine which questions are relevant by choosing how to distribute property rights.

In one 1972 case involving Odessa Junior College, a state-owned institution in Texas, the Supreme Court considered the claim of a professor who had what the Court characterized as "de facto" tenure. Although the college did not have a formal tenure system, it stated that professors would continue to be employed so long as "[t]eaching services are satisfactory and . . . [the professor] displays a cooperative attitude toward his co-workers and his supervisors." When the professor was fired, the Court held that he had a right to a hearing at which he could contest whether he had satisfied these requirements.[29]

On the same day, the Court decided a different case involving Wisconsin State University and came to the opposite conclusion. In this case, the legislature had determined that professors did not have tenure and could be fired "at will." Under these circumstances, the Court held that the professor did not have a property right in his job and, therefore, had no due process right to a hearing.[30] This holding makes a kind of sense: if professors can be fired for no reason at all, then there are no issues to dispute at a hearing, and therefore no point to the hearing.

The two cases taken together nonetheless demonstrate that differences in property entitlements transform civil liberties protection. Just as a constitutional skeptic would predict, the civil liberty right to a hearing cannot be protected in circumstances where the government can redistribute property. If the legislature chooses to give one professor tenure—conferring a form of property on the professor—then it must adhere to the due process clause and provide a hearing. If the legislature hires another professor "at will," with no "property right" to her job, then the due process clause loses its force, and there is no right to a hearing.

The Court has used a similar technique of property redistribution when it has wanted to limit the Fifth Amendment privilege against self-incrimination. The Amendment prohibits the government from compelling a person to provide incriminating information that can be used in a criminal prosecution. Someone who is suspected of a criminal offense has a constitutional right to remain silent and cannot be compelled to cooperate in a procedure that might lead to his criminal conviction.

But what constitutes compulsion? It turns out that in many

cases, the word can be given meaning only if we assume fixed property-like distributions. For example, if a mugger threatens to harm you if you don't hand over your wallet, you're *compelled* to yield your property. In contrast, if a realtor offers you the opportunity to buy a house, that's a choice; you are not compelled to buy it. In this situation the distinction between compulsion and choice rests on ownership of the property: in one case the wallet is yours, but in the other the house is not.

What implications does this understanding of compulsion hold for issues of self-incrimination? It means that whether one is compelled or not depends on whether one has a property right. And that means that the Court can either fix property distributions and protect the right or allow property redistribution and sacrifice the right. Either solution is inconsistent with the idea that issues about civil liberties and issues about the distribution of property can be separated.

In ways that seem unprincipled, the Court has alternated between at times fixing the property distribution and protecting the privilege against self-incrimination and at other times allowing property redistribution and sacrificing the privilege.

Consider the pay-to-play case of *Lefkowitz v. Turley*.[31] New York was understandably worried that private firms were bribing state officials to gain lucrative contracts with the state. In order to stop the practice, the state enacted a statute providing that contractors were barred from entering future contracts with the state unless they waived their right to self-incrimination and testified about alleged bribery before a grand jury. Turley was a contractor who was called to testify. He claimed that if he did so, he would have to incriminate himself, and that the state's threat not to contract with him in the future amounted to compulsion in violation of the constitutional privilege against self-incrimination. The Supreme Court agreed and invalidated the statute.

The decision rested on the implicit assumption that Turley had a constitutional right to contract with the state—a property interest in doing so. Threatening to take this right away was like a mugging—Turley would be *coerced* to incriminate himself. The ruling therefore provides an example of how the Court must rely on the distribution of property to make civil liberties, such as those protected by the Fifth Amendment, meaningful.

To see the point, compare *Lefkowitz* with an imaginary case in which the state required contractors to submit vouchers requesting reimbursement for legitimate expenditures. Suppose a contractor claims that the government should reimburse her for a large sum of money, but when she is asked what the money was spent on, she claims the Fifth Amendment privilege. Until she proves that she has incurred legitimate expenses, she cannot claim a property right to reimbursement—she hasn't been mugged if she doesn't yet own the wallet. So she is not being coerced to incriminate herself. The question of property ownership, as defined by the government, is key to the contractor's ability to invoke her Fifth Amendment right against self-incrimination. The civil right is contingent on the government's definition of property ownership.

The Supreme Court has captured this intuition by stating that the Fifth Amendment privilege can be used as a shield, but not as a sword.[32] It can be claimed to prevent the government from taking something away from you that you already have a right to, but it cannot be claimed in order to demonstrate that you are entitled to something that you do not yet own.

In reaching conclusions like these about civil liberties, however, the Court is effectively determining what people do and do not own. A real case, *McKune v. Lile*,[33] illustrates how the trick works. The state "asked" convicted inmates to participate in a "rehabilitation" program that required inmates to confess to crimes of which they had not been convicted. Prisoners who refused to participate were transferred to a different facility, where work and wage opportunities were more limited and where exercise equipment was not readily available. Lile claimed that the "threat" to transfer him to the less desirable facility constituted unconstitutional compulsion to provide evidence about crimes that could be used in a prosecution against him.

At first it would seem that the prisoner's claim in *McKune* was analogous to the contractor's claim in *Turley*. Both insisted that they were "compelled" by a government threat to take something away from them—the right to contract with the state in *Turley*, the right to better living conditions in *McKune*. But although the Court accepted the contractor's claim, it rejected the prisoner's. It reached these results by implicitly manipulating the definition of property rights. According to the Court, the prisoner had no "right" to be in the better facility. Instead, he bore the burden of proving that he was entitled to remain there by participating in the program. The program therefore constituted an "offer" of a benefit rather than a "threat" of a detriment to someone's property, and the prisoner was trying to use the self-incrimination clause as a sword, to obtain something that wasn't his, rather than a shield to protect something that was. Lile was not "compelled" because he was free to decide whether he would demonstrate his worthiness to remain in the better facility by participating in the program.

What are we to make of all these examples? They demonstrate that protection of civil liberties cannot be separated from questions of distribution. Civil liberties ultimately rest on determinations about who owns what. By constitutionally enforcing—or failing to enforce—civil liberties, the courts are effectively making rulings about property rights. The post–New Deal settlement that purported to draw a sharp distinction between property and human rights therefore fails.

As a good skeptic, I am doubtful of any final, constitutionally based answer to the question of which distribution of wealth serves the "general welfare." Part of the human condition is being caught between conflicting and inconsistent universalist and particularist impulses. I regularly vote for candidates who promise to raise my taxes, but when I fill out my annual 1040 form, I never make a voluntary contribution to the federal government. I think that all human beings are entitled to my equal concern and respect, but I regularly buy presents for my wife and children and not for strangers.

I do think that as things stand now, our country's policies are too weighted toward the welfare of the rich, and that authentic pursuit of the general welfare would require reallocation of resources toward those who have been left behind. But a real skeptic will be ready to concede that there are powerful arguments on the other side—arguments, for example, that particularism is morally justified and perhaps even mandatory, that redistribution tends to weaken incentives, and that unfettered markets allocate goods toward people who have the initiative and skill to produce things of value.

However one comes out on the substantive question, a constitutional skeptic will insist that the outcome should not be foreordained by constitutional text. What counts as "the general welfare" is the most important political question that any society faces. It is at the very center of our political arguments. In a free and vibrant society, it simply cannot be that the question is permanently resolved by a particular understanding of a vague and ancient legal document.

To some extent, so long as we treat the Constitution's ground rules entrenching the structure of the state and federal governments as sacrosanct, they will bias outcomes toward a certain distributional pattern. Different ground rules would produce different distributional patterns that conformed to a different conception of the general welfare. That is why a constitutional skeptic rejects the proposition that these commands and the other detailed commands contained in the Constitution's text should be sacrosanct. A skeptic's constitution would embrace the Constitution's broad and aspirational Preamble, but leave the detailed ground rules open to disputation, with all sides appealing to their conception of the general welfare.

Even if we take the detailed structure as a given, though, that provides no excuse for the Supreme Court to further entrench a conception of the general welfare that favors citizens with the most economic power. Yet that is what the Supreme Court has done since the founding of the republic. There was a time when at least it did so openly—when it publicly and vociferously defended free markets and status quo distributions. But during the Roosevelt administration, that honesty led to a strong and, for the Court, devastating, political counterreaction. The justices have learned their lesson. There is nothing honest or straightforward about their current manipulation of the post–New Deal settlement. The Supreme Court now hides economic rulings behind a veil of misleading civil liberties rhetoric. When it wants to, the Court secretly entrenches status quo distributions of property rights while pretending to enforce civil liberties. At other times, it secretly undermines civil liberties by relying on the power of the political branches to redefine and redistribute property rights.

The protection of civil liberties disguises patterns of distribution that, in a democratic society, should be politically contestable rather than judicially imposed. If we were really to respect the post–New Deal settlement that leaves distributional issues to the political sphere, we would have to give up entirely on judicial protection for civil liberties.

No doubt many will find this prospect frightening. But the fear ultimately stems from a misguided belief in some wise, omnipotent institution designed to protect our liberties for us. The Supreme Court is not omnipotent, and it is not particularly wise. If we want to live as a free people, we will have to do the hard work ourselves. That means engaging with our fellow citizens about the meaning of "the general welfare," the definition of civil liberties, and the disguised distributional questions that lie at the core of those definitions.

Removing the layers of obfuscation that surround these issues will not settle them. It is, instead, the first step toward allowing the argument to proceed in an honest and straightforward fashion. Ironically, draining the idea of the general welfare of specific distributional content might serve to give the phrase real meaning. The Constitution's clause does not mandate any particular distribution, but it does remind us that we arc all in this together, that we have things in common, and that we share a commitment to a concept of welfare that transcends our own particular needs and desires. In other words, it reminds us of our obligation to respect the skeptic's constitution.

A shared promise to respect and work for the generality of our welfare, even as we disagree about the implications of that promise, is a necessary precondition to a good-faith debate about actual distributions. Constitutional skeptics believe that Americans have the decency and discipline to conduct this debate without the assurance of a predetermined outcome. Of course, constitutional skeptics are *skeptics*, so they must acknowledge the possibility that they might be wrong. At least, though, we should give authentic self-governance a real try.

FIVE

Securing the Blessings of Liberty, Part 1

The Problem of Civil Liberties and Cultural Power

In the summer of 1925 two titans of the American left—William Jennings Bryan and Clarence Darrow—showed up in the small town of Dayton, Tennessee. Under a blazing sun, they battled over the conflicting populist and progressive strands of American liberalism in *Tennessee v. Scopes*—what became known as "the Scopes monkey trial."

The struggle concerned a newly enacted Tennessee statute that had the effect of prohibiting the teaching of evolutionary theory in public schools. Bryan, the populist, argued that the statute should be enforced. He did so in the name of the dignity of ordinary people and of evangelical Christianity. Darrow, the progressive, argued against the statute. He did so in the name of science and enlightenment values. The struggle ended inconclusively. John Scopes, a young high school teacher, was convicted of violating the statute, but an appellate court reversed his conviction on a technicality.[1]

The trial was originally the brainchild of community leaders in the small Tennessee town of Dayton. They had little ideological interest in either evolution or biblical literalism. Instead, their objectives were secular. They thought that hosting a "test case" involving the state's new statute prohibiting publicly funded schools from teaching "any theory that denies the Story of the Divine

Creation of man as taught in the Bible" would attract tourists and be an economic boon to Dayton. (They turned out to be right!)[2] At the beginning, everyone understood that there would be no hard feelings. John Scopes himself may never even have actually taught evolution, and he openly cooperated with the prosecution so as to put on a good show.[3]

The emotional temperature went up when, over the opposition and doubts of some of the original participants, Bryan and Darrow arrived on the scene. Ironically, Bryan and Darrow had been allies for many years, fighting for workers, outsiders, and the economically oppressed. But now they found themselves locked in a fierce battle.

Bryan was a hero to many populists. He had run for president three times and served as Woodrow Wilson's secretary of state, but had since retired from politics.[4] He nonetheless retained a huge following and had spent years of his life campaigning against evolutionary theory and arguing for laws that prohibited the teaching of the theory in public schools.[5] Darrow, the most famous trial lawyer of his time, had prevailed in many seemingly hopeless cases. He was a tireless defender of labor and of radicalism and a notorious religious skeptic and advocate of material determinism.[6]

When these two giants showed up, the case turned into a media circus climaxed by Darrow's dramatic decision to call Bryan himself to the stand as an expert on the Bible. In the suffocating heat, Darrow mercilessly badgered Bryan about biblical literalism. A huge throng watched on an outdoor platform, where the trial had been moved for fear that the courtroom floor would collapse. Millions more followed the trial through a primitive radio hookup and the print media. The jury's guilty verdict, reached after only minutes of deliberation, was anticlimactic, but high drama returned when Bryan died suddenly a few days after the trial. By the time the episode concluded, it had become the stuff of American legend.[7]

How do these events from almost a century ago relate to modern constitutional skepticism? Constitutional skeptics are skeptical about our "civil liberties" tradition so celebrated by traditional constitutionalists. For the skeptic, civil liberties are not what they seem to be. Part of this skepticism is rooted in the realization that traditional conceptions of civil liberties, such as the protection of free speech and due process, are inextricably linked to an unjust distribution of economic power. But, Marxists notwithstanding, economic power is not the only power that matters. Claims to civil liberties also mask the assertion of cultural power—the ability of some Americans to present themselves as smarter, more dispassionate, and more worthy of being taken seriously than other Americans. For this reason, skeptics reject the embrace of civil liberties as enshrined in the Constitution. Intentionally or not, adulation for these aspects of the Constitution disguises law and behavior that have cemented in place both an economic and a cultural hierarchy out of step with current American values.

Superficially, the argument in Dayton was about civil liberties. Clarence Darrow presented himself as the avatar of free speech and free thought. But William Jennings Bryan understood the real stakes. Bryan was an opponent of evolutionary theory, but he was at least as motivated by opposition to the sneering condescension that cultural elites and "experts" directed toward the views and lifestyles of ordinary people.

Darrow and Bryan were representatives of a much broader argument between progressives and populists about the true meaning of the "blessings of liberty" promised in the Constitution's Preamble. For progressives at the time, the realization of these blessings required a government controlled by well-educated "experts" who understood complex social and economic issues. These experts had to be shielded from mass opinion, which was too often uninformed, bigoted, and shortsighted. Progressives used the heavy armor of constitutional civil liberties to provide protection from what they thought of as mass irrationality—irrationality exhibited, for example, by the effort to stamp out the teaching of evolutionary theory. For populists, the blessings of liberty meant that ordinary people should control their own government. A government dominated by elites who had little understanding of how most people lived, and one that was corrupted by big money, was the problem, not the solution. For them, conventional "civil liberties" sometimes stood in the way of popular control.

Whereas the fight over economic distribution pitted leftists against conservatives, the argument about cultural hegemony was originally mostly an intramural fight on the left. Progressives and populists agreed about the need for economic redistribution, but their cultural disagreement translated into radically different views about constitutional law. For most of the twentieth century, conservatives, preoccupied with economic issues, stood on the sidelines as this argument played out. In recent years, though, there has been a dramatic change in the political valence of populism. In a shift that has upended our law and our politics, conservatives have managed to co-opt the populist movement, taking advantage of populist distrust of governments dominated by wealthy elites. The cultural divide has led populists to believe that these elites don't actually care about people like them. The result has been that they have joined forces with conservatives to block redistributive measures that would actually be in the interest of populists.

Constitutional skeptics offer a powerful strategy for counteracting these unfortunate developments: stop relying on the Constitution to settle questions of what "the blessings of liberty" actually means. The skeptic's constitution does not permit top-down dictation about civil liberties or anything else by an elite Supreme Court pretending to interpret a centuries-old document. Instead, it prizes respectful and equal discussion between people with opposing views—discussion that will not be resolved by disingenuous reference to what the Constitution does and doesn't allow.

Comparing two key civil liberties cases that came before the courts two years apart—the *Scopes* case about teaching evolution in 1925 and *Buck v. Bell*[8] in 1927, about eugenics and forced sterilization—shows that there is in fact no "correct" reading of the Constitution with respect to civil liberties. Indeed, those on both sides of the progressive/populist divide flip-flopped completely from *Scopes* to *Buck* in their stances on civil liberties. Hence the skepticism.

What, exactly, was at stake in the Scopes trial? On one level, the answer is not much. Even after Darrow and Bryan became involved, there were many indications that the participants were not playing for keeps. There was never a risk that Scopes would be incarcerated or even lose his job.[9] Bryan, who had always opposed attaching penalties to antievolution statutes, graciously offered to pay Scopes's modest fine.[10] Even had he lived, Bryan would not have had to make good on the offer because the Tennessee Supreme Court found a technicality that allowed it to reverse the jury's verdict.[11] The court urged the prosecution not to retry the case,[12] and the prosecutors promptly acquiesced.[13]

The absence of the high personal stakes that often accompany criminal trials serves only to emphasize the symbolic stakes. But what, exactly, were those stakes? On conventional accounts, the trial pitted Bryan's belief in majority rule against Darrow's defense of civil liberties. These accounts take at face value the standard story about constitutionalism: that it mediates between democratic majorities on the one hand and minority rights and civil liberties on the other.

On a few occasions, Bryan himself described the stakes this way. He repeatedly and eloquently defended democratic self-government as it pertained to the rights of communities to decide for themselves what was taught in their own public schools.[14] On the other side, Darrow's co-counsel from the American Civil Liberties Union, Arthur Garfield Hays, also embraced this framing. According to his characterization, John Scopes represented free thought, inquiry, and expression—the freedom to resist majority pressure in the name of minority rights and civil liberties.[15] On this view, it was Darrow, rather than Bryan, who was the supporter of dignity and freedom.

But this characterization fits awkwardly with the positions

actually taken by each side. There is no doubt that Bryan's belief in democratic self-rule by majority was sincere, but there is good reason to doubt that it provided his primary motivation. It is hard to imagine that he would have traveled hundreds of miles and spent weeks in unbearable summer heat to defend, say, the right of a popularly elected school board to ban *biblical* accounts of the creation and *require* the teaching of evolutionary theory, if that's what the majority of the voters had wanted.

On the other side, Hays's individual rights stance provides an even more procrustean fit with the ACLU's actual position. It is deeply implausible that Scopes's defenders really believed that individual schoolteachers had the right to teach *whatever* they wanted to schoolchildren. No one claimed that a school board had to permit teachers to tell their students that mathematics was the work of the devil or that totalitarianism is the best form of government.

These examples of inconsistent positions taken by both sides illustrate the constitutional skeptic's point: despite appearances, "civil liberties" are not really about reconciling democracy with individual rights. There was an argument going on, all right, but it was not *that* argument. If we are to have any hope of settling the argument, we first need to understand what it was actually about.

On occasion, Darrow provided a more honest answer. He often characterized the trial as pitting religious ignorance and obscurantism against free inquiry and scientific rationalism. This is the way that famed journalist H.L. Mencken described the trial in his dispatches from Dayton,[16] and how Frederick Lewis Allen presented the case in his best-selling book published six years after the trial.[17] It was the dramatic focal point for *Inherit the Wind*, the Broadway play and movie based on the trial. It was how Darrow framed the controversy when his cross-examination of Bryan revealed Bryan's scientific illiteracy and the absurdities produced by biblical literalism.[18]

Unfortunately for Darrow, though, this more accurate framing— the ostensible superiority of educated elites—actually undermined his point. Instead of demonstrating the superiority of elite knowledge, it showed the dangers of elite arrogance.

Consider first the "scientific" basis for Darrow's position. If not still in its infancy, evolutionary biology was undergoing a turbulent adolescence in 1925. Its scientific status was contested and shaky.[19] Evolutionists themselves were divided between Darwinian and Lamarckian versions, and the Lamarckian theory, now discredited, was still endorsed by important scientists in 1925.[20]

It gets worse. Perhaps the most important archeological evidence in support of Darwinian theory was Piltdown Man, discovered some thirty miles from Darwin's home in 1909 on the fiftieth anniversary of the publication of Origin of Species. The discovery was hailed by the leading experts on human development.[21] According to the highly regarded biologist Boyd Dawkins, "The evidence was clear that this discovery revealed a missing link between man and the higher apes."[22] Paleontologist Arthur Smith Woodward of the British Museum stated that "the Piltdown skull representing a hitherto unknown human species, is the missing link[.] I for one, have not the slightest doubt. . . . [W]e came from a species almost entirely ape."[23] In a debate with Bryan three years before the Scopes trial, Henry Fairfield Osborn, the president of the American Museum of Natural History, relied on the discovery to refute Bryan's claim that evolutionary theory was unproved.[24]

It should come as no surprise, then, that when Darrow submitted affidavits of leading scientists to the Scopes court in support of evolutionary theory, some of them relied heavily on the Piltdown discovery.[25] There was only one problem: years later, investigators revealed that Piltdown Man was a crude fake, produced by burying together a human skull, the jaw of an orangutan, and chimpanzee teeth.[26] When it came to Piltdown, it turned out to be conservative Christians who asked the skeptical questions, and much of the scientific establishment that was guilty of ingenuous faith.

If Darrow's claim to speak for science was exaggerated, so too was his assertion that Bryan was the voice of mindless biblical literalism. No doubt, Bryan believed biblical accounts of miracles that cannot be explained by modern science,[27] but at a crucial stage of Darrow's examination, he conceded that at least some biblical passages should be read figuratively and even managed to joke about biblical literalism: when Darrow asked whether Bryan believed that "all the living things that were not contained in [Noah's Ark] were destroyed," Bryan replied, "I think that the fish may have lived."[28] At many other points in the examination, Bryan commendably refused to express an opinion without studying the matter in greater detail.[29]

On a broader level, much of Bryan's opposition to evolution was political rather than theological. Of course, his Christian faith was important to him, but he was never a "fundamentalist" in the modern sense of the word. His religion was instrumental. Christianity was important because he saw it as supporting the political commitments that had shaped his adult life: the insistence on individual dignity and on the necessity of taking seriously the needs and beliefs of ordinary people.[30] For Bryan, mechanistic and deterministic evolutionary theory put these commitments at risk, especially in an environment where opponents of these commitments were using "survival of the fittest" to justify laissez-faire economic policies that in his view were incompatible with individual dignity.

All of this, in turn, throws new light on Darrow's famous cross-examination of Bryan. Here is the emotional climax of Darrow's questioning and Bryan's responses:

THE WITNESS [BRYAN]: These gentlemen . . . did not come here to try this case. They came here to try revealed religion. I am here to defend it, and they can ask me any question they please.

THE COURT: All right.

(Applause from the court yard.)

MR. DARROW: Great applause from the bleachers.

THE WITNESS: From those whom you call "yokels."

MR. DARROW: I have never called them yokels.

THE WITNESS: That is the ignorance of Tennessee, the bigotry.

MR. DARROW: You mean who are applauding you?

(Applause.)

THE WITNESS: Those are the people whom you insult.

MR. DARROW: You insult every man of science and learning in the world because he does not believe in your fool religion.[31]

As this exchange illustrates, the main dispute was not about majority rule or individual rights. It was about the conflict between progressive and populist versions of the blessings of liberty. For progressives, the blessings of liberty required protecting government from the influence of a biased and ignorant populace and their "fool religion." For populists, the blessings of liberty required shielding powerless "ordinary" people from elite denigration — from being labeled as "yokels."

For constitutional skeptics, then, the struggle illustrates the way in which standard constitutional arguments about majority rule and individual civil liberties obscure what is actually going on. These concepts are stand-ins for a battle over cultural power — over what counts as "knowledge" and what is mere "superstition," over whom we listen to respectfully and whom we make fun of. And the skeptic knows that, no matter how hard advocates may search for it, nothing in the text of the Constitution provides a resolution to this tension.

Nevertheless, cases pitting majority rule against civil liberties have come to the courts repeatedly over the years, often with the proponents taking precisely the opposite positions that Bryan and Darrow took in the *Scopes* case. A clear example of this came a mere two years later, when progressives and populists locked horns again over the right of the state of Virginia to tie Carrie Buck's fallopian tubes. This time, the roles were reversed.

Although there was none of the hoopla or press coverage that marked the Bryan-Darrow confrontation, the 1927 trial in another southern, rural community—Amherst County, Virginia—was also mostly for show.[32] Counsel for the defense was a longtime friend and supporter of the plaintiff and put up only token opposition to the plaintiff's case.[33] The result was again a foregone conclusion, and, as in Dayton, the purpose of the trial was to establish a broader point only tangentially related to the personal interests of the participants. But whereas the personal stakes for John Scopes were negligible, the stakes for Carrie Buck—the eighteen-year-old Amherst County woman at the heart of the trial—were huge. Her loss, ultimately ratified in a notorious opinion written by Oliver Wendell Holmes Jr. for the United States Supreme Court,[34] resulted in compelled surgery that permanently deprived her of the ability to give birth.

The Amherst County trial grew out of the eugenics craze that engulfed the country in the early twentieth century.[35] At the height of the craze—which promoted selective reproduction to increase desirable characteristics in the population—Virginia enacted a statute that permitted the forced sterilization of individuals found to be "afflicted with hereditary forms of insanity that are recurrent, idiocy, imbecility, feeble-mindedness or epilepsy."[36] By 1931, twenty-eight states had enacted similar statutes authorizing eugenic forced sterilization, and laws along these lines had been endorsed by some of the leading scientists and intellectuals in the United States.

Carrie Buck was an early victim of the craze. She was the descendant of destitute white farmers who had been forced off their land, the sort of people who might have supported William Jennings Bryan's presidential campaigns. Her mother's economic difficulties made it hard to care for the child, and Buck was taken in by John and Alice Dobbs, who treated her as a servant.[37] When Buck became pregnant as a result of being raped by Alice's nephew, John and Alice filed a petition to commit Buck to the Colony for Epileptics and Feeble-Minded.[38] Buck had been a good student, and there is little or no evidence that she suffered from mental deficiencies.[39] Despite this fact, the judge granted the petition.[40]

When the head of the Colony was looking for a test case to establish the constitutional validity of Virginia's new eugenics statute, he selected Buck.[41] After she lost at trial and in the United States Supreme Court, she was involuntarily sterilized,[42] and eventually released from custody.[43] People who knew her late in life had no doubt about her intelligence. One visitor found her reading the newspaper daily and "joining a more literate friend to assist at regular bouts with the crossword puzzles." The visitor reported that Buck was "not a sophisticated woman, and lacked social graces," but that "she was neither mentally ill nor retarded."[44]

The eugenics fad resulted in personal tragedy for Carrie Buck and for many others, but the fad and the judicial reaction to it also illustrate important facts about the struggle between populists and progressives and about the elusive meaning of "civil liberties." The eugenics movement that victimized Carrie Buck was actually related to the Darwinism that Bryan had attacked in Scopes. Charles Darwin himself understood the attraction of eugenics. For example, he suggested that smallpox vaccinations were problematic because they preserved people of "weak constitution." The result, he wrote, "must be highly injurious to the race of man." Darwin, though, came down against sacrificing those with "weak constitution[s]." He thought that "the noblest part of our nature" meant that "we must bear without complaining the undoubtedly bad effects of the weak surviving and propagating their kind."[45]

Many of Darwin's supporters were uninhibited by these moral reservations. His half cousin Francis Galton coined the word "eugenics" and produced "scientific" work linking Darwinian insights to a program of promoting "the more suitable races or strains of blood . . . over the less suitable."[46] Darwin's son Leonard was the president of the Eugenics Education Society.[47] Ronald A. Fisher,

perhaps the leading evolutionary biologist in Europe, was motivated by the desire to prove the worth of eugenics.[48]

Many evolutionary biologists in the United States held similar
views. Although Clarence Darrow himself was a strong opponent
of eugenics,[49] six of the experts that he summoned to support
him in the Scopes trial had endorsed eugenics.[50] The textbook
from which John Scopes taught linked evolutionary theory to eugenics and endorsed both.[51] (When the Scopes trial ended, the
textbook's author removed references to evolution but retained a
discussion of eugenics.)[52] Scopes made a public appearance with
Charles B. Davenport, one of the country's leading eugenicists,
who was also a fierce defender of evolutionary biology.[53] Harry
Laughlin, a tireless campaigner for eugenic sterilization, held a
doctorate in biology from Princeton.[54] Every article on eugenics
published in medical journals between 1899 and 1912 favored
selective sterilization.[55]

Conversely, much of the opposition to eugenics came from
Christian opponents of Darwinism. Bryan himself opposed evolutionary theory in part because it led to eugenic conclusions.[56]
When Nebraska's governor vetoed a sterilization bill, he stated
that the bill was "more in keeping with the pagan age than with
the teachings of Christianity" and that "man is more than an ani-
mal."[57] Billy Sunday, the leading evangelist of his day, insisted on
a similar linkage. "Let your scientific consolation enter a room
where the mother has lost her child," he said. "Try your doctrine
of the survival of the fittest. And when you have gotten through
with your scientific, philosophical, psychological, eugenic, social
service, evolution, protoplasm and fortuitous concurrence of at-
oms, if she is not crazed by it, I will go to her and after one-half
hour of prayer and the reading of the Scripture promises, the tears
will be wiped away."[58]

The second important fact about the eugenics movement was
that it was largely a progressive project.[59] Theodore Roosevelt, the
progressive hero of the "Bull Moose" campaign in 1912, was also
the country's most famous advocate for eugenics. "Feeble minded

persons," he insisted, should be "forbidden to leave offspring behind them."[60] While serving as reform governor of New Jersey,
Woodrow Wilson, a strong supporter of eugenics, signed into law
a statute permitting surgery on the "feebleminded (including idi-
ots, imbeciles, and morons), epileptics, rapists, certain criminals
and other defectives."[61] Oliver Wendell Holmes Jr., the author of
the majority opinion in Buck v. Bell confirming Virginia's right to
sterilize Carrie Buck against her will, was a longtime proponent of
eugenics;[62] he was also a progressive hero, although his relationship to the progressive movement was complex and ambivalent.[63]
The same could not be said of Louis Brandeis, an unabashed
progressive,[64] or of Harlan Fiske Stone, who was rapidly moving
toward progressive positions.[65] Both joined Holmes's opinion in
the Buck case.

More broadly, eugenics fit seamlessly into a progressive program that emphasized rationality, social hygiene, science, and the
seemingly limitless potential for reform that could be produced
by intelligent use of government power to correct social ills.[66]
Of course, a strong current of racism and xenophobia also ran
through the eugenics movement. It was no coincidence that its
triumphs came at a time when there was growing panic about immigration and a change in the country's ethnic mix. But given this
fact, it is all the more striking that eugenics never gained a foothold in the Deep South. The reason seems to be that progressive
elitism was almost entirely a northern phenomenon. The eugenics movement was populated by white, middle-class, northern,
and urban reformers, who were also attracted to progressivism.
Where populism reigned, eugenics mostly failed.[67]

Given this association, it is easy to see why Carrie Buck's case,
like John Scopes's, pitted progressive and populist versions of constitutionalism against each other—but on opposite sides this time.
Once we see that trying to find rationales for civil liberties in the
Constitution yields completely contradictory outcomes in two
cases within two years of each other, we should be very skeptical
indeed!

Holmes might have based his opinion in *Buck v. Bell* on any number of arguments. For example, he might have supported Carrie Buck's claim to protect her ability to become pregnant on the ground that the Constitution protects minority rights — the standard explanation for civil liberties. This is the Holmes of his famous dissent defending free speech rights eight years before *Buck* in *Abrams v. United States.*[68] There, in the context of criminal prosecutions of opponents of World War I, he warned that we should be "eternally vigilant against attempts to check the expression of opinion that we loathe."[69] It is also the way that Arthur Garfield Hays characterized what was at stake in the Scopes trial, where he argued John Scopes had the right to have his minority opinion on evolution protected.

Holmes also might have ruled in Buck's favor on the ground that eugenics was "junk science." Although many contemporary scientists supported eugenics, there was enough contemporary dissent to form the basis for doubt.[70] In *Scopes*, Darrow had argued against the unthinking acceptance of received wisdom — in that case the biblical creation story. Holmes was a well-known critic of conventional ideas. In *Abrams*, he had warned that "time has upset many fighting faiths."[71] The Holmes of the *Buck* decision might have directed some of his famous skepticism against the state's "science."

Conversely, if Holmes were determined to rule against Buck, he might have done so on the grounds that democratic majorities should prevail. This stance would have aligned him with Bryan's assertion in *Scopes* that, whether or not biblical creation accounts were accurate, the majority had the right to have its way. This was also the view Holmes expressed in his famous dissent in *Lochner v. New York*,[72] a 1905 case in which the Supreme Court invalidated a state law designed to protect workers from having to work more than ten hours per day. Here Holmes, defending majority rule, wrote, "If it were a question whether I agreed with that theory, I should desire to study it further and long before making up my mind. But I do not conceive that to be my duty, because I strongly believe that my agreement or disagreement has nothing to do with the right of a majority to embody their opinions in law."[73]

But Holmes wrote none of those opinions. After a brief and perfunctory obeisance toward the principle of judicial deference to majority will,[74] he wrote the following:

> We have seen more than once that the public welfare may call upon the best citizens for their lives. It would be strange if it could not call upon those who already sap the strength of the State for these lesser sacrifices, often not felt to be such by those concerned, in order to prevent our being swamped with incompetence. It is better for all the world, if instead of waiting to execute degenerate offspring for crime, or to let them starve for their imbecility, society can prevent those who are manifestly unfit from continuing their kind. The principle that sustains compulsory vaccination is broad enough to cover cutting the Fallopian tubes. . . . Three generations of imbeciles are enough.[75]

This is not the language of skepticism, of deference to majority judgments, or of conventional civil liberties. It is a full-throated defense, on the merits, of the eugenics program.[76] That defense is consistent with broad strands in the progressive tradition that celebrated public policy produced by unsentimental, rational, and clear-eyed balancing of costs and benefits, a posture that leads naturally to an uncritical acceptance of scientific expertise — evolution in the case of Darrow and *Scopes*, but eugenics in the case of Holmes and *Buck*.

What "civil liberties" amount to for these progressives is not immunity for an individual who dissents from majority views, but immunity for government from the threat of unreasoned and biased mass opinion. Darrow and Hays opposed the unreasoned and biased mass opinion that valued biblical literalism. They thought that experts who favored evolution needed protection from this sort of ignorance. Holmes opposed unreasoned and biased mass

opinion that obstructed sensible progressive schemes like eugenics. Indeed, he thought the country as a whole needed protection
from the idiocy that threatened the gene pool.

To understand how far progressives were willing to go in order
to provide this protection, we need to grasp the breadth of the
eugenics project that *Buck v. Bell* endorsed. A report funded by
the Carnegie Institution suggested that sterilization might be insufficient and that euthanasia should be considered as a method
of dealing with disabled individuals.[77] Harry Laughlin, the head
of the Eugenics Record Office and a leading spokesperson for
the movement, wrote that the "lowest ten percent of the human
stock are so meagerly endowed by Nature that their perpetuation
would constitute a social menace."[78] Intelligence tests administered to newly arrived immigrants in 1913 found that 79 percent
of Italians, 80 percent of Hungarians, 83 percent of Jews, and
87 percent of Russians were feebleminded.[79] Tests administered
to 1.75 million army enlistees in 1917 found feeblemindedness
in 47.3 percent.[80] One leading eugenicist thought that it might be
necessary to sterilize some fifteen million people.[81]

In light of all this, it is easy to see why William Jennings Bryan
thought that eugenics and the evolutionary theory that buttressed
it were an existential threat. The eugenics project was nothing
less than an attempt to extirpate the portion of the population
most likely to be his supporters. The reasonableness of that fear,
in turn, makes understandable both Bryan's support for the majority's right to ban the teaching of evolution and, had he lived,
what undoubtedly would have been his support for the individual
right of Carrie Buck to bear children. The thread that connects
the two positions is not a concern for either majority rights or individual rights as we understand these concepts today, but rather a
determination that "ordinary people" not be belittled, subjugated,
and, ultimately, eliminated by an arrogant and heartless elite.

Thus the progressive and populist stances in *Scopes* and *Buck*
are internally consistent if one focuses on the question of cultural
power—the true issue at stake. But both sides flip-flop completely,

from one case to the other, in terms of where they stand on civil liberties. For the constitutional skeptic, this raises a large red flag. If both progressives and populists waffle on what the Constitution promises in terms of the blessings of liberty, how can we possibly rely on that document to resolve conflicts in that arena?

SIX

Securing the Blessings of Liberty, Part 2

Civil Liberties and Cultural Power Today

The *Scopes* and *Buck* trials occurred a century ago. What do they have to do with the modern status of constitutional law? Remarkably, the battles over cultural primacy that preoccupied Bryan, Darrow, and Holmes one hundred years ago—and the inconsistencies they reveal about interpretations of civil liberties—still influence how modern jurists characterize the "blessings of liberty." Progressives continue to use civil liberty arguments to paper over elitist power grabs, and populists use the rhetoric of majority rule to try to wrest power back for "ordinary Americans." Both parties continue to claim adherence to the text of the Constitution, even as they make inconsistent and spurious attempts to read into its tea leaves counsel on the putative topic of "civil liberties." What is really at stake is a culture war, and the Constitution provides little true guidance to either side.

But although much has remained the same, one crucial thing has changed: in recent years, populists have changed their allegiance from the left to the right. Instead of uneasy allies with progressives in the fight for economic equality, they have become uneasy allies with conservatives in the fight for cultural power.

The following romp through some of the major civil liberties cases of the twentieth and early twenty-first centuries follows the through-line of progressives turning to the Court under the guise of protecting civil liberties in order to cement their cultural hegemony. These efforts created a populist backlash, rooted in a sense of disempowerment. Ultimately, that sense led many populists to ally themselves with conservatives at the expense of populists' own economic interests.

What is the solution to this problem? Constitutional skeptics counsel progressives to stop insisting that disputes about values can be definitively resolved by disinterested, expert, lawyerly exegesis of the Constitution. They need to stop pretending that their constitutional positions are ones that all rational and sensible people must accept. That insistence again mistakes partial, elite viewpoints for universal principle—the mistake made a hundred years ago by people like Darrow and Holmes. The mistake will be corrected only when progressives stop demanding adherence to civil liberties orthodoxy and give up their authoritarian insistence that the Constitution simply requires the results that they favor.

Buck v. Bell has never been overruled, and the Supreme Court continued to cite it into the twenty-first century.[1] America's love affair with efforts to control the genetic pool continued as well. Polls in the late 1930s found that 84 percent of Americans favored sterilization of "habitual criminals and the hopelessly insane."[2] In 1974, a federal judge found "uncontroverted evidence" that in the recent past "minors and other incompetents have been sterilized with federal funds and that an indefinite number of poor people have been improperly coerced into accepting a sterilization operation under the threat that various federally supported welfare benefits would be withdrawn unless they submitted to irreversible sterilization."[3] As late as 2010, California was sterilizing large numbers of female prisoners without their full consent.[4]

But although support did not die out, cultural, scientific, and legal developments reversed the momentum favoring eugenics. The cultural change resulted from popular revulsion with the Nazi eugenics program.[5] That revulsion, in turn, fueled a growing scientific skepticism about the claims made for eugenics. The legal change came in the key case of *Skinner v. Oklahoma*,[6] decided in 1942. In *Skinner*, progressives and populists ended up on the same side of the case, albeit for very different reasons. Because of changes in science and culture, each side was motivated to adopt a legal position that used the Constitution's text as a means of opposing a eugenics program.

At issue was a state statute providing for involuntary sterilization of persons who had committed three or more "felonies involving moral turpitude." Justice Douglas's opinion for the majority cited *Buck* several times and purported to leave its holding intact.[7] It nonetheless found that the Oklahoma statute violated the equal protection clause because it excepted from its coverage "offenses arising out of the violation of the prohibitory laws, revenue acts, embezzlement, or political offenses." Chicken thieves risked sterilization, Douglas pointed out, but corrupt politicians did not.[8]

The first paragraph of Justice Douglas's opinion, apparently added late in the drafting process,[9] invoked neither the populist nor the progressive tradition. Instead it seemed to endorse the standard story about civil liberties. "This case touches a sensitive and important area of human rights," Douglas wrote. "Oklahoma deprives certain individuals of a right which is basic to the perpetuation of a race—the right to have offspring."[10]

But here, as in *Scopes* and *Buck*, we should not be misled by individual rights rhetoric. If the "important" "right to have offspring" really had constitutional stature, then *Buck* would have been overruled, or at least sharply limited, and there would have been no need to resort to equal protection analysis.

To understand what actually drove the outcome, we need to view the case through the prism of populist and progressive constitutionalism. It turns out that, whereas populists and progressives disagreed in *Scopes* and *Buck*, they could join in an overlapping consensus in *Skinner*.

From the progressive point of view, an important change occurred between 1927 and 1942. In large part because of the Nazis' brutal experiment with eugenics, elite opinion had changed sides.[11] Although eugenics remained popular among the populace as a whole, experts increasingly doubted eugenics claims.[12] Academics now saw the program as thinly disguised racism based on myth and pseudoscience, in much the way that experts had denigrated biblical creation stories fifteen years earlier in the *Scopes* trial.[13]

There are hints throughout the *Skinner* litigation that the justices were influenced by this shift. At oral argument, Chief Justice Stone asked skeptical questions about whether criminal traits were subject to genetic transmission,[14] and Justice Jackson asked whether environment rather than genetics produced crime.[15] Douglas's majority opinion purported to express no conclusions on the topic of the "inheritability of criminal traits" and on whether scientific skepticism about it was a sufficient basis for invalidating the law.[16] Yet Douglas took the trouble to cite seven studies suggesting that the eugenics argument was deeply flawed.[17] And when he turned to the equal protection analysis, he mocked Oklahoma's claim that there was scientific evidence supporting the notion that chicken thieves but not embezzlers had a genetic propensity to crime.[18] Justice Jackson's concurring opinion called "the present state of knowledge" about the transmissibility of characteristics "uncertain."[19] Chief Justice Stone likewise based his concurrence on the failure of the state to provide a hearing to discover whether "[the defendant's] criminal tendencies are of an inheritable type."[20]

In light of this shift in expert opinion, the progressive stance in *Scopes, Buck,* and *Skinner* is entirely consistent with the constitutional skeptic's theory about cultural power. In each case, progressives treated the Constitution as shielding government from ignorant and prejudiced mass opinion. The fact that elite opinion about eugenics flipped between *Buck* and *Skinner* might have given more perceptive progressives pause about their ingenuous faith in expertise. But because that faith remained unshaken, progressives were willing to change their views to conform to a shift in the scientific consensus.[21] Because that consensus now condemned eugenics, the preservation of government as the domain of experts now required courts to condemn it as well.

That condemnation, standing alone, might have led to the outright overruling of *Buck*. But by preserving *Buck* and shifting to a theory about discrimination, Justice Douglas was able to make a second point, this time appealing to populists. For populists, the invocation of a right against discrimination served to emphasize the class bias inherent in the eugenics project. No doubt because of the Nazi experience, Douglas mentioned race and nationality rather than class. Still, the statutory distinctions that he emphasized—between chicken thieves on the one hand and embezzlers and corrupt politicians on the other—made the point about class distinctions clearly enough. "Strict scrutiny," he wrote, was necessary "lest unwittingly or otherwise invidious discriminations are made against groups or types of individuals in violation of the constitutionality of just and equal laws." [22]

For populists, this language could easily be read as endorsing the proposition that the lifestyles, customs, and beliefs of "ordinary Americans" were not sources of shame and should not be the target of derision and condescension. They were certainly not a cancer to be removed from the American body politic. Instead, they were sources of pride to be valued and respected—the underlying point that Bryan was making in *Scopes*, and, indeed, throughout his public life.

Just as *Skinner* required a reinterpretation of *Buck*, the Court's decision a year later in *West Virginia Board of Education v. Barnette*[23] required a reinterpretation of *Scopes*. But whereas *Skinner* produced a populist-progressive détente, Barnette demonstrated that the conflict between those two groups could not be resolved permanently, giving the lie to the idea that the Constitution could settle the issues that divided the combatants.

According to conventional constitutionalists, *Barnette* is one of the great cases in the Supreme Court's history—one in which the justices courageously defended the rights of a small and vulnerable minority. Constitutional skeptics see the case very differently. It marks the disguised victory of progressive condescension and arrogance against populist demands for the rights of ordinary people to dignity and respect. As such, it offers a clear example of progressives pretending to locate directives in the Constitution about civil liberties, when what is really at stake is cultural power.

At issue was a school district's expulsion of children who, as adherents to the Jehovah's Witness faith, refused to participate in a flag-saluting ceremony. In a case a few years before *Barnette*, the Court, in *Minersville School Dist. v. Gobitis*, had endorsed, with only one dissent, the school district's right to expel the children.[24] A scant three years later, it reversed itself and endorsed the children's free speech challenge to the school district's rule.

Justice Jackson's opinion in *Barnette* is famous for his powerful endorsement of individual rights, and Justice Frankfurter's lengthy and sprawling dissent rings all the changes of majority rule and judicial restraint. Once again, though, one needs to look beneath the surface to find the cultural struggle that was actually at the center of the dispute.

Consider first the Jackson opinion. In its most famous passages, Jackson proclaims, "One's right to life, liberty, and property, to free speech, a free press, freedom of worship and assembly, and other fundamental rights may not be submitted to vote; they depend on the outcome of no election"[25] and, "[i]f there is any fixed star in our constitutional constellation, it is that no official, high or petty, can prescribe what shall be orthodox in politics, nationalism, religion or other matters of opinion."[26]

This is strong rhetoric, but it presents two difficulties. First, the rhetoric conflicts with the more general progressive position on government power, and represents a flip-flop from the progressive stance in *Buck*, where the "science" of the day called for extreme government intervention, even on the very bodies of women. Recall also that progressives, like populists, favored a government strong enough to enact economic regulations that more fairly distributed wealth. The kind of individual constitutional rights that

Jackson celebrates in his *Barnette* opinion had in fact been used by conservatives to erect constitutional barriers to government redistribution.

To his credit, Jackson himself conceded that the tension existed. He admitted that the principles of individual liberty that he relied on in *Barnette* seemed more consonant with government restraint than with the traditional progressive embrace of government intervention. He recognized that his endorsement of the Witness children's civil liberties "grew in a soil which also produced a philosophy that the individual was the center of society, that his liberty was attainable through mere absence of governmental restraints, and that government should be entrusted with few controls and only the mildest supervision over men's affairs."[27] Progressives like Jackson had spent generations fighting *against* this philosophy. And, on Jackson's account in *Barnette*, they had finally won the battle: "[The] laissez-faire concept or principle of non-interference has withered at least as to economic affairs, and social advancements are increasingly sought through closer integration of society and through expanded and strengthened governmental controls."[28]

These musings amount to a remarkably (and in Jackson's case characteristically) candid acknowledgment of progressive confusion over civil liberties. But they leave a key question unanswered: why should progressives, who trust government power everywhere else, worry about it in the context of requiring students to salute the flag?

The confusion is especially pronounced because *Barnette* dealt with children, where doubts about whether "liberty [is] attainable through mere absence of governmental restraints" are most intense. Jackson must have understood that withdrawing government compulsion did not leave the children free to decide for themselves whether to salute the flag. As Justice Frankfurter wrote in *Gobitis*, the pledge might serve to "awaken in the child's mind considerations as to the significance of the flag contrary to those implanted by the parent."[29] Viewed from this angle, it is easy to see the progressive point that state compulsion sometimes *promotes* freedom of thought, as when, for example, it dissipates the effect of parental indoctrination.[30]

This point, in turn, leads to a second problem. Whatever the merits of Jackson's eloquent attack on compelled orthodoxy in other contexts, it is hard to reconcile with the way that public education actually functions. Public education is shot through with compelled orthodoxy. Indeed, the transmission of a unifying body of common knowledge and belief is the central aim of the enterprise.[31] Children who write essays defending white supremacy in their civics classes or insist on the Ptolemaic system in their science classes do not tend to get good grades. Jackson wrote that "[f]ree public education, if faithful to the ideal of secular instruction and political neutrality, will not be partisan or enemy of any class, creed, party, or faction."[32] But Jackson could make this assertion only by wrongly associating secularism with "political neutrality" and his own contestable beliefs with nonpartisanship. Jackson could not see the water in which he swam; conflating one's own stance with "neutrality" is incompatible with the very intellectual freedom that the opinion celebrates—but it is fully consistent with progressive elitism.

For these reasons, *Barnette* fits awkwardly both with conceptions of individual rights and with traditional progressive support for a strong government. Looking at events that transpired between the first flag-saluting case, *Minersville School Dist. v. Gobitis* in 1940, where the Court endorsed the compulsory flag salute, and *Barnette* in 1943, where the Court changed its mind, helps us to understand what the *Barnette* opinion is really about—to see how it fits with the story that constitutional skeptics tell about the unreliability of our mainstream civil liberties tradition.

As law professors Vincent Blasi and Seana Shiffrin detail in their riveting account,[33] in the immediate wake of *Gobitis*, hundreds of violent attacks were perpetrated on Jehovah's Witnesses. In one incident, Witnesses were "forced . . . to drink large quantities of castor oil, roped . . . together, then paraded . . . through town." In two Wyoming incidents, Witnesses were beaten, tarred, and feathered. In still another incident, "vigilantes pulled [a] Witness . . . from his car, draped a flag over the hood, and when he refused their demand that he salute the flag, slammed his head against the hood for nearly thirty minutes as the chief of police looked on."[34] Altogether, 1940 saw attacks against almost fifteen hundred Witnesses in 335 incidents in forty-four states.[35] Over two thousand Witness children in forty-eight states were expelled from school for refusal to salute the flag.[36]

Barnette does not explicitly mention any of these events, but there is no doubt that the justices were aware of them. Jackson's original draft referred to the post-*Gobitis* violence, but Chief Justice Stone warned Jackson that the allusions might promote "the impression that our judgment of the legal question was affected by the disorders." At Stone's strong urging, Jackson removed the direct references.[37] Instead, he made his point inferentially by detailing "the Roman drive to stamp out Christianity, . . . the Inquisition, . . . the Siberian exiles, . . . down to the fast failing efforts of our present totalitarian enemies."[38]

Jackson's concern was rooted in progressive fears about populism unchained—a fear more than justified in the case of the Jehovah's Witnesses. Despite populist claims to the contrary, "the people" do not always speak the truth. Indeed, the very idea of a unified "people" is often a myth. In any case, this situation was not solely or even primarily about government impingement on individual rights; the Jehovah's Witnesses were victimized by *private* violence.

This background helps reconcile Jackson's defense of schoolchildren's civil liberties in *Barnette* with his more general commitment to the progressive belief that social advancement could be achieved "through expanded and strengthened governmental controls." His concern was not so much about the right of people to a liberty unconstrained by government as about the ignorance and intolerance of ordinary people *unchecked by the government*—the very fear that motivated Darrow during the

Scopes trial and Holmes when he decided the fate of Carrie Buck. Here, as in *Scopes* and *Buck*, progressives' true concern was not the traditional idea of civil liberties, but the notion that popular irrationality required active government intervention. To Jackson, when he was ruling that Jehovah's Witness children had a right not to salute the flag, government intervention meant getting rid of the legislation that was fueling the violence.

In this case, progressive concern about mob violence was reinforced by elite disdain for empty, symbolic ritual. Jackson was willing to tolerate flag-saluting ceremonies designed to promote nationalism when they were purely "voluntary." He nonetheless wrote that the ceremonies were "a primitive but effective way of communicating ideas . . . a short cut from mind to mind."[39] This shortcut was no substitute for the hard intellectual work necessary to reach the kinds of conclusions that merited respect. True national unity was the product of "persuasion and example,"[40] not compelled ritual. Jackson was confident of the "appeal of our institutions to free minds" and protective of "intellectual individualism and the rich cultural diversities that we owe to exceptional minds."[41]

This rhetoric fits uncomfortably with the Witnesses' actual objections to the flag salute, based as they were on religious faith rather than on secular, intellectual analysis. But it is hardly a surprise that progressive justices would use arguments like these to support their position. The arguments are rooted in a commitment to rationality and Enlightenment values. They implicitly discount the roles of history, culture, habit, ritual, and indoctrination as sources of value and methods by which values are transmitted. Put differently, the civil liberties arguments enshrined in Jackson's majority opinion in *Barnette* do not actually describe the ways in which many Americans come to their views. His opinion reflects the way that elites would like Americans to think, not how many people actually form their deepest commitments.

Justice Frankfurter, joined by Justices Roberts and Reed, dissented in *Barnette*. Frankfurter argued that the state had the right to compel students to salute the flag. But his opinion was hardly a defense of populism. Instead, the argument between the dissent and the majority amounted to an intramural quarrel between progressives. Frankfurter did not defend mass opinion, much less mass violence. As a Jew who had immigrated from Austria and, in his own words, "belongs to the most vilified and persecuted minority in history,"[42] he hardly could. As a personal matter, his opinion noted, he "whole-heartedly associate[d] [himself] with the general libertarian views in the Court's opinion, representing as they do the thought and action of a lifetime."[43] But for Frankfurter, the lesson to be drawn from the progressive triumph that he helped bring about was that judges should generally abstain from interferences with the political branches, which could, on the whole, be trusted to produce wise and humane public policy.

Of course, self-restraint of this sort depends on a faith that political institutions will be mostly a force for good even if they occasionally adopt retrograde policies. But as a lifelong progressive, Frankfurter understood that a failure of this faith doomed the progressive platform as a whole. He was prepared to resolve progressive confusion over civil liberties by an unambiguous embrace of government power. Accordingly, he warned that the majority's support for freedom of speech and religion might also support "[t]he right not to have property taken without just compensation"[44]—a right that had notoriously stood in the way of progressive economic redistribution. For him, the proper analogies were not to the Roman suppression of Christianity or the Inquisition. Instead, like Holmes in *Buck*, he invoked standard progressive programs for public betterment like "compulsory vaccination" and "food inspection regulation."[45] And in a chilling, if perhaps unintentional, reminder of *Buck*, he added "compulsory medical treatment" to his list.[46]

On this reading, then, both Jackson's and Frankfurter's opinions defended progressivism against populist rivals. For Jackson, that defense meant standing up to mass pressure and unregulated private violence that threatened sensible, unbiased government institutions like the public schools. Channeling Federalist support for a large republic at the time of the framing, Jackson warned that "small and local authorit[ies]" might be more susceptible to mass pressure.[47]

For Frankfurter, progressivism meant defending government against claims of individual rights. Frankfurter might have responded by celebrating local, direct democracy, as populists and Antifederalists before him often did. Instead, he made the opposite point, emphasizing that "[t]he flag salute requirement . . . comes before us with the full authority of the State of West Virginia. . . . To suggest that we are here concerned with the heedless action of some village tyrants is to distort the augustness of the constitutional issue."[48]

No one on the Court suggested that "some village" might be the best venue for determining school policy. Neither Jackson nor Frankfurter was sympathetic to the view that smaller units of government might allow ordinary citizens more direct control over their rulers, that citizens of such a village might feel legitimately threatened by challenges to the sacred ceremonies that defined their culture, or that their school curricula might be rooted in something other than the "ideal of secular instruction and political neutrality." In *Barnette*, as in *Scopes* and *Buck*, "civil liberties" proves to be a shape-shifting concept that means what progressives say it means at any given moment.

One can draw a direct line from *Skinner* and *Barnette* to a flowering of progressive constitutionalism that occurred after Earl Warren—a liberal who embraced progressive ideas, occasionally crosscut by a particular strain of populism—became the chief justice of the United States in 1954.

In the *Skinner* case, the justices had announced that laws impinging on civil liberties with respect to basic rights should be subject to what it called "strict scrutiny." The Warren Court seized on this rhetoric to expand protection for civil rights and liberties, subjecting additional categories—including racial classifications and classifications impinging on "fundamental interests" like the right to vote and to a lawyer in criminal cases—to heightened review.[49] Relying on *Skinner's* invocation of reproductive rights, the Warren Court began an inquiry[50] that culminated in the abortion right announced in *Roe v. Wade*.[51]

Barnette's emphasis on secularism and rationality in public education led to banning prayers in public schools,[52] imposing limits on the funding for parochial schools,[53] enabling the teaching of evolution in public schools,[54] and outlawing school segregation.[55] Justice Jackson's concern that populist hysteria might destroy establishment institutions led the Warren Court to oppose McCarthyism.[56] *Barnette's* embrace of free inquiry led to the Warren Court's free speech activism, including its defense of academic freedom[57] and of erotic literature.[58]

As law professor Lucas A. Powe has powerfully argued,[59] Warren Court progressive activism rested on two pillars: an effort to bring rural and southern America into the mainstream northern, suburban, and urban political culture;[60] and an unbridled faith in the power of government-led reform.[61] Although Powe himself does not put it this way, both pillars illustrate the victory of progressive over populist constitutionalism. They provide an additional way to understand the fight over civil liberties as a fight over cultural power.

The effort directed at mainstreaming what were perceived to be backward regions of the country is illustrated by the reapportionment decisions. In famous cases decided in the 1960s, the Warren Court outlawed legislative districts with unequal populations and proclaimed the principle of one person, one vote.[62] At first it may seem that this outcome flows naturally from democratic premises, but, in fact, matters are more complicated. Conventionally, a democratic system balances majoritarianism against minority rights. What if granting additional legislative power to rural districts is necessary to protect their inhabitants from systematic discrimination? Or suppose that a majority of citizens in a state actually favored malapportioned districts. One might think that the principle of "majority rules" would require the Court to uphold this judgment, but, to the contrary, in a Colorado case the Court struck down the results of a statewide referendum that mandated a malapportioned upper house of the state legislature.[63]

Because of difficulties like these, political theorists have continued to argue about whether the one-person-one-vote principle really follows from democratic premises. What is beyond dispute, though, is the fact that the reapportionment cases massively shifted electoral power from the countryside to the emerging urban and suburban areas.[64] As a cultural matter, reapportionment was a triumph for the educated and cosmopolitan middle and upper classes—the natural constituency of progressives. Its victims were the already isolated and downwardly mobile rural voters—the natural constituency of populists.

In still more obvious ways, the Court's desegregation decisions attacked what was then thought of as southern exceptionalism. No one should deny the fact that the vicious system of southern apartheid denied equal citizenship—indeed, equal humanity—to people of color. Nor should anyone deny the Warren Court credit for its role in dismantling that system. Still, it did not escape the attention of southern populists that the Court quickly lost its zeal for the integration process when the battle moved from the rural South, where populists ruled, to the urban North, where progressives were more powerful.[65]

It is also worth thinking about the different ways that a hypothetical *populist* court, devoted to racial justice, might have approached the problem. Instead of requiring desegregation, the Court might have required massive public investments in Black communities and institutions. This approach would have embraced the kind of localism and community power compatible with a populist worldview. Instead, the Court nationalized the struggle. It effectively mandated the destruction of African American primary and secondary schools and embraced the progressive view that emphasized the irrationality of racial differences and the need to assimilate African Americans into a "sensible," "meritocratic," and "rationalistic" white culture. In that sense, the desegregation decisions were not just a victory for racial justice over southern bigots. They were also a victory for the cultural power of white elites over Blacks who resisted assimilation into white culture.

The Warren Court's criminal justice decisions—its insistence on *Miranda* warnings and judicially approved warrants for police searches—stemmed from similar impulses. As many have pointed out, the justices thought of criminal justice reform as a branch of its racial justice project.[66] The target was mostly southern, racist police forces that used state violence to enforce racial subjugation. The objective was to "modernize" and "professionalize" policing by making it more scientific and rational.[67] A populist approach might, instead, have focused on democratizing policing and providing for direct community involvement and control.

Many Warren Court decisions also illustrate the second of Powe's two hallmarks of Warren Court activism: unconstrained optimism about the possibilities of social transformation through the vigorous and "rational" application of constitutional law. Justices on the Warren Court appear to have actually believed that racism could be eradicated by the integration of public education; that *Miranda* warnings and suppression of illegally seized evidence could eliminate police violence and professionalize law enforcement; that a speech marketplace that was "robust" and "wide open"[68] would yield sensible public policy; and that disputes about matters like birth control, pornography, and prayer in schools could be settled by calm study of the empirical evidence.

With the advantage of hindsight, it is now clear that these predictions were wildly optimistic. For present purposes, though, it is important to emphasize that they were connected to the general progressive faith in progress and rationality, and rejection of populist fears about elitism and condescension. And progressives thought they found that faith in the text of the Constitution.

Occasional populist strands did show up in Warren Court jurisprudence. For example, the Court's efforts to deal with the problem of poverty reflected a populist sensibility. Decisions that guaranteed the right of poor people to representation in criminal trials,[69] that prohibited jailing of defendants too poor to pay fines,[70] that abolished the poll tax,[71] and that protected the rights of welfare recipients[72] all suggested a concern about class-based exclusion from full citizenship.

It is nonetheless striking that the Warren Court was at its most tentative when it embraced the class problem. The Court never quite got around to saying that wealth discrimination was a suspect classification or that there was a fundamental interest in the means of subsistence. Reforms to protect the poor and powerless in the criminal justice system were linked to the rise of plea bargaining, which made the reforms more theoretical than real.[73] For all the civil liberties the progressive Warren Court purported to find in the text of the Constitution, this one continued to elude them.

The inevitable conservative counterrevolution began slowly and tentatively, but eventually it picked up steam and achieved its apotheosis in 2020 when Donald Trump jammed through his third conservative appointment to the Court. There are many explanations for this shift, including Warren Court overreaching, macro-level political and economic changes, and luck in the timing of Supreme Court vacancies.

Whatever the explanation, though, the result, with respect to the progressive-versus-populist battles over civil liberties, has been a bizarre and momentous political realignment. Conservatives have managed to co-opt populist concerns about the distribution of cultural power and meld them to right-wing concerns about the distribution of economic power.

This transformation has had its most profound effect on our general political culture, but it has also influenced modern constitutional culture. Counterintuitive as it might seem, we stand at the threshold of a populist constitutional moment. For constitutional skeptics, this shift is as predictable as it is unfortunate.

Sooner or later, it was inevitable that conservatives would take advantage of the progressive insistence on using civil liberties rhetoric to cement elite cultural power. Now that conservatives have co-opted populists, skeptics offer a way out of our difficulty: a renunciation of constitutionally based "civil liberties" as a means of forcing all people to accept value judgments held only by some people.

In recent years, conservatives have cleverly seized upon populist tropes to reinforce their new coalition with populists. Consider Justice Thomas's startling rediscovery of the debates over evolution and eugenics, and his use of these disputes to challenge progressive orthodoxy. In a separate opinion defending abortion restrictions, he devotes ten pages of the official reports of Supreme Court opinions to an extended essay about abortion, eugenics, and Darwinian thought. All three are identified with "progressives, professionals, and intellectual elites."[74]

The analogy between state-mandated sterilization and individual choices about childbearing is far from perfect,[75] but that fact should not distract us from the way in which Justice Thomas takes advantage of early twentieth-century populist rhetoric. Like William Jennings Bryan before him, Justice Thomas reinterprets progressive support for individual rights as an effort to control subordinate groups that in his view make progressives uncomfortable. He thinks that progressive support for abortion rights is connected to their historical support for eugenics and to the belief that some groups are genetically inferior to others.

Similarly, the Court's emerging concern for the rights of conservative Christians[76] echoes in obvious ways the worries about elite denigration of traditional religion that brought Bryan out of retirement almost a century ago.[77] The Court has moved strongly to protect prayer in public places,[78] funding for religious schools,[79] religious monuments and displays on public land,[80] and, somewhat less strongly, Christian businesspeople who do not want to provide service to gay customers or contraception coverage to their employees.[81]

The Court has also moved to restrict affirmative action programs thought to harm the white middle and lower classes.[82] Instead of conceptualizing these programs as remedying centuries of racism, it has focused on powerless, economically vulnerable whites, whose victimhood amounts to the unnoticed byproduct of elite, racial condescension.[83]

When the Court announces these decisions, it typically utilizes the dry language of constitutional exegesis and statutory construction, but occasionally the raw rhetoric of populism seeps through. Consider, for example, Justice Scalia's attack on his colleagues for their efforts to constitutionalize gay rights:

[T]he Federal Judiciary is hardly a cross-section of America. Take, for example, this Court, which consists of only nine men and women, all of them successful lawyers who studied at Harvard or Yale Law School. Four of the nine are natives of New York City. Eight of them grew up in east- and west-coast States. Only one hails from the vast expanse in-between. Not a single Southwesterner or even, to tell the truth, a genuine Westerner (California does not count). Not a single evangelical Christian (a group that comprises about one-quarter of Americans), or even a Protestant of any denomination. . . . [T]o allow the policy question of same-sex marriage to be considered and resolved by a select, patrician, highly unrepresentative panel of nine is to violate a principle even more fundamental than no taxation without representation: no social transformation without representation.[84]

With appropriate modifications, William Jennings Bryan might have said the same thing almost a century earlier. Like Bryan before him, Scalia voiced the suspicion that what progressives think of as protection for minority rights is actually a cover for elite denigration of the beliefs of ordinary Americans.

Similarly, consider how Justice Thomas defends his position that the University of Michigan has failed to demonstrate

a "compelling state interest" justifying its affirmative action program. Like populists of the late nineteenth and early twentieth
centuries, Thomas worries that wealthy and powerful interests
are systematically devaluing the welfare of the middle and lower
classes. On his view, "[t]he [University of Michigan] Law School's
decision to be an elite institution does little to advance the welfare
of the people of Michigan or any cognizable interest of the state
of Michigan. . . . With the adoption of different admissions methods, such as accepting all students who meet minimum qualifications, the Law School could achieve its vision."[85]

Many progressives correctly believe that conservatives use this
rhetoric to manipulate populists. On this view, those on the right
are cynically weaponizing grievances about the distribution of
cultural power so as to entrench their views about the appropriate
distribution of economic power. But faced with the choice between "free" markets and rule by corrupt government elites who
have no understanding of their culture and values, many modern
populists are prepared to choose the former.

Because the economic interests of conservatives and populists
clearly diverge, the alliance may be more fragile and vulnerable
than it seems. That said, the view that populists are merely being
used by conservatives ignores the real sense of cultural grievance
that modern populists feel. It also reflects the long-standing progressive inclination to believe that ordinary people do not know
what is best for them and must be guided by elites who better
understand their interests. Finally, and perhaps most disturbingly,
the view distracts attention from the role that progressives themselves have played in producing the alliance—a role that becomes
more apparent if one understands the constitutional skeptic's view
of "civil liberties" as enabling progressive elitism.

Historically, populist distrust in government was countered or at
least leavened by successful progressive social reform. From Theodore Roosevelt's Square Deal through Lyndon Johnson's Great
Society, progressives met populist claims that the government was
irretrievably corrupt with actual programs that improved the lives

of vulnerable people. That success, in turn, reinforced the strains in populist thinking that had always been sympathetic to at least some forms of government activism.

Two trends beginning in the 1960s and reaching a climax in our own period have sharply limited this ability of progressives to temper populist distrust of government.

The first trend relates to the progressives' turn toward racial justice. Throughout the history of progressivism, extending into the New Deal period and its immediate aftermath, race was far from the center of the progressive agenda. As the eugenics controversy illustrates, some early progressives believed in "scientific racism." Even when elite opinion changed, New Dealers were willing to embrace a bargain that exchanged white southern support of New Deal programs for acceptance of segregation and racial subordination.[86]

In the wake of the New Deal, the left made sporadic attempts to break the stranglehold that southern Dixiecrats held over the Democratic Party. President Roosevelt made a spectacularly unsuccessful attempt to purge southern conservatives from his coalition in 1938,[87] and northern Democrats were willing to accept a southern walkout from the 1948 convention in order to enact a civil rights plank in their platform.[88] But it was not until the Warren Court period and the election of Lyndon Johnson that progressives broke decisively with the racist South.[89]

When they did so, progressives provoked a huge populist backlash, as Johnson himself had predicted.[90] Unfortunately, populism had a long, if not entirely unbroken, history of racism. With the emergence of progressive support for racial justice, many populists now saw the economic redistribution programs that they had previously supported through the lens of racial division. The upshot was a reinforcement of populist distrust of government and increased suspicion of progressive elites.

The second trend involved a retrenchment of progressive ambition. Progressivism was never as radical as populism. Historically, progressives tended to be insiders rather than outsiders and reformers rather than revolutionaries. Still, programs like Medicare, Social Security, and the GI Bill provided material evidence of government's capacity to improve the lives of ordinary citizens. Progressives were able to temper populist concerns about cultural power by enacting measures that at least modestly redistributed economic power.

In recent years, however, progressive enthusiasm for large-scale reform has declined. When progressives were actually in office, they ended "welfare as we know it,"[91] embarked on a massive program of deregulation,[92] and promoted a "free trade" system that some perceived as decimating American labor.[93] Many progressives made their peace with Wall Street and with a regulatory regime that is more facilitative than disruptive. Piecemeal reform, exemplified by the Affordable Care Act,[94] the Dodd-Frank banking reforms,[95] and the McCain-Feingold campaign finance reforms,[96] has marginally improved the functioning of economic and political markets but exponentially increased their complexity and opacity.

The reforms have provided a kind of jobs program for elite experts who are necessary to interpret and apply these complex regulatory regimes. Faith in government has remained, but it is faith in a government staffed by policy experts who are resistant to "simplistic" redistributive schemes and paralyzed by their understanding of the complexities of market regulation and the possibilities of unintended consequences. This stance, reinforced by the dependence of the Democratic Party on large and wealthy donors, makes many modern progressives suspicious of "demagogic" proposals that in their view are likely to make things worse rather than better and are, in any event, politically unattainable.

Like the evolution of populism, the changed focus for progressives is most evident in the general political culture. Unsurprisingly, though, it, too, manifests itself in constitutional doctrine. Progressives on the Supreme Court continue to defend "expert agenc[ies]" who engage in "sensible regulation."[97] They worry about the ability of juries to evaluate pseudoscientific evidence not derived from "the scientific method" and not exposed to peer review by other, recognized scientists.[98] They still rail against public policy that endorses what they identify as religious rather than secular purposes.[99] In other words, they continue their long-running project of vindicating elitist views against the forces of popular democracy.

For the constitutional skeptic, all of this suggests that one should be suspicious of top-down, judicial efforts to bring about social reform based on perceived constitutional promises. As Justice Scalia proclaimed, the Supreme Court is itself a culturally elite institution, with few members who have much understanding of the lives of ordinary Americans. As the experience of the Warren Court demonstrates, judicial and constitutional efforts to impose solutions to our social problems risk creating a backlash rooted in populists' sense of cultural disempowerment.

It does not follow, though, that constitutionalism more broadly conceived—skeptical constitutionalism—has no role to play in reviving a populist-progressive coalition and healing our body politic. A skeptical constitutionalist takes seriously the Preamble's commitment to the blessings of liberty as an invitation to an open-ended, pragmatic dialogue about how that promise might be realized. Part of that dialogue will be about how economic power should be distributed so as to enhance the general welfare. But the dialogue also requires taking seriously issues about the distribution of cultural power.

None of this means that progressives should silently acquiesce to the worst impulses embedded in the populist tradition. They can and must stand strong against racism, misogyny, xenophobia, and homophobia. Progressives have much to learn from populists, but populists, too, must do some learning. Importantly, though, the learning will come only when progressives are willing to defend their position on the merits and not rely on faulty constitutional compulsion.

Once these goals are accomplished, progressives and populists can begin to have a real discussion about the prerequisites for a decent society. It would be expecting too much to suppose that these conversations will produce a permanent détente. The gap between progressive and populist sensibilities is too wide and the history of conflict too fraught to produce a lasting coalition. At some future point, frustration, resentment, and anger will again drive the two sides of liberalism apart, as it always has in the past.

But if periods of rupture are part of the history of modern liberalism, so too are periods when contradictions have been papered over and old divisions patched up. An overlapping consensus has emerged in the past, and the skeptic's constitution can facilitate its emergence in the future. Temporary though it may be, such a consensus is more important now than ever before, as we face the looming possibility of social and constitutional disintegration.

SEVEN

Establishing a More Perfect Union

The Problem of Rights and Rhetoric

The Framers of the Constitution made a syntactical mistake: "perfect" is an absolute, so there cannot be "more" or "less" perfect unions. A mistake—but a generative one. The phrase "more perfect" suggests the potential for perfection already immanent in the enterprise, but it also suggests an ongoing striving for perfection never actually achieved. In other words, the phrase captures the constitutional skeptic's attraction to radical possibilities close enough at hand to motivate political action but always just out of reach. Like Sisyphus, the constitutional skeptic must create meaning out of the striving itself, but like Zeno, he understands the paradoxical fact that Achilles will never catch the tortoise.

What kind of constitution would a skeptic endorse to facilitate this endless striving? Assuredly not a constitution that pretends to have already created a perfect union. Not one that provides pre-fabricated answers that allow us to escape from striving. Not one that purports to predetermine the final outcome of our struggle, as if any outcome could be final.

Instead, a skeptic's constitution provides a framework for a polity whose citizens can live in relative peace even as they argue over unsettled, fundamental issues. It is a constitution that permits all of us to pledge allegiance to it precisely because it does not resolve the hard questions that divide us. If those questions were finally resolved, there would no longer be union, perfect or otherwise. A constitution that settled the argument in one way or another would produce losers who have no incentive to remain in the game. A skeptic's constitution forms a more perfect union by leaving the outcome permanently unsettled even as it provides hope to people with divergent views that they might eventually prevail.

Fragments of our constitutional tradition support this version of constitutionalism, but for the most part, our constitutional impulses have pushed us in the opposite direction. Instead of viewing the Constitution as facilitating discussion with no predetermined outcome, we have weaponized it and used it as a cudgel against our political opponents. Instead of encouraging humility, skepticism, and engagement with others, the Constitution has made us more self-righteous, less tolerant, and more isolated from our fellow inhabitants.

The rhetoric of constitutional rights contributes in important ways to these unfortunate outcomes. By their very nature, claims of constitutional rights shut down the kinds of respectful discussion that should go on in a healthy democracy. An argument over rights is not likely to be friendly. Saying, for example, that there is a right to carry a gun is very different from saying that, all things considered, we would live in a better society if people carried guns. The latter claim invites us to talk about consequences and empirics. People can have friendly, if vigorous, disagreements about questions like that. The former claim directs our attention to something much more basic that is disconnected from actual outcomes—to what it means to be an American or even a human being. Constitutional "rights" are foundational. They invoke "self-evident truths" and therefore implicitly raise questions about the moral capacity of skeptics, for whom the truths are not self-evident.

To see the point, consider a controversial law review article written twenty-five years ago by two social conservatives, Robert

George, a political science professor at Princeton, and Gerald Bradley, a law professor at Notre Dame.[1] They believe that gay marriage is a very bad idea. Why? Well, because, they say, legitimate sexual intercourse is "of the procreative type," and it "may [not] legitimately be instrumentalized to any extrinsic end."[2] Gay sex, they think, does just that.

Because they are academics, their article is filled with dense argumentation. Ultimately, though, they make a startlingly honest admission:

> Intrinsic value cannot, strictly speaking, be demonstrated. . . . [T]he value of intrinsic goods cannot be derived through a middle term. Hence, if the intrinsic value of marriage, knowledge, or any other basic human good is to be affirmed, it must be grasped in noninferential acts of understanding. . . . In the end, we think, one either understands that spousal genital intercourse has a special significance as instantiating a basic, noninstrumental value, or something blocks that understanding and one does not perceive correctly.[3]

Now, to be clear, like many others (or at least like virtually all of the people I hang out with), I find this "argument"—the scare quotes make the point—question-begging and unconvincing. Indeed, I would use stronger words. It is ridiculous, bigoted, small-minded, and authoritarian. But whether I am right about this or not, it is important to explore the fact that I and many others will feel called upon to use these adjectives. A discussion about gay marriage at the foundational level is not likely to be friendly.

Nor is a foundational response by supporters of gay marriage likely to make things better. We say that gay sexual relationships, like straight sexual relationships, have the potential to promote love, connection, and human flourishing, and that these, too, are noninstrumental goods. We add, for good measure, that "one either understands that [gay relationships] have a special significance as instantiating a basic, noninstrumental value, or something blocks that understanding and one does not perceive correctly." And where are we then?

The point is not that people in ordinary political discourse should always avoid claims like these. And the point is certainly not that people should abstain from using political means to achieve ends grounded in foundational beliefs. There is nothing wrong with gay rights advocates pushing to advance their agenda in the political realm, and nothing wrong with cultural conservatives pushing theirs.

But advancing claims based on constitutional *rights* imposes a cost on our polity, and the cost does not always outweigh the benefit. When we get to the level of foundational rights, the liberal discourse that we depend upon gives out. I believe to my core that gay rights advocates are correct and that Bradley and George are deeply and tragically wrong. But, when it comes down to it, I cannot offer Bradley and George a reason for that belief that I can credibly expect them to accept—what the political philosopher John Rawls called a "public reason."

Perhaps rights claims would be worthwhile if they actually changed people's minds. In fact, millions of Americans have changed their minds about gay rights. But that change has not come about because of constitutionally based arguments about rights. Instead, and just as Bradley and George claim, the change is rooted in "noninferential acts of understanding." With the collapse of the closet, many straight people have come to see and appreciate the humanity of their gay, lesbian, trans, bi, and queer friends, neighbors, and relatives. These changes in attitude are the result of experience, not constitutional exegesis. The process has proceeded in much the way that cultural conservatives and pro-choice advocates have advanced their respective agendas: by forcing us actually to see fetuses and the abortive procedures that kill them, or by showing us what a coat hanger can do to a woman's internal organs.

The general point, then, is that the assertion of constitutional rights tends to divide rather than to convince, to block rather than to encourage the "noninferential acts of understanding" that do have the power to convince. Rights talk is often abstract and disengaged from actual experience. Foundational beliefs are not things that people can be talked into. And focusing on foundations tends to distract us from the possibility of seeing the results of our laws in concrete and specific terms. Arguing about foundational beliefs obstructs agreement on less basic matters, like what effect a policy actually has and how it changes the lives of real people. In short, rights talk gets in the way when we try to create a more perfect union. Looking at two basic categories of rights claims—the claim to equality and the claim to liberty—helps to illustrate the idea that invoking constitutional "rights" impedes constructive discussion of what would actually advance equality and liberty in contemporary America.

At the most abstract level, a commitment to equality is neither controversial nor useful in resolving real-world disputes. We can all agree with Shylock that he, too, has "hands, organs, dimensions, senses, affections, passions," and that if you prick him, he, too, bleeds.[4] We can all also agree to disagree about what, as a logical matter, follows from this commonality. As we've seen, a core commitment to the moral equality of all humans (and what about animals?) tells us nothing about conflicting particularist preferences, nothing about unequal distribution, and nothing about how to account for differences in need and desert.

Equality arguments typically start with a question about why two people—or, more often, two groups of people—should or shouldn't be treated differently.[5] "Johnny can stay up until nine o'clock. Why can't I?" "Straight people can marry. Why can't gay people?" Answers are always possible: "Johnny can stay up later because he is older than you. When you are older, you can stay up, too." Different treatment is justified if the people or groups of people are differently situated. The problem, though, is that any two people or any two groups of people are both the same and different in an infinite number of ways. It follows that equality arguments hinge on whether the differences are relevant. "Johnny can stay up later because he is older than you" feels relevant. "Johnny can stay up later because his first name begins with *J* and your first name begins with *L*" does not.

It follows that to make an equality argument, the advocate must appeal to some uncontroversial standard of relevance. Suppose, for example, the response is "Straight people can marry because they engage in marital sexual intercourse of the procreative type. Gay people can't marry because they don't." That's a difference, all right, but is it a relevant difference? As we've already seen, its relevance turns on questions of "noninferential understanding" that are not part of the tool kit for constitutional argumentation.

This turns out to be a big problem for equality arguments. If they are meant to settle questions that are truly controversial, they are bound to fail, because the arguments themselves cannot separate relevant differences from irrelevant ones. Foundational equality claims replicate the underlying dispute and exacerbate it. They cannot settle the argument.

Suppose that all agree that two groups of people are relevantly similar, and that the equality argument therefore succeeds. There is an additional problem with advancing an equality claim. The claim can be resolved in one of two ways: we can make the disadvantaged group better off, or we can make the advantaged group worse off. Insofar as we are concerned solely with equality, both responses are equally effective.[6]

Years ago, Georgetown University, where I teach, prohibited college students from forming a recognized student organization to promote gay rights. Outraged students went to the university president and pointed out to him that the law school recognized similar organizations. They asked the equality question: if promotion of gay rights is compatible with the university's mission on one campus, why isn't it so on another campus? The president was momentarily stumped and responded that he would have to think about their point. The next day, he had an answer: "I've thought about it, and you are completely right. There is no relevant difference. From now on, gay rights organizations at the law school won't be recognized either."

On occasion, the Supreme Court has answered equality questions in a similar fashion. In the nineteenth century, during the days of "separate but equal," African American parents filed a lawsuit premised on the equal protection clause. They claimed that their community funded a white high school but no Black high school. The Court rejected the claim on the ground that the equality argument would be fully satisfied by closing the white school. And that result, the Court insisted, would make African Americans no better off.[7]

It would be comforting to dismiss this argument as the kind of tendentious claptrap that we have outgrown. A much more recent Supreme Court case demonstrates that this problem has not gone away. In 2017, the Supreme Court decided *Sessions v. Morales-Santana*,[8] where it confronted a statute dealing with the citizenship of children born to unmarried parents when only one parent was a United States citizen. The law provided that if the child's father was a United States citizen, the child was entitled to citizenship if the father had lived in the United States for five years prior to the child's birth. By contrast, if the mother was a United States citizen, she could transmit citizenship to her child if she had lived in the United States for only one year.

In an opinion written by Justice Ginsburg, the Court held that this gender-based distinction violated equal protection. But, having found that the unequal treatment was unconstitutional, the Court nonetheless refused to mandate the more generous standard. Instead, it imposed the more restrictive standard on the children of mothers who were citizens as well as on the children of fathers who were citizens. Thus, even though the plaintiff "won" his case, people like him did not benefit from the victory. Tragically, citizenship is now available to a smaller number of people than enjoyed the benefit before the Court acted.

Economists have a term for how to make decisions in situations like this, derived from the name of the Italian economist Vilfredo Pareto. "Pareto efficiency" mandates that we should make a change when at least one person will be better off and no one will be worse off.[9] So a change that makes at least one person worse off while making no one better off flunks the Pareto test, and presumably no rational person would favor such a change. At least at first, it seems that the Court's decision in *Morales-Santana* flunks the Pareto test. It makes some people worse off and no one better off.

But, like much economic theorizing, the Pareto standard begs an important question. Couldn't one say that a person is made better off simply by the fact that the person is no longer treated unequally? Even though men like Morales-Santana failed to get citizenship for their children, perhaps they are better off because their suffering is now shared by women whose children are also denied citizenship.

This claim can't be dismissed entirely. Who is to say that being treated as an equal does not make a person better off, even if it is not accompanied by any material change?[10] A common complaint about the death penalty is that it is imposed discriminatorily on African Americans. Suppose that the government responded to this complaint by executing more people who were not African Americans. Would this response violate the Pareto standard? Perhaps not. If the change conveyed the social message that Black lives matter, executing more people who were not African Americans might make Black people better off.

Still, it quickly becomes clear that, in many contexts, this resolution of equality claims will seem irrational and mean-spirited. Does anyone suppose that Georgetown college students were made better off by the knowledge that Georgetown law students were now prevented from forming groups defending gay rights? Schadenfreude is a powerful emotion, particularly with respect to sibling rivals, so perhaps Johnny's younger brother will feel some immediate satisfaction if Johnny, too, must go to bed early. But these feelings are premised on the ancient fallacy that two wrongs make a right. The same point holds even in the context of capital punishment. If, as I believe, the death penalty is an evil, can we really feel better about things if the evil is imposed on more people?

People who make foundational equality arguments are essentially making a political wager: yes, it is possible that the government might ratchet benefits down for everyone, but "equalizers" are willing to bet that the government will instead choose to ratchet benefits in the other direction, essentially "truing them up." If put to the choice of executing more non–African Americans or fewer African Americans, these people predict, the government will choose to execute fewer African Americans.

Like all bets, this one may not pay off. The other side might call the bluff of equality's advocates by making things worse for everyone. That is what happened in *Morales-Santana*. When equality advocates miscalculate, they end up making the world worse for everyone. In many situations, however, the risk that the political calculation will fail is vanishingly small. Theoretically, the government could have responded to an equality argument for gay marriage by abolishing marriage for straight people, but few people thought that this was a serious risk.[11] Often, the political bet is more than worth taking.

The important point for the constitutional skeptic, though, is that when people make this bet, they are not really making equality claims. An authentic advocate of equality would be equally satisfied by ratcheting up or by ratcheting down. Both moves fully satisfy the demand for equal treatment. If an advocate will be satisfied only by ratcheting up, she is not actually making an equality claim. The argument is therefore dishonest. People who make it are using equality to advance some other end. The end might be worthy, but advocates for it ought to defend it on its merits. For example, if, as I believe, the death penalty is evil, then I have an obligation to defend that position when challenged by advocates of capital punishment. Making phony equality arguments that purport to rely on the text of the Constitution's equal protection clause illegitimately relieves me of this obligation. For this reason, claims to constitutional equality often distract us from the issues that ought to engage us.

Assertions of constitutional *liberty* rights also obstruct the kind of dialogue necessary to make our union more perfect. We cannot have an organized society if people are at liberty to do whatever they want. Assertions of a liberty right to torture innocent children, drive on the wrong side of the road, or refuse to pay taxes are ridiculous on their face. Advocates for a constitutional liberty right therefore need a metric to determine *which* liberty interests have the status of "rights" and which are relegated to the realm of "mere license."

Constitutionalists embrace three different solutions to this problem, none of which passes the skeptic's sniff test. First, and most obviously, they argue for deference to a canonical text that makes the decision for us. The United States Constitution explicitly protects certain liberties—freedom of speech, freedom of religion, and freedom from unreasonable search and seizure, for example. It does not explicitly protect other liberties—the liberty to raise one's family free from unreasonable government interference, to obtain an abortion, or to pursue an ordinary occupation, for example. Perhaps the Framers made the wrong choices, constitutionalists will say, but we might avoid the problem of trying to make the right ones by simply deferring to their judgment.

For all the reasons that Constitution-worship in general is a bad idea, this example of it fails. The Framers had some very good ideas, but they also had some very bad ones, beginning with the idea that some people should be at liberty to own other people. The Framers were not infallible, and they also could not have known how the choices they made several centuries ago would intersect with modern conditions that they did not contemplate. They should not be permitted to rule us from the grave.

Furthermore, it turns out that the Framers themselves did not mean to bind us to their judgments about which liberties were fundamental. The Constitution's Ninth Amendment provides that "[t]he enumeration in the Constitution, of certain rights, shall not be construed to deny or disparage others retained by the people." A large scholarly literature disputes the meaning of this opaque sentence, but, at a minimum, it must mean that the Framers left open the possibility of rights "retained by the people" that are not specifically enumerated in the Constitution. Other clauses of the Constitution lead to a similar conclusion. For example, the Fourteenth Amendment guarantees that "the privileges or immunities of citizens of the United States" will not be subject to state abridgment, and the Fifth and Fourteenth Amendments prohibit deprivations of liberty without due process. These capacious phrases are not self-defining and pretty obviously invite modern supplementation. Indeed, the Preamble's promise of "a more perfect union" suggests, if it does not compel, modern definitions of liberty that will make the union more perfect.

A second solution put forth by advocates of the Constitution asks us to make determinations about which liberty interests are "fundamental" or required by "natural law" or essential to human flourishing. A long and not entirely happy history of efforts along these lines runs from Thomas Aquinas in the Middle Ages through philosophers including John Rawls,[12] John Finnis,[13] Martha Nussbaum,[14] and Amartya Sen[15] in the modern period. These thinkers have tried to identify which liberties human beings are entitled to simply because of their status as humans.

One obvious difficulty with this effort is that these thinkers have been unable to agree on an answer to this question. Are individuals entitled to resist taxation that supports programs they oppose on religious grounds? To keep and control property that they rightfully own? To speak words that harm others? Do they have the liberty to marry (and if so, what about marrying a close relative or more than one person)? What about the liberty to raise children as they choose (and if they have this liberty, does that mean that they can subject their female children to genital mutilation—and if that is an abuse of liberty, then what about male circumcision)? Do they have the right to drink water that does not contain fluoride? To drink water that does not contain lead?

A popular and intuitively appealing way to settle this disagreement is by resort to what political philosophers call the "harm principle." Often traced to the writings of the nineteenth-century reformer and political theorist John Stuart Mill,[16] the principle asserts that individuals have the right to engage in conduct that does not harm others. Modern economists make a similar point when they talk about "negative externalities." If an individual's conduct imposes injury on others (say, by releasing noxious fumes that poison his neighbors), then the state may intervene. But neoclassical economists think that the preferred method of intervention is by making the individual "internalize" the costs of his conduct (say, by paying the victim to compensate for the injury). If all the costs are "internalized"—if the individual imposes no *uncompensated* harms on others—then the individual has the liberty to engage in the activity.

Mill thought that for the most part, individuals knew what was best for themselves and that, even if they didn't, government intervention was likely to be badly motivated and to make things worse rather than better. But modern libertarians have turned Mill's insight into a matter of rights. For them, human liberty means the ability to be free from external constraints except in circumstances where one's conduct is imposing unjustified constraints on others.

Unfortunately, though, the principle doesn't really afford the Court much guidance in deciding rights cases. It is too narrow to be of much use, because it fails to recognize important rights claims that do impose burdens on others. If a poor person has a right to be free from starvation, then a rich person must be taxed in order to purchase the necessary food. Does it really violate core constitutional principles to deprive the rich person of the liberty of owning a third vacation home by taxing her to feed the poor person?

The harm principle is also too broad because it elevates to the status of a right harmless conduct that no one would claim is especially valuable or important—say, the "right" to pick one's nose or to purchase a useless product. As a prudential matter, it may be a waste of valuable time and resources to regulate conduct like this. It does not follow that the regulation is always foolish or that it implicates foundational questions concerning our humanity.

Finally, and most importantly, the harm principle is indeterminate. By itself, it provides no definition of what constitutes "harm" or a logical stopping point for recognizing claims of injury. The Supreme Court, for example, has held that a person who has devoted her career to the study of endangered species suffers no constitutional harm if the species goes extinct,[17] and that African Americans suffer no harm when other members of their race suffer from discrimination.[18] On the other hand, the Court has also held that white individuals suffer a constitutionally recognized injury when denied admission to a college that has an affirmative action plan, even though the plan had nothing to do with their rejection (they would have been rejected anyway).[19]

Many observers believe that these decisions are incoherent and unprincipled, and, indeed, they are. Yet one can't help sympathizing with the justices, who have given themselves an impossible task. On the one hand, they do not want to acknowledge that anyone who feels unhappy about a situation has suffered the kind of injury that deserves constitutional recognition. On the other hand, there is no metric readily at hand to separate worthy instances of injury from unworthy ones.

Consider again the case of gay marriage. When Elizabeth Warren was asked how she would answer an "old-fashioned" supporter who thought that marriage should be between one man and one woman, she replied, "Well, I'm going to assume it's a guy who said that. And I'm going to say, then just marry one woman. I'm cool with that." After the audience laughed and applauded, she added "Assuming you can find one."[20] Warren's joke invoked the harm principle. The implicit claim is that consensual marriages do no harm to outsiders, and therefore people are at liberty to form them.

But one could argue that "old-fashioned" opponents of gay marriage do experience harm. For starters, some of these opponents live in sincere dread of the punishment that God will inflict on our country for allowing these marriages to occur. Perhaps we can treat these claims to harm as too fanciful to take seriously, but there are other sorts of "harm" that are more difficult to dismiss. The recognition of gay marriage and of the more general legitimacy of gay relations changes our culture in subtle but real ways that some people experience as harmful. Anyone who doubts this might think about the changes in how all of us live produced by, say, the invention of the television or the ubiquity of computers and cellphones. Not purchasing a television, computer, or cellphone is no defense against these dramatic changes. People who yearn for a culture that no longer exists undoubtedly experience the changes as inflicting harm.

What we need for the harm theory to work, then, is a definition of the types of harm that are legitimate. One might say, for example, that it is legitimate for African Americans to feel injury when they see their brothers and sisters murdered in the street by the police, but illegitimate for religious conservatives to feel harm when they are forced to live in a society where gay marriage is common. In obvious ways, however, these judgments merely reintroduce the disagreement about foundational rights that causes the problem in the first place.

It is worth reemphasizing that claims to constitutionally conferred rights are not usually invitations to a friendly conversation. The assertion that certain harms "don't count" because the rights at stake are "fundamental" or "self-evident" precludes the possibility of reasonable disagreement. The claim that a right is fundamental excuses the proponent from the ordinary civic obligation of offering reasons in support of her conclusions. As legal philosopher Ronald Dworkin asserted years ago, rights are "trumps."[21] They do not permit the kind of balancing of one interest against another that is common when what is at stake is mere public policy. Instead, rights must be respected, if not quite "though the

heavens may fall," then at least in the absence of a truly compelling and unusual interest on the other side.

This claim for rights is what gives them their power and dis-
tinctiveness, but the claim also makes rights problematic. For
example, philosophers have plausibly argued that health and
freedom from hunger, pain, and despair are basic goods necessary
for human flourishing. But at what cost? If protection of a small
percentage of the population from disease requires a permanent
shutting down of the U.S. economy, does it really follow that we
are obligated to incur the cost? Does the right to freedom from
pain entail a requirement to devote a huge percentage of the gross
national product to the development of more effective analgesics?

A related difficulty emerges when rights run into each other.
The problem becomes especially acute if, as many modern rights
advocates argue, the Constitution mandates positive rights to government assistance. The Supreme Court's well-known decision
in *DeShaney v. Winnebago County Department of Social Services*[22] illustrates the point. Social workers in Winnebago County
received repeated reports that four-year-old Joshua DeShaney
was being abused by his father. With Kafkaesque efficiency, they
carefully documented the reports but didn't actually do anything
about them. Eventually, the father beat Joshua so severely that the
child suffered permanent brain injury that left him with profound
developmental disabilities and in an institution for life.

Joshua and his mother sued, claiming that the state's failure
to act violated Joshua's constitutional due process right to liberty.
The Court rejected that claim, but many progressives have attacked the decision on the ground that the right to liberty should
include protection from private violence.

Suppose that the Supreme Court had upheld the claim. The
result, no doubt, would be that future social workers would be
much more ready to intervene when confronted with evidence
of abuse. The very purpose of the holding would be to provide
incentives for government employees to intervene.

But what if the incentives are too strong? Might a social

worker, worried about the possibility of a large damage award, act against parents who in fact had done nothing wrong?[23] The risk is especially worrisome if, as is often the case, social workers are dealing with parents from marginalized or minority communities or who choose nonstandard methods of child rearing. Might not this overreaction threaten another constitutional right—the right of parents to raise their children free from undue government interference?

Other rights claims pose similar problems. There are few things that are completely predictable in life, but here is one of them: when the governor of Rhode Island threatened to prevent New Yorkers from entering the state so as to reduce transmission of the coronavirus, within nanoseconds Harvard law professor and civil libertarian Laurence Tribe was on MSNBC asserting that the ban violated the constitutional right of New York citizens to travel. The point is fair enough, but what about the right of Rhode Island citizens to effective government protection against a serious health risk?

The same problems attach to rights that the Constitution explicitly guarantees. Consider the Fourth Amendment right of the people "to be secure in their persons, houses, papers, and effects against unreasonable searches and seizures." The Supreme Court has interpreted the provision to mean that police must obtain warrants (unless the case comes within an exception to the general rule) and demonstrate probable cause before searching or seizing.[24] But suppose the most serious threat to the security of persons, houses, papers, and effects comes not from the police, but from burglars, robbers, and rapists. In that event, rigid warrant and probable cause requirements might obstruct, rather than vindicate, constitutional rights.

What all these examples have in common is that they require balancing. An economist would say that we should continue "purchasing" units of one good until the "price" of the forfeited unit of the second good exceeds the additional value that we receive in return. Needless to say, this is not the rhetoric of rights. Instead, it is the sort of cost-benefit analysis that rights rhetoric is designed to avoid.

To be clear, there may well be optimal solutions in these cases. Indeed, economists make their living by trying to find optimal solutions. With carefully calibrated damage awards, we might encourage social workers to take abuse claims just seriously enough without also encouraging them to overreact. Perhaps there are other, effective ways to protect public health without impinging on rights to travel. Smart policing might actually reduce crime rates by showing respect for the privacy of neighborhood citizens, thereby enlisting their cooperation.

In a well-functioning republic, pursuing a more perfect union, citizens should engage in good-faith debate about solutions like these. Not every game is zero-sum. Even strong claims on both sides can often be accommodated, so long as compromise and imperfect reconciliation are on the table. The problem with rights talk is that it has a tendency to take these sorts of solutions off the table. Because constitutional rights present themselves as absolutes, they lead to nonnegotiable demands. If not totally vindicated, then "rights" turn out not to be rights at all, but mere interests that can be sacrificed for the greater good. The very thing that makes rights talk attractive—the resistance of rights to ordinary interest group deals—also makes the talk profoundly dangerous.

Perhaps, then, we should adopt a third solution to the liberty problem: rather than flee from the contingent nature of rights, we should embrace contingency. We might dethrone rights claims from their absolute status and treat them as no more than a demand that government provide a good reason before they are disregarded. This approach is important in European constitutional law. For example, the European Court of Human Rights has developed the idea of a "margin of appreciation," which balances rights claims against national interests.[25] Similarly, the Canadian Charter of Rights and Freedoms contains a "notwithstanding clause," which permits governments to override rights claims for renewable five-year periods.[26] And even in our own constitutional culture, which purports to treat rights as absolutes, there are none-theless many circumstances where, implicitly or explicitly, the Court balances these rights claims against other interests.

The difficulty with this approach is that it solves the problem by so diluting rights claims that they turn into mere claims of interest. It makes decisions involving rights no different from ordinary decisions. After all, whenever the government acts or fails to act, it is appropriate to call it to account by asking whether there is sufficient reason for its decisions. That is true for decisions large and small—when the government does something as unimportant as changing the name of a local post office or as important as going to war.

True, recognizing the contingent nature of rights deems certain sorts of claims quite important and therefore counts them for more when balanced against other claims. But this is the same approach we use to deal with ordinary interests: if farmers have depended on wheat subsidies for generations, there is a presumption that they have an interest in the subsidies, and that the subsidies should not be suddenly terminated absent a strong reason. Yet no one would say that they have a "right" to the subsidies. If this is all that rights claims amount to, then they have become mere claims of interest.

When we are talking about depriving farmers of subsidies they have long enjoyed, we generally expect the political branches to make the decision. The special status of rights claims might still be salvaged if we gave courts the power to decide when rights, rather than mere interests, are at stake. For example, law professor Randy Barnett has proposed a "presumption of liberty" frame, in which the government would have to convince judges to overrule rights claims, while mere "interests" would be within the purview of the political branches, not the courts.[27]

But giving nonelected justices the duty to make final determinations about government policy amounts to a wholesale abandonment of representative democracy. The problem is especially acute if one recognizes (as Barnett does not) positive rights. The government fails to do an infinite number of things that it might do to promote human flourishing. Giving courts the authority to determine what laws the government should enact would, literally, turn the courts into legislatures. We can avoid this problem only if we could agree on a more limited domain where "rights" and not merely "interests" were at stake. For all the reasons explored earlier, there is little hope of achieving such an agreement.

And even if we could limit the courts to deciding issues about truly fundamental rights, the claim that this sort of interest balancing can be scientific and uncontroversial is ridiculous. Balancing necessarily implies a unit of conversion between the two goods being balanced. We can't decide how many apples we should give up for a specified number of oranges without first deciding how much we value apples and oranges. There is no "scientific" way to do that. Nor is there a scientific answer to the question of, say, whether the prevention of tooth decay is worth more than the deprivation of the liberty not to ingest fluoride, or whether a marginal decrease in highway deaths is worth depriving people of the right to drive faster than sixty miles per hour.

Because these are not scientific questions, judges who purport to answer them are necessarily imposing their values on the rest of us. They are, in other words, invading space that we Americans should occupy when we strive to make our union more perfect. Worse yet, they are doing so in a fashion that discourages real dialogue. It is not, after all, just the opinion of the justices that, say, the costs of campaign finance regulation outweigh the benefits. That judgment instead is said to reflect a balance commanded by the Constitution. When the Court decides issues in this way, it is hardly inviting a discussion among equals. Instead, it is demanding obedience. Americans should not put up with the arrogance of that demand.

Human beings are not about to stop claiming that certain rights are fundamental and grounded in the Constitution, nor should they. Law professor Patricia Williams has written movingly about how the assertion of rights transformed the consciousness of African Americans who had been deprived of their very right to be human.[28] From John Hancock to Martin Luther King Jr. to Edith Windsor, we have a long tradition of Americans who have inspired and mobilized others with rights claims. There are times when and places where it is appropriate to make rights claims. There are times when and places where we can do no other.

But not every time or place is appropriate for a rights claim, and making such a claim should be the last resort rather than the first. Before making such claims, we need to understand that the claims have at best a limited capacity to persuade. Moreover, when we make these claims, we encourage others to make similar claims. Too many such claims, advanced with too much moral fervor, have the potential to destroy the polity. For that reason, before resorting to the rhetoric of constitutional rights, we should be certain that the issue cannot be resolved by other means of persuasion, and by the ordinary give-and-take of political bargaining.

Suppose someone heeds all these cautions but nonetheless decides that she must make a claim based on her constitutional rights. Even then, a constitutional skeptic will argue for the virtues of humility and doubt. Pursuing a more perfect union means that when we fight for our own conception of rights, we also recognize that the conception is held contingently, and that no one has full access to immutable truth. It means insisting that elite institutions have no right to dictate our future and that no piece of parchment contains all the answers. Most of all, it means understanding that we share our union with others who disagree with us about basics and that, for that reason, even as we pursue perfection, actually achieving it will not be our destiny.

EIGHT

Insuring Domestic Tranquility

The Problem of Violence

The first responsibility of government is to avoid chaos—what seventeenth-century political philosopher Thomas Hobbes called "a war of all against all."[1] It is therefore no surprise that the Constitution's Framers included a promise to "insure domestic tranquility" in the Preamble.

So how are we doing? Have the dialectical grants of and restrictions on government power that the Framers embedded in the constitutional text ensured domestic tranquility? Of course, no one wants complete tranquility. As constitutional skeptics understand, progress comes from tumult and discord, and an end to struggle means paralysis and decline. Still, for the struggle to be useful, some boundaries and inhibitions are necessary. Unrest is productive, but chaos and violence are not.

The right question, then, is whether the Constitution provides boundaries, powers, and restrictions that make struggle productive instead of a "war of all against all." Do we have sufficient freedom from fear, violence, and oppression to go about our ordinary lives and participate in political and other projects? Unfortunately, for many Americans, the answer is no. Most of us are not in a "state of nature" where, as Hobbes put it, life is "nasty, brutish, and short."[2] But some of us have been historically, and, shockingly, some of us still are. Many other Americans simply do not enjoy sufficient tranquility to allow for full human flourishing. It's no surprise to the constitutional skeptic that, despite the Preamble's promise, the text of the Constitution hasn't actually ensured domestic tranquility for all Americans.

This problem is not new. The men who gathered in Philadelphia had some particular and contemporary reasons for worrying about domestic tranquility. The new republic was fragile and founded on revolutionary ideals that encouraged resistance to established authority—sentiments that could not be quickly extinguished once the war against Great Britain ended. The country was in the midst of a severe economic downturn that produced serious social unrest. The Framers were badly shaken by Shays's Rebellion, an uprising by financially pressed farmers in Massachusetts that ended in a full-blown military confrontation. The rebellion contributed to the more general sense that things were coming apart at the seams and that the Articles of Confederation had to be replaced.

So the Framers backed their promise to "insure domestic tranquility" with provisions that created a much stronger central government. Specific constitutional language required the president to "take care that the laws are faithfully executed,"[3] and to serve as "the Commander in Chief of the . . . Militia of the several States, when called into the actual Service of the United States."[4] The Constitution also guarantees to the states "[protection] against domestic Violence."[5]

These measures were designed to protect the country from the sort of private violence that threatened domestic tranquility. But opponents of the Constitution feared that the newly empowered federal government might, itself, threaten domestic tranquility by abusing its citizens. They were concerned about the risk of *public* violence, in the form of abuse by the government of suspected criminals, dissidents, and other outsiders. At first, defenders of the Constitution including James Madison and Alexander Hamilton thought that constitutional protections against government abuse were unnecessary or might even be harmful. Ultimately, though, Madison changed his mind and, in the first Congress, introduced amendments that balanced the new empowerment of the central government with a guarantee of rights designed to control abuse.

A surprising number of the rights were attempts to regulate use of the national military and criminal prosecutions—means of state violence that might threaten domestic tranquility. Among the most prominent: the Second Amendment's protection for state militias, the Third Amendment's limitations on quartering soldiers in private homes, the Fourth Amendment's guarantee that the people would be "secure in their persons, houses, papers, and effects from unreasonable search and seizure," the Fifth Amendment's privilege against self-incrimination, and the Sixth Amendment's guarantee of a right to counsel and jury trials in criminal cases.

Clearly, however, the original Constitution did not ensure domestic tranquility for people of color. In that sense, the text of the Constitution fails utterly to live up to the Preamble's promise. From the country's founding, African Americans have been the targets of both private and public violence, bought and sold, forced to work against their will, raped, lynched, killed by the police, and subject to other state-sanctioned forms of terror. While in recent decades we have made important progress in correcting these evils, the ongoing disproportionate targeting of communities of color by law enforcement, mass incarceration, and police killings of unarmed Black men and women underscore the ineffectiveness of words on a piece of paper to make high-minded ideals a reality on the ground.

For the majority of Americans exempt from this discriminatory treatment, one could argue that our Constitution has created a more or less stable framework within which we can argue about our disagreements without resorting to violence. More broadly, defenders of our constitutional structure will point out that in the almost two and a half centuries since the Constitution was ratified, we have had only one civil war. There have been no military coups. At least so far, officeholders have willingly given up their offices at the end of their terms. People are not (usually) rioting in the streets. Most Americans, most of the time, are able to go about their daily lives calmly and peaceably.

And yet . . .

Perhaps most contemporary Americans are not haunted by anxieties as serious as those that influenced the Framers, but it would be ignoring obvious facts to say that our domestic tranquility is altogether secure. According to an NBC/*Wall Street Journal* poll released in June 2020, 80 percent of voters thought that the nation was "out of control."[6] In recent years, widespread commentary has addressed the unraveling of the American experiment and the collapse of democratic norms. If not quite mainstream, speculation about secession and about resistance to a peaceable change in power has become much more plausible. The theoretical possibility of violent resistance to democratic outcomes became a frightening reality on the afternoon of January 6, 2021, when angry insurrectionists stormed the Capitol and temporarily delayed the certification of Electoral College votes for president. Around the same time, revulsion against the spectacle of white police officers murdering unarmed Black men in the streets produced not only peaceful and lawful protests, but also significant acts of violence.

Of the many reasons for our current worries about domestic tranquility, an important one relates to the extraordinarily high level of both public and private violence that still exists in this country. Perhaps the Founders' creation of a strong central government and the first Congress's approval of the Bill of Rights made things better at the beginning, but they hardly solved the problem. It is true that most Americans, most of the time, can go about their daily lives without immediate fear for their personal safety. But many Americans all the time and virtually all Americans some of the time cannot. This is not a normal or necessary state of affairs. For too many of us, the promise of domestic tranquility has not been kept. Many of us feel threatened by criminals, by the police, or by both. How can one avoid skepticism about a constitution that fails to protect us from these reasonable fears?

The evidence of this failure is all around us. We can start with the crime rate. The United States has the 45th highest rate of crime among 132 surveyed countries in the world. We do worse than every other Western democracy, as well as worse than many non-Western countries including Egypt, Iran, Iraq, Indonesia, and Botswana.[7] We rank 11th out of 126 for the most rapes[8] and 18th out of 107 for the most robberies.[9]

Crime statistics in general are notoriously imprecise, and these particular statistics may be distorted by under- and overreporting in some countries. Moreover, in the last few decades, the American violent crime rate has declined significantly. Politicians and local news outlets regularly exaggerate the risk of crime for their own selfish purposes. Still, many Americans remain rightly fearful of criminal violence. The fear is made worse by the fact that the violence is not evenly distributed among the population. Americans who live in urban areas—especially Black Americans who live in urban areas—suffer from astonishingly high rates of criminal depredation and homicidal gang violence.

We have also paid an unacceptable price for whatever success we have had in controlling crime. From 1975 to 2009, the number of people incarcerated in the United States grew from 380,000 to 2.25 million, an increase of almost 600 percent.[10] On a per capita basis, these numbers put us far ahead of any other nation in the world.[11] And for the latter part of this period, when most of the increase has come about, the growth in incarceration actually occurred against the backdrop of a declining crime rate.[12]

As disturbing as these outcomes are, they understate the impact on the African American community and the violence that has been perpetrated against people of color from the country's founding. Today, Black men are six times more likely to be incarcerated than white men.[13] Twenty percent of Black men born between 1965 and 1969 have been imprisoned by the time they reach their early thirties.[14]

Hyperincarceration is part of the problem, but not all of it. African Americans live in the worst of both worlds. They are disproportionately harmed by crime, but they are also dispropor- tionately harmed by police misconduct. In 2015, *The Guardian* built a comprehensive database of police killings in the United States. During the first twenty-four days of that year, U.S. police killed fifty-nine people. By contrast, police in the United King- dom killed fifty-four people over the past *twenty-four years*. Po- lice in Stockton, California, killed three people in the first five months of 2015. Iceland, with a slightly larger population, has had one police killing in the seventy-four years of its existence.[15]

The outrages of police officers murdering Black people in the streets, along with the daily indignities produced by discrimina- tory traffic stops, stop-and-frisk, and harassment for minor "quality of life" offenses, are facts of life for millions of African Americans and other people of color, who would scoff at the idea that our contemporary government ensures their domestic tranquility.

Other disquieting signs of pervasive violence disrupt the coun- try's domestic tranquility as well. The United States has approxi- mately ten million cases of intimate partner violence per year.[16] An estimated one in five women attending college is sexually as- saulted while there. We have approximately 120 privately owned guns per 100 residents[17]—more guns than are owned by the next twenty-five countries with the highest gun ownership combined, and 46 percent of the total number of privately held guns in the world.[18] We also lead the world in mass shootings. According to the Gun Violence Archive, there have been 2,128 mass shootings in this country since 2013, or approximately one per day.[19] And we host a large number and wide variety of armed militia groups, some of whom have been involved in well-publicized standoffs with government authorities, including the siege of the Capitol on January 6, 2021.

It would be silly to claim that our Constitution is responsible for all of these problems. Social scientists have long studied the causes of crime and violence, but proof of causation has been elusive. No doubt American violence—famously as American as apple pie—has multiple roots in our culture and history: It is related to racial and ethnic divisions as old as America itself, to our frontier heritage, to a culture of individualism, and to the economic insecurity that results from weak social programs.

Still, if the Constitution has not caused the threats to our domestic tranquility, neither has it remedied them. In fact, it has actually obstructed remedies that might make things better. The standard liberal story about this obstruction claims that the problem is not with the Constitution itself, but with distortions of the Constitution produced by conservative Supreme Court justices, who misread the Second Amendment concerning gun rights,[20] interpret the Fourth Amendment to give police almost unlimited discretion,[21] and have turned the Fourteenth Amendment on its head to protect practically everyone *but* African Americans.[22] If only we could go back to the halcyon days of the Warren Court, the Constitution would do a much better job of guaranteeing the peace and security that America deserves.

There is more than a little truth to this story. The modern Court has hampered efforts to control both private and public violence. Consider first private violence. With questionable textual support, and contrary to years of precedent, the Court has invented a constitutional right to own guns that complicates enactment of effective gun control legislation.[23] It has also invalidated federal legislation creating civil penalties for violence against women[24] and prohibiting possession of guns near schools.[25]

But it is the modern Court's reaction to public violence that most worries Warren Court defenders. They point out that the modern Court has expanded the stop-and-frisk doctrine in a fashion that has turned it into a program of systematic harassment of African American males.[26] It has eviscerated constitutional protection against "no knock" warrants.[27] It has sharply limited the protections against unreasonable searches and seizures[28] and against coerced confessions.[29] And it has tolerated grossly incompetent and hopelessly overworked and underfunded criminal defense attorneys, turning the right to counsel in criminal trials into a bad joke.[30]

Perhaps most egregiously, even when undisputed constitutional violations occur, the Court has too often held that the law provides no remedy for them. The absence of meaningful remedy, in turn, leaves police violence unchecked, and so undermines domestic tranquility for the portion of our population vulnerable to police misconduct. For example, together with Congress,[31] the Court has sharply limited the availability of the ancient writ of habeas corpus, which allows prisoners to challenge the reasons for their confinement. Today, a complex web of procedural rules prevents prisoners from raising legitimate constitutional claims, even when they are about to be executed.[32]

Similarly, the Court has made it next to impossible to get legal redress for discriminatory police practices. For example, it has held that evidence should not be excluded at trial even when it is seized by an officer motivated by racial animus.[33] In the civil context, it has demanded an extraordinarily high level of proof before a plaintiff challenging discriminatory policing can even see the evidence necessary to prove the claim.[34] It has dismissed as irrelevant a convincing and well-conducted study demonstrating racial discrimination in administration of the death penalty.[35] And, remarkably, in one case the Court even held that the police can constitutionally stop an individual where part of the basis for the stop is an explicit generalization about the ethnicity of the suspect.[36]

The interplay between still another set of Court rulings about remedying police abuse provides a shocking example of the Court's hypocrisy. The Court has played a cynical game of whack-a-mole, withholding one remedy on the theory that another is available, but then withdrawing that remedy when plaintiffs try to use it.

Under the Fourth Amendment, the Court has developed an "exclusionary rule" as one means of protecting citizens against public violence in the form of police misconduct. The rule prevents the prosecution from using evidence the police gained as the result of an unlawful search and seizure. But the exclusionary rule has long been the whipping boy of law-and-order conservatives, and for obvious reasons: The image of a clearly guilty defendant smirking as he leaves the courtroom a free man because the police made some technical mistake in filling out a warrant application understandably angers many Americans.

In fact, conservatives have greatly exaggerated the cost of the rule. For the most part, it deprives the government only of evidence it is not entitled to in the first place under the Fourth Amendment—evidence obtained through truly unconstitutional behavior. What critics claim to be the cost of the rule is therefore actually the cost of effective enforcement of the Fourth Amendment itself.

That said, the argument in favor of the rule is complicated, and its optics can be terrible. Conservatives on the Court have not had the gumption to completely overturn the rule, but they have added so many exceptions to it that it has become toothless. To give just a few examples, the Court has held that the exclusionary rule is unavailable when an officer relies in good faith on a constitutionally deficient warrant,[37] on an unconstitutional statute,[38] on an erroneous police database,[39] or on an erroneous judicial decision.[40] The police do not have to worry about the exclusion of illegally seized evidence used to cross-examine a defendant at trial[41] or to deport an undocumented person,[42] or in a civil case,[43] or when they unconstitutionally fail to knock before entering.[44] Evidence need not be excluded if it has an "independent source,"[45] or if it would have been discovered anyway,[46] or if its discovery is "attenuated" from the constitutional violation.[47] The bottom line is that if an officer is thinking about violating the Constitution, he can be reasonably confident that he will still be able to make some use of the evidence that he finds.

Not to worry, the justices have said. We don't need to exclude evidence in these cases. There are better and less costly methods to curb police abuse. And what are the better methods? The Court has said that the exclusionary rule is much less necessary today than it once was, because we have developed effective civil damage remedies to punish and deter unconstitutional police behavior. An injured citizen can sue police officers and recover compensation, thereby deterring wrongdoing without letting guilty criminals escape justice through the exclusion of valuable but illegally obtained evidence.[48]

In the abstract, this is a defensible position. Yet, even as they have made this claim, conservative justices have undermined the civil damage remedy by devising the doctrine of qualified immunity, which makes it next to impossible for a citizen to get a judgment against a police officer. To understand the doctrine of qualified immunity, one must first understand that police-officer defendants already enjoy all the protections available to ordinary civil defendants. They have the right to a jury trial, often before juries that are sympathetic to law enforcement. The plaintiff bears the burden of proof, and the jury must find for the police officer if the force used was reasonable under the circumstances or, even if it was not, if the officer made a reasonable mistake of fact.

Qualified immunity is a special doctrine for government officials, layered on top of all these protections. It provides that even if the officer is guilty of a constitutional violation, he cannot be held liable for money damages unless the plaintiff demonstrates violation of a right that was "clearly established" at the time the officer acted.[49]

One might think that the Fourth Amendment itself clearly establishes a right to be free from unreasonable searches and seizures, but the Court has interpreted the requirement to require a much more specific before-the-fact articulation of the right; there must be some specific prior case that, on similar facts, found a rights violation. The problem, of course, is that every case is different in some respects from every other case. The upshot, then, is that, except in the unlikely event that a plaintiff can point to a case that is essentially identical to her case, overcoming qualified immunity is an uphill battle.

The main argument for qualified immunity is that without it, the police will be "overdeterred." Fear of large monetary damages will prevent the police from engaging in perfectly lawful activity that, police officers worry, a judge or jury might later find unlawful. There is much less to this argument than might first appear. Recall that to be liable in the first place, the police must act "unreasonably." Thus a "reasonable" police officer will have nothing to fear. Moreover, officers found to be liable for damages are usually reimbursed by the governments for which they work. They are therefore free to vigorously enforce the law, confident that if they inadvertently go too far, their employer will bear the risk.

Beyond that, though, the argument again reveals the Supreme Court's stunning hypocrisy. For someone worried about overdeterrence produced by damage awards after the violation has already occurred, there is an obvious alternative solution: Why not tell the police before the fact what they may and may not do? The law has a method for accomplishing this. It is called injunctive relief. Instead of punishing officers for offenses that have already occurred, an injunction orders them not to repeat the abuse in the future.

One might think, then, that the Supreme Court would have enthusiastically embraced injunctive relief. In fact, though, nothing could be further from the truth. The Court has made injunctions against police misconduct all but impossible to obtain by holding that in most cases, plaintiffs lack "standing" to bring the action. The standing requirement is complex, but as a general matter it means that the plaintiff is not permitted to complain about an abstract grievance not personally affecting her. Instead, she must show that there is a realistic risk that she, herself, will be harmed.[50]

At first, it might seem that this requirement is clearly met in a case where the plaintiff, for example, has already been victimized by an illegal chokehold when arrested. But the Supreme Court didn't see things that way. It dismissed a request for injunctive relief by such a plaintiff. Why? In order to have standing, the Court said, a plaintiff must demonstrate not just that he had already been victimized, but also that he was *likely in the future* to again be arrested and again be subjected to a chokehold—an impossible hurdle to get over.[51]

Let's step back and look at the overall picture. The Supreme Court thinks that the exclusionary rule is unnecessary because citizens can sue the police for damages if the citizens' rights are violated. But the Court also disfavors a damages remedy because that unfairly punishes police officers after the fact. That suggests the Court would prefer a before-the-fact remedy, but no—those, too, are disfavored, because no one has standing to ask for them.

For many liberals, the conclusion to draw from all this is obvious: the Court is simply not serious about preventing widespread and serious constitutional violations by the police. If the Court were being honest with us, it would say that it actually opposes the constitutional protections. Because it is too cowardly to tell us the truth, it hides what it is doing behind the patently false argument that any remedy that might actually work imposes costs that are too great.

Unsurprisingly, this tolerance for police violence produces widespread abuse by the police and widespread cynicism on the part of the victims of the abuse. The abuse and cynicism, in turn, contribute to racial tensions and social fracture, which feed back into private violence. If we would simply resurrect Warren Court protections for constitutional rights, liberals claim, we will be back on the road to domestic tranquility.

Are the liberals correct? There's force to their argument, but the argument also ignores important problems with Warren Court solutions. For the constitutional skeptic, the problems run very deep and raise doubts about the overall project of looking to the Constitution to guarantee domestic tranquility.

We can start with guns. It is true that the Supreme Court badly misinterpreted the Second Amendment to create a right to private gun ownership. It is hard, though, to claim that the Court is the source of our gun problem. Gun ownership was extraordinarily widespread before 2008, when the Court in *District of Columbia v. Heller* upheld a constitutional right to gun ownership. Gun control measures were going nowhere in Congress. The Court's intervention has marginally complicated the task of passing effective legislation, but to date the Court has limited its holding to protecting possession within a home. It has all but invited legislation to ban particularly dangerous or uncommon weapons, to ban possession in sensitive locations, to impose restrictions on sales such as effective background checks, and to ban certain classes of people from owning weapons.[52]

The real problem, then, is not with the Court's decision. Instead, there are legitimate questions about whether any politically plausible gun control measure would have much real-world effect. A prior effort to prohibit assault weapons was widely regarded as a failure and was allowed to expire. Registration, background checks, and limits on who can own a gun are already on the books. Yes, loopholes might be closed and prohibitions strengthened, but short of politically impossible mass confiscation or compulsory buyback measures, we are likely to live for the foreseeable future in the most heavily armed country in the world.

That does not mean that constitutional law is irrelevant to the issue, though. The American habit of formulating public policy questions in terms of absolute and inviolable constitutional rights has unnecessarily inflamed the debate and made reasonable compromise difficult. More broadly, a combination of Madison's mistakes—establishing a government deliberately shielded from popular participation and disabled by checks and balances—has fostered distrust of government's capacity to act in the public interest. That distrust, in turn, encourages a culture of individualism and a belief that individuals who feel threatened by crime must rely on self-protection.

These are problems, all right, but they are not problems created by a conservative Supreme Court. Instead, they are difficulties imposed by the Constitution itself, or at least by our constitutional culture, which treats archaic attitudes and institutions as unchangeable objects of veneration.

What about other forms of violence, including police violence, street violence, and domestic violence? A fair assessment of the Constitution's role in ensuring domestic tranquility should begin with a recognition that the violence problem in America is both public and private. The police violate the rights of Americans when they stop people for no reason, when they enter homes without warning or probable cause, when they use excessive force, and when they use trickery or coercion to secure false confessions. But criminals also violate the rights of Americans when they assault domestic partners, burglarize houses, commit drive-by murders, or rape innocent individuals on the streets.

Public and private violence are linked in complex ways. Sometimes, reducing public violence can increase private violence. If the Constitution requires police to secure a warrant before they search and seize, there are likely to be fewer searches and seizures, and fewer crimes will be solved. It is also plausible, though, that a reduction in public violence might lead to a reduction in private violence. A police force that does not behave like an occupying army is more likely to engender the trust and cooperation necessary to combat crime.

Unfortunately, our constitutional tradition allows the Court to manipulate only one of the relevant variables. It can reduce police violence, but it cannot force the government to reduce private violence. The Constitution takes status quo distributions of power and wealth as its baseline. A person wealthy enough to live in a gated community and hire private security guards need not worry much about burglars. A person living in a dilapidated apartment building with no burglar alarm and no private security has to depend on the government for protection. The Constitution puts limits on what the government can do to harm the rich person through the exercise of public power, but it puts almost no limits on the government's ability to ignore the private violence that harms the poor person.[53]

The Warren Court did nothing to remedy this fundamental problem with American constitutionalism. It established rules restricting what the police could do, but it claimed that it lacked power to establish constitutional requirements on government to limit what criminals could do. The result was that the Court ended up vulnerable to the charge that it was protecting criminals at the expense of ordinary citizens—a charge that Richard Nixon made with great effect during his successful run for the presidency in 1968.

Suppose, though, that counterfactually, the Court were able to manipulate both variables. Fighting both public and private violence requires complex empirical judgments. We need to know whether, when, and to what extent the magnitudes of police violence and private violence move in opposite directions. When will more vigorous policing reduce crime, and when will it only generate community alienation that causes an increase in crime? The answer is unlikely to be the same at all times and in all places.

Even if the Court somehow got all the empirics right, that would not end the difficulties. We are also confronted with questions of value. Suppose it turns out that more police activity leads to less private violence. Is the trade-off worth it? We are confronted again with an apples-and-oranges question. People have different "tastes" about the risks posed by the police as compared to the risks posed by criminals. Who is to say what balance is correct?

For these reasons, it is unsurprising that the Constitution leaves unanswered important questions about controlling violence. For example, the Fourth Amendment bans "unreasonable" searches and seizures. One might say that a search or seizure is "unreasonable" if it is not cost-justified—that is, if the police violence is not paid for in the currency of reduced private violence. But constitutional text says nothing about what the appropriate trade-off is.

Given that silence, one must ask what justification judges have for imposing their personal trade-off on the rest of us.

Similarly, the Fifth Amendment contains a naked prohibition on compelled self-incrimination. It says nothing about when pressure makes what would otherwise be a free choice into a compelled act. One might say, as the Court has said, that the tipping point comes when a suspect's "will is overborne." But this formulation begs the question rather than answering it. No one acts in a vacuum without various pressures influencing their decision. How much and what kinds of pressures amount to "overbearing" requires a value judgment left unresolved by the Constitution.

To vindicate its own value judgments, the liberal Warren Court ended up creating a large number of complex rules that the police were obligated to follow. In the Fourth Amendment context, the Court thought that the appropriate trade-off could be achieved by requiring warrants and probable cause for searches and seizures and by excluding evidence when the police acted without these.[54] With regard to the Fifth Amendment, the Court banned confessions when a defendant was questioned without the famous *Miranda* warnings and when he did not knowingly and voluntarily waive his right to remain silent.[55]

But the constitutional text does not support these requirements either. The Fourth Amendment requires probable cause for a warrant, but it doesn't actually have a requirement that police obtain a warrant, and it doesn't say anything about warrantless searches or excluding wrongly obtained evidence. The Fifth Amendment privileges a defendant from being a witness against himself, but it says nothing about stationhouse interrogations and nothing about *Miranda* warnings. For decades, academics have engaged in an arcane and inconclusive argument about whether the Court's holdings can nonetheless somehow be wrung from the constitutional text. But even if one thinks we should be bound by century-old judgments about appropriate trade-offs between public and private violence, the Court was hardly compelled to read the text in the way that it did.

And why, anyway, should we be so bound? The Fourth and Fifth Amendments were written at a time when there were no organized police forces in the United States. It applied only to the federal government, at a time when there were virtually no federal crimes. There were no semiautomatic weapons, no stop-and-frisk, no police manuals detailing subtle means of psychological coercion, no hyperincarceration—indeed, no prisons in the modern sense. The notion that the cost-benefit analysis that seemed appropriate then should bind us now is ludicrous.

In its attempt to deal with this dilemma, the Court has vacillated between an approach that focuses only on deciding the individual case that comes before it and an approach that uses individual cases to formulate general rules designed to resolve many future cases. The constitutional skeptic rejects both approaches as deeply flawed.

In *Marbury v. Madison*,[56] the first Supreme Court case invalidating a federal statute, Chief Justice John Marshall endorsed the first approach. He argued that constitutional holdings are only the incidental consequence of deciding individual cases that come before the Court. But this American habit of thinking about constitutional law in terms of individual cases has done the country considerable damage. We can see the consequences of the approach in the rhetoric surrounding police misconduct. Almost always, the rhetoric centers on a particular instance of egregious police abuse—the beating of Rodney King, say, or the murder of George Floyd. That focus has two unfortunate consequences. First, it holds the general point about police abuse hostage to the facts of a particular case. Suppose a later-discovered video makes clear that what the police did in the particular case was justified. As a logical matter, that fact in no way impeaches the general argument about systemic racism in policing. As a rhetorical matter, though, the discovery could be devastating. Having put their eggs in the individual-case basket, advocates for reform have no choice but to watch the eggs break when the basket won't hold them.

Second, and relatedly, the focus on individual cases obscures the systemic nature of the problem. It leaves advocates for change vulnerable to the "few bad apples" defense. Instead of leading us to confront the deep and pervasive racism in policing, it promotes symbolic but ineffective measures like punishing an individual officer or providing sensitivity training.

Almost two hundred years later, the liberal Warren Court tried to address these shortcomings in the realm of crime and violence by formulating general rules based on the precepts laid out in the Constitution. To its great credit, the Court recognized that criminal and police violence is a systemic problem that requires a systemic solution; police departments are large bureaucracies that need clear guidance from above. But skeptics recognize that, ultimately, an approach based on general rules predicated on the Constitution is doomed as well.

The Warren Court's approach is best illustrated by its famous decision in *Miranda v. Arizona*.[57] For decades, the justices had wrestled with the problem of coerced confessions using the vague "Was this particular defendant's will overborne?" test.[58] This meant that the Supreme Court itself had to examine the particular facts of the particular case in order to reach a judgment—an impossible task. Every year, there are thousands of stationhouse confessions; at most, the Court could hear only one or two confession cases. Its Delphic musings about the facts of these individual cases gave lower courts no real guidance about how to decide the next case. More significantly, the Supreme Court gave no real guidance to police officers operating in good faith who wanted to secure confessions but also felt duty-bound to obey the limits that the Court imposed.

The Warren Court thought that it could do better, so instead of continuing to decide individual cases that came before it by asking whether the defendant's will had been overborne, it used *Miranda v. Arizona* as a vehicle for announcing a general rule. A striking fact about the *Miranda* decision is that the Court did not get around to discussing the individual facts of the case until the very end of the opinion. Even then, the discussion was cursory. The facts hardly mattered.

Instead, *Miranda* was about a new approach that could be applied to large numbers of cases without regard to their individual facts. From now on, the Court held, confessions were automatically deemed coerced unless the defendant was given the famous *Miranda* warnings—that he had a right to remain silent, that what he said might be used against him, that he had a right to a lawyer, and that a lawyer would be provided for him if he could not afford one. Once these warnings were provided, the Court added, the confession was admissible only if the defendant knowingly and voluntarily waived his rights.

Miranda is only the most famous of a large number of Warren Court decisions that took this form. For example, the Warren Court abandoned an approach to the right to counsel in state cases that looked to the individual facts[59] in favor of a general rule that required defendants to be provided with lawyers in all serious cases.[60] Instead of asking whether a search "shocked the conscience,"[61] it held that evidence gained through Fourth Amendment violations must *automatically* be excluded in state cases.[62] Instead of asking whether it was "reasonable" for the police to search or seize without a warrant,[63] it reinforced a general principle that warrants were almost always required.[64]

These rule-like decisions were designed to make constitutional rights meaningful, but the Warren Court's efforts to solve the violence problem were bound to fail for at least two reasons. The first reason is practical: over 95 percent of criminal cases are resolved by plea bargains under which, in exchange for a reduced sentence, a defendant waives both his right to make the government prove his guilt and his right to contest the constitutionality of his treatment. That bargain may be in the interests of individual defendants, but, as a systemic matter, it effectively sidesteps the rules, which come into play only if a case goes to trial.

The second problem with general rules is that they invite exceptions, because one size really doesn't fit all. One characteristic of rules is that they must be enforced even if, on the individual facts of an individual case, they are counterproductive. As a result, judges are regularly confronted with the distasteful necessity of enforcing the rule when it seems like pointless formalism to do so. The natural reaction to this situation is to invent an exception to the rule that leads to a just result in the case the judge confronts. But if this process is repeated often enough, we end up with all exception and no rule—in other words, back where we started with unadministerable, all-things-considered, individual-case adjudication.

This difficulty is not just hypothetical. It is what happened to most Warren Court rules. To take only one example, consider the rule that police must get warrants before they conduct searches and seizures. Over the years, as the Court administered this rule, it encountered more and more cases where, on the facts of the case, the requirement made no sense. In response, the Court announced a series of subrules. Yes, warrants are generally required, but there is an exception for when there isn't time to get a warrant,[65] and another one for when the police search an automobile,[66] and another one for when the defendant consents to the search,[67] and another one for when the search is for noncriminal purposes,[68] and another one for when the search is part of an administrative program directed at a highly regulated industry,[69] and so on. Taken separately, each of these exceptions may make sense. Each may be necessary to avoid absurd results in individual cases. Taken together, they have eviscerated the warrant requirement and left us more or less back where we started.

A courageous judge might insist on holding the line and enduring the criticism that comes with deciding a case in a way that appears absurd. But when the Warren Court consistently ordered the suppression of voluntary admissions of guilt because of a technical violation of the *Miranda* rules or suppressed the results of an entirely reasonable search because of minor defects in a warrant application, the result was a collapse of public support that, rightly or wrongly, ultimately doomed the entire project.

To summarize, liberals are correct when they complain that conservative justices have dismantled Warren Court reforms that had some potential to make our country less violent and to secure domestic tranquility. What they have failed to see, though, is that it is not just conservative justices who are to blame. There are also important difficulties internal to the project of trying to ensure domestic tranquility by enforcing constitutional law. Among them:

- Relying on the Constitution allows the Court to try to control public violence by the police, but offers no tools to regulate private violence by criminals.
- Constitutional law purports to be permanent and rigid, but effective policies for minimizing violence vary from time to time and place to place.
- Controlling violence inevitably requires contestable value judgments that the constitutional text cannot provide and that should not be resolved by unelected judges.
- Regulating the huge police bureaucracy requires formulation of bright-line rules, but the rules have little textual support in the Constitution and are always under pressure because application of the rules to individual cases often produces (or at least appears to produce) absurd results.
- Our entrenched constitutional ideology requires thinking about the problem in terms of individual cases and thereby discourages systemic solutions.

One might have supposed that liberal constitutionalists would have learned their lesson from this sad episode. Instead, nostalgic yearning for the Warren Court years has diverted needed attention from taking the steps that might actually make things better. What sort of steps? It is striking that we are in the midst of the most serious engagement with the problems of violence and policing in a half century, yet that engagement has nothing to do with the Supreme Court or, except in the most general sense, with constitutional law. The important actors have been not lawyers arguing in ornate palaces of justice, but ordinary Americans demonstrating on the streets. The discussion has not been about the exclusionary rule or *Miranda* warnings, but ground-level policies to control police racism and violence. Put simply, the engagement has been political rather than legal.

The initial impulse for the demonstrations came from specific acts of police misconduct, but the ultimate response must extend and has extended beyond the initial impulse. The political discussion is about systemic racism, violence, hopelessness, and rage. There is no legal doctrine and no court case that can deal with those problems. Instead, they are subjects that must be addressed through dialogue, political pressure, legislation, administrative action, and compromise.

The same point holds if we address violence more broadly conceived. Going forward, our domestic tranquility is threatened by more than just police and criminal violence. We will not have domestic tranquility if we do not address problems associated with climate change, disparities in wealth, migration, disease, globalization, and automation. These are not constitutional issues, at least as constitutional issues are generally understood. There are no elite, top-down solutions that lawyers and judges can provide. Looking to constitutional law, as ordinarily understood, to resolve such dilemmas promises only diversion and disappointment. Instead, we need serious political engagement and thoughtful policy solutions.

It does not follow, though, that the skeptic's constitution has nothing to contribute. Constitutionalism, understood as an attitude, a set of aspirations, and an invitation to dialogue, is essential. The attitude required is skeptical engagement—a persistent doubt about conventional wisdom, simple solutions, and the inevitability of the status quo. The aspirations are for a tranquility that is founded on justice, decency, and experimentation. The dialogue is between people of different views who nonetheless share a commitment to achieving the common good and are willing to engage in free discussion with no guaranteed outcome.

No doubt, many people will think it dangerously romantic to suppose that constitutionalism so conceived will solve our problems. But recent events have provided hopeful examples of how such a dialogue might actually take place. In the wake of George Floyd's murder, some communities have begun a systematic review of policing. The reviews have been open-ended and inclusive, and the proposed solutions creative and frankly experimental. There have been serious efforts to rethink the problem from the ground up, unbounded by conventional (or "constitutional") ways of doing things.

Will these efforts work? Are they scalable? Perhaps not, but we might instead ask what the plausible alternatives are. Not arid constitutionalism marked by reverence for ancient and archaic text. Not elite policy prescriptions masquerading as constitutional commands and forced upon an unwilling populace. And certainly not a self-centered free-for-all, where no one is willing to listen to others or to sacrifice anything for the benefit of all of us.

Perhaps skeptical constitutionalism is impractical and the skeptic's faith in such a constitution is foolish. If that is true, though, it is hard to see how there is much hope for the future. Some current events suggest that the skeptic's constitution is less impractical than it might first seem. Moreover, if one looks to the past, it turns out that there have been important moments in our history where skeptical constitutionalism has actually driven events and moved us closer to domestic tranquility. The following chapters explore those moments and how we might build upon them.

NINE

Ordaining and Establishing This Constitution, Part 1

Early American Skepticism

How do constitutions get off the ground? How are they "ordained and established," in the words of the Preamble? Every constitution asserts its own legitimacy. For example, the American Constitution proclaims itself to be "the supreme Law of the Land." But no constitution can pull itself up by its own bootstraps. The Constitution's declaration of its own supremacy has force only if we treat the declaration itself as supreme. Ultimately constitutions are "ordained and established" only when ordinary people treat them as law.

That fact poses a problem for advocates of the skeptical constitution. As things stand now, ordinary people seem to treat the version of the Constitution preserved under glass at the National Archives as law. They do so, according to conventional accounts, because of the lessons learned from several centuries of American history. On this view, for hundreds of years, the standard Constitution has kept us together as a nation. Its goodness has been the organizing ethos that has allowed Americans to prosper and the American experiment to survive. Establishing and ordaining the skeptic's constitution requires dislodging that perception — no small task.

In fact, there is a seldom-told version of American history that presents a very different story. Surprisingly, the American

Constitution's legitimacy has never been fully and finally ordained and established. Through two centuries of hagiography
for the Founders and worship of the text that they have produced,
atheists and agnostics have survived. Indeed, some of the most
important and inspiring figures in our nation's history have been
constitutional skeptics. Bringing this alternative account to light
is an essential first step if the skeptic's constitution is to be ordained and established. This chapter and the two that follow begin the task of recounting the centuries-long story of American
constitutional skepticism.

The story starts before there was an American Constitution. Late
eighteenth-century Americans had views about constitutions that
were quite different from those of the Constitution's modern defenders. On the one hand, they took constitutionalism and constitutional violation seriously.[1] Rhetoric of the period is full of
constitutional claims and assertions of constitutional rights. On
the other hand, Americans seemed quite content with a system
that lacked a clear means of constitutional enforcement or authoritative resolution of constitutional controversy. As law professor Larry Kramer summarizes the prevailing zeitgeist:

> [The] constitutional system . . . was self-consciously legal in
> nature, but in a manner foreign to modern sensibilities about
> the makeup of legality. . . . Eighteenth-century constitutional-
> ism was less concerned with quick, clear resolutions. Its notion
> of legality was less rigid and more diffuse—more willing to tol-
> erate ongoing controversy over competing plausible interpreta-
> tions of the constitution, more willing to ascribe authority to an
> idea as unfocused as "the people."[2]

This is constitutionalism of a sort, but it is a constitutionalism
at war with the standard story as we have come to understand
it. It provided neither settlement nor hierarchical ordering. It
was a site for contestation and civic engagement, not a means of

permanently resolving disputes and defusing destabilizing controversy. In other words, it was the skeptic's constitution.

As foreign as it may seem to us today, this view of constitutionalism appears to have been quite common in the late eighteenth
century. For example, it was a common assumption that state constitutions could be drafted and amended by ordinary legislative
means,[3] and some leading authorities believed that they could be
repealed by statute.[4] Constitutional enforcement was the job not
of politicians or judges, but of the people themselves. Popular enforcement, in turn, was facilitated by the very short terms of office
for legislatures, narrow jurisdiction for courts, and truncated powers for executives.[5]

Eighteenth-century Americans were able to conceptualize
constitutionalism in this way because they lived in an era of constitutional creation, rather than constitutional obedience. The act
of creating a constitution is exhilarating and liberating. It is an
assertion of generational autonomy.

So long as Americans were creating constitutions for themselves, there was no contradiction between constitutionalism and
popular sovereignty. But a problem arose when constitutional
creators began writing not just for themselves but also for their
children. When constitutional aspirations congealed into a text
immunized from easy revision, the struggle for generational autonomy began to seem like a zero-sum game.

American constitutionalism was therefore founded on a contradiction. Late eighteenth-century America was a revolutionary
state. When the Framers met in Philadelphia, memories of the
uprising against British rule were still fresh. Importantly, and despite the colonists' assertion of the "rights of Englishmen," that
uprising was illegal under then-existing law. It therefore had to
be justified by theories that rejected the binding force of that
law—theories like the one outlined in the Declaration of Independence.[6] These theories did not magically disappear with the
victory at Yorktown. A generation formed by rebellion against
British authority was not about to accept meekly the claims of

new rulers. Hence the free-form, populist, nonauthoritarian constitutionalism that dominated America's early years.

But the country also needed stability to grow and thrive. It therefore could not avoid the dilemma faced by all revolutionary states: How does one establish that the revolution is over? How can law and order be reestablished once it has been disrupted? Ruling elites somehow had to make clear that rebellion against the British was one thing, but rebellion against the new status quo—Shays's Rebellion, for example—was another thing altogether. The country had to find a way to suppress, compartmentalize, or rationalize the illegality of its own birth in order to establish the new legality.

On conventional accounts, the drafting and ratification of the Constitution resolved this contradiction. Popular ratification put an end to the fluidity and destabilization of revolutionary constitutionalism and legitimated rigid rules that established fixed boundaries between different branches, governments, and spheres. Writing within a decade of ratification, Justice James Iredell explained how text congealed the law and put an end to disputation:

> It has been the policy of all the American states, . . . and of the people of the United States, . . . to define with precision the objects of the legislative power, and to restrain its exercise within marked and settled boundaries. If any act of congress, or of the legislature of a state, violates those constitutional provisions, it is unquestionably void. . . . If, on the other hand, the Legislature of the Union or the Legislature of any member of the Union, shall pass a law, within the general scope of their constitutional power, the Court cannot pronounce it to be void, merely because it is, in their judgment, contrary to the principles of natural justice.[7]

No doubt, some of the Constitution's Framers hoped that constitutional text would produce this sort of certainty and stabilization.

Their success in accomplishing this goal is less clear. In fact, the effort to fix constitutional discourse had something like the opposite effect. For all its imprecision and destabilizing potential, pre-ratification constitutionalism reconciled the demands of popular sovereignty and constitutional law. When the Constitution was stabilized by a legal text and immunized from easy revision, this reconciliation unraveled. The result was the emergence of a variety of worries, critiques, and contradictions that remain with us today—and give us reason for skepticism.

We can begin with the Constitution's opponents. The Anti-federalist campaign was the most sustained and unambiguous attack on the American Constitution in our history. Leaders of the campaign created a huge volume of argument and theory, some of which deserves to be ranked among the classics of political thought.[8] And the campaign almost succeeded.[9]

It is no surprise, then, that the Antifederalist campaign produced a treasure trove of argument against the Constitution—argument that still resonates some two centuries later. The Antifederalist distrust of the federal power, celebration of localism and decentralization, worry about militarization and high taxes, and fear of a remote political class, all play important roles in modern American politics.

Antifederalists also complained repeatedly and vociferously about the Constitution's legality. The Constitutional Convention had blatantly ignored the legal requirements imposed by the Articles of Confederation.[10] The problems of fairness and legality grew only more serious as the ratification process proceeded. Individual state conventions were marred by serious irregularities, efforts to short-circuit or terminate debate and deliberation, and, in a few cases, violent intimidation. After a critical mass of states had voted to ratify the Constitution, the holdouts were threatened with economic retaliation and collapse if they did not go along.

These difficulties support the modern argument for displacing the standard Constitution and embracing constitutional skepticism. Throughout American history, the original sin of the Framers has destabilized the myth of immaculate conception. As legal scholar Bruce Ackerman has forcefully argued, there is no reason to suppose that only one generation had the wisdom and intelligence to break with the past.[11] The ratification process therefore raised deeply destabilizing questions about whether we should emulate the Framers' own example of disobedience to others or slavishly follow their hypocritical insistence on obedience to them.

Antifederalist arguments also support modern constitutional skepticism in another way. The most basic Antifederalist objection to the new Constitution was that it expanded federal power at the expense of local politics. In the late eighteenth century, state governments were remarkably responsive to the views of the electorate. State legislators served very short terms, and, by modern standards, executives and courts were relatively powerless.[12] These arrangements were justified by belief in republican governance and the sort of free-form constitutionalism described earlier. On this view, politics was something more than a spectator sport. Direct and regular involvement in the institutions of government built civic virtue and contributed to the good life.[13]

The Framers wanted to change this state of affairs. On the specific level, the Constitution's Framers and supporters were deeply frightened by the threats to property and contract posed by state governments. On the more general level, they disparaged direct popular rule and believed that democracy led inevitably to faction and denial of minority rights.

The Antifederalist desire to keep the general population involved in the political sphere meshes seamlessly with modern constitutional skepticism. Because all formal and written constitutions channel politics and constrain the range of possible outcomes, they are all enemies of the sort of free-form, participatory democracy that some Antifederalists favored. If one truly believes in republican deliberation—in the ability of the people to transcend their differences and engage in self-rule—then fixed constitutional commands that predetermine outcomes and control politics are an evil.

Of course, the Antifederalists lost and the Federalists won. Surprisingly, though, some Federalist writings in support of the Constitution also support the modern skeptical stance. In particular, the Federalist Papers, authored by Alexander Hamilton, James Madison, and John Jay, and doubtless the most sophisticated defense of the new Constitution, express themes that support constitutional skepticism.

The themes find clearest expression in Madison's and Hamilton's dismissal of what they both called "parchment barriers."[14] Ironically, the Framers themselves understood how parchment turns to dust. Their complaint supports the modern skeptical argument that mere words on a piece of paper do not protect our freedoms. Hamilton justified the refusal of the Framers to provide for a bill of rights partially on the ground that mere textual guarantees were worthless.[15] In a letter to Jefferson during the ratification struggle, Madison seemed to agree. Experience with state constitutions demonstrated that "repeated violations of these parchment barriers have been committed by overbearing majorities."[16]

In the Federalist Papers, Madison extended this argument and made it central to his defense of the Constitution more generally. Because men were not angels, he insisted, they were unlikely to respect limits on their power simply because of legal commands. Instead, these limits had to be bolstered by self-interest. This could be achieved, Madison insisted, by "setting ambition against ambition" and building conflict between self-interested actors into the structure of government.[17] It was for this reason that "checks and balances" were essential to the preservation of liberty.

This classic argument in favor of the American Constitution also serves as the starting point for a skeptical critique. The argument suggests that constitutions are either ineffective or unnecessary. Government officials who are public-spirited enough to obey constitutional commands will also be public-spirited enough not to use their power to oppress others. In a world where men are angels, constitutions are unnecessary.

The source of concern is about government officials who are not angels and who will be tempted to misuse their power. But officials of this sort will also be tempted to disobey constitutional commands. They will not be restrained by mere "parchment barriers," and so for them the Constitution will be ineffective.[18]

In Federalist 78, Hamilton argued that this problem might be remedied by an independent judiciary with authority to invalidate unconstitutional acts.[19] The argument is the source of an enduring puzzle. The judiciary had to be independent, Hamilton argued, if it was to resist pressure from the other branches of government and from the public to trample on constitutional rights.[20] But unless we are to suppose that judges are angels, this very independence meant that these judges would be free to defy rather than enforce the Constitution. As an anonymous Antifederalist using the pseudonym Brutus wrote, a powerful judiciary lodged power "in the hands of men independent of the people, and of their representatives, . . . [with] no way . . . left to controul [sic] them but with a high hand and an outstretched arm."[21]

Hamilton's response to this worry was to point out that a judiciary with "no influence over the sword or the purse" and possessed of "neither FORCE nor WILL" was "the least dangerous branch."[22] But at best this observation demonstrates only that judges acting alone would not themselves threaten liberty. It does not explain why they might not form a coalition with another branch to do so, how they could enforce the Constitution when they had neither force nor will, or what motive they would have to attempt such enforcement. Our experience with the judiciary in the two centuries since Hamilton wrote demonstrates that these problems are not merely theoretical.

Madison's effort to deal with the problem of enforcement was at once more sophisticated and more skeptical.[23] Instead of trusting any particular institution or group of people to act in a public-spirited fashion, he argued for structural protections. The Constitution's byzantine system of overlapping and conflicting powers provided built-in mechanisms to discipline official misconduct. On his view, officials responsible to different constituencies and elected at different times will have different interests. These interests will inevitably conflict with each other and provide an incentive for different branches of government to check each other. In this fashion, "the private interest of every individual [would] be sentinel over the public rights," and the Constitution would become self-enforcing.

Madison's theory has been strongly criticized on a variety of grounds, but for our purposes, the important point is that it is in serious tension with the usual arguments for constitutionalism. First, notice that the theory says nothing about direct constitutional protection for individual rights, about judicial review, or about the enforcement of the legal minutiae contained in all constitutions. Madison's point is that the broad structures of the American Constitution will protect public rights, not that enforcement of specific commands is either possible or necessary. Put differently, his argument has nothing to do with, for example, the constitutionalization of issues about affirmative action, gay rights, abortion, or racial discrimination.

Nor does it speak to enforcement of specific constitutional commands about questions like when the president's term of office begins or what the line of succession should be in the case of presidential death or incapacity. In short, it has nothing to do with the principal role that the Constitution plays in contemporary American life.

Of course, modern constitutional issues occasionally arise about the general structure of government. But here, too, Madison's argument is at best ambivalent about the role of constitutional text. A common modern argument for constitutional obedience rests on the value of stability and predictability. But

Madison argued for a fluid, ill-defined government structure that would invite contestation between the branches and so counteract ambition with ambition.[24]

Finally, Madison never successfully resolved the "parchment barriers" problem. This phrase first appears in Federalist 48, which starts with the observation that "powers properly belonging to one of the departments, ought not be directly and completely administered by either of the other departments."[25] Madison then turns to the question of how to enforce this requirement. A decade later, Supreme Court justice James Iredell, reflecting the standard defense of constitutionalism, wrote that the Constitution "define[d] with precision the objects of the legislative power, and [restrained] its exercise within marked and settled boundaries." Remarkably, Madison used almost identical language to reject this ambition. "Will it be sufficient to mark, with precision, the boundaries of these departments, in the constitution of the government, and to trust to these parchment barriers against the encroaching spirit of power?" he asked.[26] His response was a resounding no: "This is the security which appears to have been principally relied on by the compilers of most of the American constitutions. But experience assures us, that the efficacy of the provision has been greatly overrated."

Madison then proceeded to provide numerous contemporary examples of the failure of constitutional law to constrain the evils he identifies. The next several Federalist Papers address other inadequate mechanisms of enforcement, including constitutional amendment and popular democracy.[27] Finally, in Federalist 51, he asked the question again and purported to provide an answer:

> To what expedient then shall we finally resort, for maintaining in practice the necessary partition of power among the several departments, as laid down in the constitution? The only answer that can be given is, that as all the exterior provisions are found to be inadequate, the defect must be supplied, by so

contriving the interior structure of the government, as that its
several constituent parts may, by their mutual relations, be the
means of keeping each other in their proper places.[28]

This "answer" is more than a little puzzling. Madison started out
by saying that the new government with its structure of overlapping powers will protect liberty and the public interest. He recognized that these good outcomes were dependent upon this
structure remaining intact and asked how the structural rules
could be enforced. But his answer leads to a circle: the structural
provisions, he says, will be enforced by the structural provisions.

The failure of this answer, offered by the most sophisticated
constitutional thinker of his generation, is itself evidence in favor
of modern constitutional skepticism. It points to the unavoidable
fact that ultimately constitutional limits depend for their efficacy
on the willingness of powerful, self-interested actors to exercise
restraint. The doubt that they will do so remains with us still.

But even if we focus on the parts of Madison's argument that
were more successful, his writings provide powerful arguments
against conventional constitutionalism. It is worth emphasizing
that Madison was deeply skeptical of text as a source of constraint, believed in fostering conflicts between the branches of
government rather than using the Constitution to impose settlement, and, at least at the time of the framing, thought that direct constitutional protection for civil liberties was unnecessary
and unwise.

Defenders of conventional constitutionalism rely not just on the
original text, but on the Constitution's first ten amendments,
adopted by the first Congress and then ratified by the states in
1791. Indeed, on these conventional accounts, the most important, defining attribute of American constitutionalism is the
textual protection and judicial enforcement of individual rights.
According to these accounts, the American Bill of Rights is widely
admired and copied throughout the world as a symbol of limited

government and individual freedom. It is central to the story that constitutionalists tell about the American experiment.

There are many reasons to doubt these accounts. In fact, many modern constitutions depart substantially from the American Bill of Rights model, in particular by providing for positive as well as negative rights.[29] Moreover, many contemporary constitutional scholars have shown that judicial enforcement of Bill of Rights protections did little to preserve civil liberties when they were challenged in times of crisis.[30] It has been less widely remarked, however, that the history of the writing and adoption of the Bill of Rights also supports a more skeptical account of our constitutional history.

As already noted, the original Constitution contained no Bill of Rights and many of the Framers thought that textual protection for civil liberties was unwise, unnecessary, or both. The people who wanted a Bill of Rights were not the authors of the Constitution, but their opponents.[31] Moreover, even the opponents tended to favor a Bill of Rights that applied only to the federal government. For most Antifederalists, a bill of rights was a means to limit federal power and, therefore, to leave the states free to protect or restrict the rights as they chose.[32] This conception is far removed from the modern idea of textual protection for the individual against all of government.

The battle for constitutional ratification was closely contested, and some Federalists—most prominently James Madison— promised to amend the Constitution promptly once it had been adopted.[33] Historians disagree about whether Madison authentically changed his mind and came to favor such amendments or whether his sponsorship of them was motivated solely by the political necessity of winning reelection to Congress and persuading North Carolina and Rhode Island to join the union.[34] (These states had not ratified the Constitution at the time Congress debated the Bill of Rights.) Whatever his personal motives, though, it is clear that the amendments he proposed made no one happy.

Madison himself apparently doubted the usefulness of a Bill of

Rights. Only months earlier, he had written to Jefferson that "experience proves the inefficacy of a bill of rights on those occasions when its controul [sic] is most needed."[35] The Federalists who dominated the new Congress were even more skeptical. Madison was repeatedly frustrated in his efforts to get the House of Representatives even to consider the amendments. Members thought that they had more important matters to attend to.[36] When debate finally started, many voiced strong opposition and, ultimately, adopted the provisions only grudgingly.

One might suppose that passage of the provisions therefore amounted to a victory for the Antifederalists. In fact, though, many Antifederalists felt betrayed by the proposals that Madison advanced and that Congress adopted.[37] They had hoped that the Constitution would be revised so as to more clearly limit federal power in general. In particular, they favored provisions that would have limited federal taxing power, banned a federal standing army, and made clear that there were no implied federal powers. What they got instead was nothing at all with regard to taxes; a pale, indirect, and ineffective reference to standing armies in the Second and Third Amendments; and a plainly inadequate Tenth Amendment that, far from limiting implied powers, seemed to invite them.

Thus, neither side attached much significance to the Bill of Rights. Instead, both sides seem to have had doubts about the importance or efficacy of textual protection for individual rights— doubts reinforced by what happened in the years following ratification of the amendments. Although the antebellum Court invalidated more federal statutes than commonly supposed,[38] it did not use the Bill of Rights to invalidate a major piece of legislation until over half a century after ratification, when it decided the infamous *Dred Scott* case, holding that efforts to limit slavery were unconstitutional and that even free Black Americans could never gain citizenship.[39] Remarkably, the Court did not get around to invalidating a statute under the free speech clause of the First Amendment until 1965.[40]

Controversy surrounding the Ninth Amendment further illustrates the skepticism of the founding generation. The amendment provides that "[t]he enumeration in the Constitution, of certain rights, shall not be construed to deny or disparage others retained by the people." Although the meaning of the amendment remains obscure and disputed, the history behind it is clear. In the run-up to ratification of the Constitution, some Federalists answered the demand for a Bill of Rights with the argument that the specification of rights would inevitably be incomplete and might imply that the rights not specified were unprotected.[41] When Madison introduced the Bill of Rights in the House, he acknowledged that "[t]his was one of the most plausible arguments I have ever heard against the admission of a bill of rights" but observed that it "might be guarded against" by enactment of the Ninth Amendment.[42]

Commentators have disagreed about the precise meaning of the Ninth Amendment,[43] but the key point here is that on all interpretations, the amendment reflected widespread skepticism that a written constitution could sufficiently constrain government power. Importantly, the amendment guards against the disparagement of other rights—that is, rights other than those specified in the Constitution. What, precisely, were these other rights? No doubt, people in the founding generation had opinions about what they were, but the Ninth Amendment amounts to a concession that it was impossible to reduce these opinions to constitutional text. Put differently, the Ninth Amendment embodies skepticism that any constitutional document can fully capture the norms that should govern a society. It is an express disavowal of Justice Iredell's ambition to write a constitution that "define[d] with precision the objects of the legislative power, and [restrained] its exercise within marked and settled boundaries."

Although Thomas Jefferson was not in Philadelphia and did not participate directly in either the ratification struggle or the adoption of the Bill of Rights,[44] he occupies iconic status in the standard story of American constitutionalism. According to that story,

Jefferson was a "strict constructionist" who strongly supported constitutional restrictions on federal power and constitutional protections for individual rights. As he once wrote, "Our peculiar security is in possession of a written Constitution. Let us not make it a blank paper by construction."[45] Jefferson's unsuccessful opposition on constitutional grounds to the creation of a national bank while in the Washington administration,[46] his secret authorship of the Kentucky Resolutions opposing the Alien and Sedition Acts while vice president,[47] his principled refusal to endorse "internal improvements"—what we would call an infrastructure program—without a constitutional amendment,[48] and his lifelong devotion to religious liberty[49] all contribute to his image as a fastidious constitutionalist.

This story is not false. Jefferson was a strict constructionist, a believer in limited government and individual rights (at least when it comes to white males), and a defender of constitutional fidelity. But Jefferson was also an immensely complicated figure. He was never a particularly systematic thinker, and his writings and career are full of contradictions and ambiguities that have puzzled and enraged historians ever since. As historian Joseph Ellis aptly characterizes him, he has become "the enigmatic and elusive touchstone for the most cherished convictions and contested truths in American culture," and "the Great Sphinx of American history."[50] It is therefore not surprising that there is another side to Jefferson's constitutional thought, much less often recognized and virtually never celebrated: throughout his life, Jefferson was a constitutional skeptic.

This skepticism took a variety of forms. First, and most dramatically, Jefferson denied the legitimate power of the authors of constitutions to bind the future. His first statement of this view seems to have been in a letter to his friend James Madison shortly after the Constitution was ratified. There, Jefferson defended the principle that "'the earth belongs in usufruct to the living' that the dead have neither powers nor rights over it."[51] From this "self-evident" proposition,[52] Jefferson derived his theory of generational limits on constitutional obligation. On his view, "by the law of nature, one generation is to another as one independent nation is to another."[53] It followed that constitutions should last only one generation: "[Members of the living generation] are masters . . . of their own persons, and consequently may govern them as they please. . . . Every constitution, then, and every law, naturally expires at the end of 19 years. If it be enforced longer, this is an act of force, and not of right."[54]

Jefferson seems to have held these views throughout his life. After retirement, in a famous letter to Samuel Kercheval, Jefferson proposed amendments to the Virginia constitution, including a built-in nineteen-year expiration date, which, he argued, corresponded to the life span of a single generation. He again insisted on the right of "each generation . . . to choose for itself the form of government it believes most promotive of its own happiness; consequently, to accommodate to the circumstances in which it finds itself, that received from its predecessors."[55] Eight years later, and only two years before his death, he wrote to John Cartwright that "a generation may bind itself as long as its majority continues in life; when that has disappeared, another majority is in place, holds all the rights and powers their predecessors once held, and may change their laws and institutions to suit themselves. . . . Nothing then is unchangeable but the inherent and unalienable rights of man."[56]

Second, Jefferson was deeply skeptical of judicial power in particular and of any authoritative, hierarchical system of constitutional enforcement in general. Jefferson's hatred of John Marshall and his anger at the Marshall Court's assertion of judicial power in *Marbury v. Madison*,[57] where for the first time the Court invalidated a federal statute on constitutional grounds, are well known.[58] Early in his career, Jefferson seems to have been a supporter of judicial review,[59] but his experience with a Federalist-dominated judiciary was enough to convince him that federal judges were a "corps of sappers and miners constantly working under ground to undermine the foundations of our confederated fabric,"[60] and that an independent federal judiciary was "a sole-cism, at least in a republican government."[61] At times, Jefferson suggested that there should be no federal judiciary at all.[62]

Jefferson's opposition to judicial supremacy was on full display when, while serving as vice president in the Adams administration, he secretly authored the Kentucky Resolutions in protest against the Alien and Sedition Acts.[63] The acts, adopted by a Federalist Congress and vigorously enforced by Federalist judges, sharply limited freedom of speech and led to the jailing of some leading figures in Jefferson's party.

As originally drafted by Jefferson, the Eighth Resolution stated that each state had independent authority to determine whether the Constitution had been violated and what the remedy should be. In a case where the federal government assumed unconstitutional powers, "a nullification of the act is the rightful remedy." This was so because states had a "natural right . . . in cases not within the compact . . . to nullify of their own authority all assumptions of power by others within their limits."[64]

The resolution ultimately adopted by the Kentucky legislature omitted the incendiary "nullification" language.[65] The parallel Virginia Resolutions, authored by Madison, were more temperate.[66] But when these less radical proposals failed to generate much northern support, Jefferson proposed a still more extreme remedy. In a letter to Madison, he urged that the dissenting states threaten "to sever ourselves from the union we so much value, rather than give up the rights of self-government which we have reserved, & in which alone we see liberty, safety & happiness."[67]

There is a sense in which Jefferson's radical views stemmed from his devotion to constitutional fidelity. Jefferson's allegiance was to the Constitution itself, not to mistaken interpretations of the Constitution advanced by misguided judges or legislators. From this perspective, it is modern believers in judicial supremacy who are unfaithful to the Constitution when they confuse mistaken Supreme Court interpretations of the Constitution with the Constitution itself.

In another sense, though, Jefferson's views are in deep tension with our standard constitutional story. That story rests crucially on the conflation of Supreme Court decisions with constitutional commands. Without an authoritative interpreter, "marked and settled boundaries" become impossible. Instead of providing a settlement, constitutionalism becomes a site for conflict and dissension of the sort that marked the pre-Revolutionary period.

Of course, decentralized constitutional authority still requires all actors to remain loyal to their own good-faith understandings of constitutional limits. But not even this much can be said of another branch of Jefferson's constitutional skepticism. It turns out that Jefferson also believed that under appropriate circumstances, the Constitution, even as he himself understood it, should be disobeyed. Jefferson's clearest statement of this belief came in a famous letter to John B. Colvin written two years after the end of his presidency.

A strict observance of the written laws is doubtless one of the high duties of a good citizen, but it is not the highest. The laws of necessity, of self-preservation, of saving our country when in danger, are of higher obligation. To lose our country by a scrupulous adherence to written law, would be to lose the law itself, with life, liberty, property and all those who are enjoying them with us; thus absurdly sacrificing the end to the means.[68]

From this abstract statement, one might think that Jefferson believed in constitutional disobedience only in extreme circumstances when the very survival of the state depended upon it. But Jefferson then went on to provide a "hypothetical case" suggesting that the Constitution might appropriately be violated in far less dire circumstances:

Suppose it had been made known to the Executive of the Union in the autumn of 1805, that we might have the Floridas for a reasonable sum, that that sum had not indeed been so appropriated by law, but that Congress were to meet within three weeks, and might appropriate it on the first or second day of their session. Ought he, for so great an advantage to his country, to have risked himself by transcending the law and making the purchase? The public advantage offered, in this supposed case, was indeed immense; but a reverence for law, and the probability that the advantage might still be legally accomplished by a delay of only three weeks were powerful reasons against hazarding the act. But suppose it was foreseen that a John Randolph would find means to protract the proceeding on it by Congress until the ensuing spring, by which time new circumstances would change the mind of the other party. Ought the Executive, in that case, and with that foreknowledge, to have secured the good to his country and to have trusted to their justice for the transgression of the law? I think he ought and that the act would have been approved.[69]

Two points are worth noting about this hypothetical. First, the acquisition of "the Floridas," while no doubt important, hardly rises to the level of "saving our country when in danger." Second, the hypothetical suggests that Jefferson thought it appropriate to disregard Congress's constitutional powers not just when it was impractical to consult with Congress, but also when opposition within Congress ("a John Randolph"—his cousin, incidentally) would frustrate his goals. Taken together, these points suggest that Jefferson was much more ready to disregard constitutional obligation than his general language about necessity and self-preservation suggests.

Jefferson presents this problem as if it were merely hypothetical, but in fact his administration was marked by significant decisions that, by his own lights, violated the Constitution. We can put to one side his imposition of an embargo on foreign trade. Many others thought that the embargo was unconstitutional,[70] but there is no evidence that Jefferson himself doubted its constitutional validity. The same cannot be said, however, for the Louisiana

Purchase, perhaps the most consequential act of self-conscious constitutional disobedience in our history.

Early on in the negotiations with France over the vast Louisiana Territory, Jefferson seems to have agreed with his attorney general and secretary of the treasury that "there is no constitutional difficulty as to the acquisition of territory," although he appears to have thought a constitutional amendment wise before any of the territory was granted statehood.[71] But as negotiations proceeded, he began to have doubts. In one private letter, he wrote:

> Our confederation is certainly confined to the limits established by the revolution. . . . The general government has no powers but such as the constitution has given it; and it has not given it a power of holding foreign territory, and still less of incorporating it into the Union. An amendment to the Constitution seems necessary for this.[72]

Gradually, these doubts seem to have hardened into conviction. Jefferson wrote to a close friend:

> I cannot help believing the intention was to permit Congress to admit into the union new states, which should be formed out of territory for which & under whose authority alone they were acting. I do not believe it was meant that they might receive England, Ireland, Holland, &c. into it.[73]

Accordingly, Jefferson began drafting proposed constitutional amendments to legalize the acquisition.

It soon became apparent, however, that constitutional scruples might prevent consummation of the purchase. Both France and Spain looked like they might back out of the deal, and haste in ratifying it became imperative.[74] Faced with this difficulty, Jefferson concluded that "the less that is said about my constitutional difficulty, the better; and . . . it will be desirable for Congress to do what is necessary *in silence*."[75] The proposed amendments were dropped, and Jefferson went forward with the transaction despite his own constitutional objections.

Although Jefferson himself believed his actions were unconstitutional, few contemporaries shared his doubts. In contrast, a second, albeit less consequential, action taken by Jefferson was unquestionably unconstitutional. When the British attacked an American ship in 1807, Jefferson ordered the purchase of material to build gunboats without prior congressional authorization, in clear violation of Article I, section 9, clause 7 of the Constitution, which prohibits withdrawing money from the treasury without "Appropriations made by Law."[76] Only after the purchase did Jefferson ask for and receive congressional approval, albeit over the heated objections of the aforementioned John Randolph, who complained that the president had violated his constitutional obligations.[77] In his letter to Colvin five years later, Jefferson was unrepentant:

> After the affair of the Chesapeake, we thought war a very possible result. Our magazines were illy provided with some necessary articles, nor had any appropriations been made for their purchase. We ventured, however, to provide them, and to place our country in safety; and stating the case to Congress, they sanctioned the act.[78]

How are we to reconcile Thomas Jefferson the believer in limited government, strict constructionist, and defender of constitutional purism with Thomas Jefferson the constitutional skeptic unwilling to accept the binding force of the Constitution on future generations and ready to disregard limits on his power when he viewed it necessary to do so?

Jefferson had a long career and doubtless changed his mind about some things. Not all his writings were fully thought out or grew out of deep, theoretical reflection. Like all politicians, he sometimes sacrificed his more general convictions to the necessities imposed by specific events. Ironically, his constitutional fastidiousness also contributed to his propensity to disregard constitutional limits. Few of Jefferson's contemporaries thought that there was a conflict between the Louisiana Purchase and constitutional commands. It was only because Jefferson read the Constitution so narrowly that he had to face the hard choice about whether to violate it.

But one cannot study Jefferson's career and writings without suspecting a deeper source for his ambivalence. Jefferson's own career captured the contradiction at the core of constitutional origins. Jefferson was, after all, the principal author of the Declaration of Independence. He was responsible for revolutionary defiance of legal authority in 1776, but when he was elected president of the United States in 1801, he became the embodiment of legal authority. How could a reflective person who assumed both these roles possibly escape contradiction?

One side of that contradiction—the side that prized constitutional obedience and celebrated constitutional restraint—is central to the mainstream story about constitutionalism's triumph. But Thomas Jefferson also had another side—a side that chafed at authority, abhorred stasis, and was skeptical that parchment should trump deep moral conviction. That side, too, deserves attention and respect.

With the passing of Jefferson and other members of the founding generation, sectional conflict, especially regarding slavery, became more serious. On standard accounts, southern secessionism led to the greatest threat to constitutional governance in our history. Southern radicals effectively seized control of almost half the country and mounted a treasonous war for human bondage and against the rule of law. The North responded by fighting to preserve the Union, and its victory constituted a decisive repudiation of doctrines including interposition, nullification, and a right of secession, which threatened the Constitution.

There is some truth to this account, but it is too simple. Elements of southern secessionist thought did raise important doubts about constitutional obligation, and many in the North did think of themselves as fighting to preserve the Constitution. But drawing the battle lines in this stark fashion misses the irony and paradox embedded in the arguments on both sides.

On the one hand, the case for nullification was grounded in constitutional obligation. Even secessionists often insisted that their position was based on respect for, rather than defiance of, the Constitution. On the other hand, many northern abolitionists flirted with secession and constitutional disobedience, and, when war finally came, Lincoln himself at least arguably took unconstitutional actions that privileged preservation of the union and termination of slavery over strict constitutional obligation.

The more interesting point, though, is that both northern and southern arguments blurred the line between constitutional fidelity and defiance. The strength of our constitutional tradition forced both sides to cloak their stance in constitutional rhetoric, but sometimes the rhetoric did the work of justifying revolutionary insubordination. Just as Jefferson was torn between his commitment to the Declaration of Independence and to the Constitution, so, too, northerners and southerners alike unselfconsciously mixed together the language of natural right and revolution with the language of legal obligation and constitutional precommitment.

Consider first southern secessionists. Surprisingly, they often justified their act of constitutional disobedience in constitutional terms.[79] For example, in a speech before Congress as the Fort Sumter crisis unfolded, Senator Jefferson Davis proclaimed that "[w]e claim our rights under the constitution; we claim our rights reserved to the States; and we seek by no brute force to gain any advantage which the law and the Constitution do not give us."[80] Remarkably, a few months later in his inaugural speech as he assumed office as the Confederacy's first and only president, Davis again invoked the United States Constitution. "The Constitution formed by our fathers," he asserted, "is that of these Confederate States."[81] In Davis's view, calling secession a revolution was "an abuse of language."[82] Secession was, instead, an effort "to save ourselves from a revolution."[83]

Given this stance, it is no surprise that framers of the Confederate Constitution closely followed the text of the original United States Constitution. For many southerners, disunion was a method of constitutional enforcement that, they hoped, would bring the North to its senses and lead to reunion on a sound constitutional footing.[84] According to Davis, the collapse of the union was not because of "the defect of the system," the mechanisms of which were "wonderful, surpassing that which the solar system furnishes for our contemplation." Rather, the collapse was caused by "the perversion of the Constitution"—by, for example, efforts to suppress slavery in the territories and failure to enforce the Constitution's fugitive slave clause. The result, on his view, was the "substitution of theories of morals for principles of government."[85]

The fact that the attempt to dissolve the Constitution could itself be justified in constitutional terms illustrates just how slippery the distinction is between constitutionalism and its opposite. And indeed, southern rhetoric seamlessly integrated the language of revolutionary anti-constitutionalism with the language of constitutional fidelity. In the same speech in which Davis claimed "our rights under the Constitution," he also invoked the natural right of rebellion:

> If I must have revolution, I say let it be a revolution such as our fathers made when they were denied their natural rights. . . .
>
> Washington and Jackson . . . are often presented as authority against [revolution]—Washington who led the army of the Revolution; Washington, whose reputation rests upon the fact that with the sword he cut the cord which bound the Colonies to Great Britain. . . . Washington, who presided when the States seceded from the [Articles of] Confederation, and formed the union, in disregard of the claims of the States not agreeing to it; and Jackson, glorious old soldier, who, in his minority, upon the sacred soil of South Carolina, bled for the cause of revolution and the overthrow of a Government which he believed to be oppressive.[86]

Consider, as well, a remarkably sophisticated speech defending secession given by Judah P. Benjamin, who went on to serve in the cabinet of the Confederacy. Benjamin effortlessly combined arguments grounded in constitutional obedience with arguments grounded in constitutional skepticism. Benjamin's argument begins with an echo of Jefferson's rejection of the ability of one generation to bind another:

> [T]he right of the people of one generation, in convention duly assembled, to alter the institutions bequeathed by their fathers is inherent, inalienable, not susceptible of restriction; . . . [B]y the same power under which one Legislature can repeal the act of a former Legislature, so can one convention of the people duly assembled.[87]

But Benjamin apparently saw no contradiction between assertion of this "inalienable" right to disregard the Constitution on the one hand and assertion of rights derived from the Constitution on the other:

> [T]he President of the United States tells us that he does not admit [the right of secession] to be constitutional, that it is revolutionary. I have endeavored . . . to show that [secession] . . . grows out of the Constitution, and is not in violation of it. If I am asked how I will distinguish this from revolutionary abuse, the answer is prompt and easy. These States, parties to the compact, have a right to withdraw from it, by virtue of its own provisions are violated by the other parties to the compact. . . . [88]

The speeches and writings of Davis and Benjamin are part of our constitutional tradition's anticanon. They are marginalized, discredited, or ignored because, rightly or wrongly, they are thought to embody constitutional defiance. In contrast, the words of northern abolitionists and defenders of the union are part of the canon. They are glorified because they are thought to embody the goodness and permanence of constitutional government.[89] But just as it is too simple to characterize the South's defenders as anticonstitutionalists, so too northerners were not uniform and consistent defenders of constitutional obligation.

Long before the Civil War, many northerners openly flirted with secession. According to one of his biographers, John Calhoun, the South's most prominent defender, first learned of arguments favoring secession by listening to Timothy Dwight, the president of Yale College, who was reacting to Jefferson's election as president.[90] Some leading Federalists went beyond talk and actually plotted to secede.[91]

During the War of 1812, New England states took numerous measures to obstruct the war effort. Gouverneur Morris, one of the key drafters of the Constitution, argued for an autonomous New England confederacy.[92] Toward the end of the war, Massachusetts convened the Hartford Convention, and attended it, along with other New England states, to consider secession.[93] Moderates successfully controlled the convention, and, despite the adoption of some inflammatory rhetoric, the delegates stepped back from the precipice,[94] but only after passing a resolution warning that if its demands were not met, "it will be expedient for the legislatures of the several States to appoint delegates to another convention to meet at Boston, with such powers and instructions as the exigency of a crisis so momentous may require."[95]

As tensions surrounding slavery mounted, the same schizophrenia about constitutional obedience that dominated southern rhetoric also began to appear in the North. Many radical abolitionists embraced constitutional disobedience. William Lloyd Garrison chose Independence Day to publicly burn the Constitution and denounced it as a pact with the devil.[96] Although he eventually changed his mind, Frederick Douglass originally argued for northern secession from the southern states.[97] On the eve of the Civil War, Wendell Phillips, another leading abolitionist, argued that "dissolution of the Union, sure to result speedily in the abolition of slavery, would be a lesser evil than the slow faltering disease."[98]

Even mainstream political figures on occasion embraced anti-constitutional language. During the debate over the Compromise of 1850, Senator William Seward, later Lincoln's secretary of state, argued that because "all men are equal by the law of nature and of nations, the right of property in slaves falls to the ground," and that if "the Constitution recognizes property in slaves," it would be a sufficient answer that "this constitutional recognition must be void because it is repugnant to the law of nature and of nations."[99] Similarly, William Ellery Channing, the foremost Unitarian clergyman, in the United States claimed that "[a] higher law than the Constitution protests against [the Fugitive Slave Act]."[100]

Both abolitionism and constitutional disobedience remained minority positions well into the Civil War, yet as conflict with the South intensified, willingness to stretch or ignore the Constitution increased as well. Many northerners participated in the effort to obstruct slaveholders who attempted to exercise their constitutional right to capture slaves who had fled to the North, and a courageous few participated in the Underground Railroad leading to freedom.[101] There was talk of nullification—the right of a state to override federal law—and one northern radical wrote that "we have got to come to Calhoun's ground."[102] (The reference was to John C. Calhoun, the South's notorious defender, who favored nullification to protect the South's interests.) The Republican Party platform promised a refusal to enforce the Supreme Court's *Dred Scott* decision, and some state legislatures voted to nullify it.[103] Although John Brown's violent and illegal raid of Harpers Ferry to free the slaves, in violation of the Constitution, was widely condemned even in the North, a handful of northerners treated Brown as a hero.[104]

On the spectrum of northern Republican opinion about abolitionism and the constitutional status of slavery, Abraham Lincoln was at best a moderate. A lifelong opponent of slavery, he nonetheless repeatedly promised not to interfere with it in states where it already existed. He acknowledged that southerners had the right to the return of escaped slaves and conceded that emancipation would have to be gradual and that slaveholders should be compensated for their loss.[105] Although he appears to have changed his mind at the end of his life, until then he believed that free African Americans could not successfully live with whites, and he repeatedly backed a variety of wildly impractical and immoral schemes that would lead to their departure from the United States.[106]

Moreover, throughout his adult life, Lincoln presented himself as a fervent believer in constitutionalism and a defender of constitutional government. As a young man, he first gained notoriety with his "Lyceum Address," which criticized "mob rule" and urged "every American . . . [to] swear by the blood of the Revolution, never to violate in the least particular, the laws of the country; and never to tolerate their violation by others."[107] Over two decades later, he began his campaign for the Republican nomination for president with his famous Cooper Union speech, where he made a remarkably lawyerly, constitutional argument against the result in *Dred Scott*.[108] He justified the Emancipation Proclamation as a constitutional exercise of his war power to seize enemy property, and he stubbornly and scrupulously declined to extend it to areas where, in his judgment, emancipation lacked military, and therefore constitutional, justification.[109]

But Lincoln's constitutionalism, like Jefferson's, was ambivalent and contradictory. Exclusive focus on his belief in constitutional fidelity misses much of his complexity and greatness. In fact, Lincoln's actions and words provide important support for modern constitutional skepticism.

Consider, for example, the Cooper Union speech. Lincoln began the speech rhetorically asking, "[W]hat is the frame of Government under which we live?" and responding, "The answer must be: 'The Constitution of the United States.'" It is constitutional obligation, he tells us, that "furnishes a precise and an agreed starting point for a discussion between Republicans and that wing of the [Democratic Party] headed by [his political opponent] Senator [Stephen] Douglas."[110]

Lincoln then proceeded to make a detailed, persuasive, and legalistic argument that the federal government had constitutional power to prohibit slavery in the territories. He relied upon the standard tools of constitutional interpretation: the Constitution's language, the intent of the Framers, and historical practice before and immediately after the Constitution was ratified.[111] This is unquestionably the language of standard American constitutionalism.

But then, as the speech draws to a close, comes this:

> If slavery is right, all words, acts, laws, and constitutions against it, are themselves wrong, and should be silenced, and swept away. If it is right, we cannot justly object to its nationality— its universality; if it is wrong, they cannot justly insist upon its extension—its enlargement. All they ask, we could readily grant, if we thought slavery right; all we ask, they could as readily grant, if they thought it wrong. They thinking it right, and our thinking it wrong, is the precise fact upon which depends the whole controversy. Thinking it right, as they do, they are not to blame for desiring its full recognition, as being right; but, thinking it wrong, as we do, can we yield to them? Can we cast our votes with their view, and against our own? In view of our moral, social, and political responsibilities, can we do this?[112]

Lincoln's answer is a resounding no. The last lines of his speech are far removed from the claim that dry and disinterested constitutional analysis will or should resolve the dispute over slavery. Instead, he gave full-throated endorsement to the primacy of moral obligation: "LET US HAVE FAITH THAT RIGHT MAKES MIGHT,

AND IN THAT FAITH, LET US, TO THE END, DARE TO DO OUR DUTY AS WE UNDERSTAND IT."[113]

It turns out, then, that even if, as Lincoln claimed, constitutional meaning is a "precise and agreed starting point for discussion," it is not the ending point. After all the legal argument is finished, it is not the Constitution, but the moral status of slavery, that is the "precise fact upon which depends the whole controversy."

The tension between Lincoln's commitment to constitutionalism and his commitment to extraconstitutional morality extended beyond his rhetoric. It marked his entire administration. Consider first the actions Lincoln took unilaterally immediately after assuming office. With Congress not in session and facing a military emergency, he suspended the right of prisoners to have access to a judge (habeas corpus) in particular areas.[114] When a judge had the audacity to issue an order requiring the release of an underage soldier who allegedly enlisted without the consent of his parents, the soldier's commander refused to comply and arrested the lawyer who served the writ. Not satisfied with even this result, Secretary of State Seward stopped payment on the judge's salary.[115] A few months later, Chief Justice Taney issued an order requiring the release of a Confederate supporter, John Merryman, and ruling that Lincoln had acted unconstitutionally by suspending the writ of habeas corpus.[116] Lincoln simply ignored the order.[117]

The Constitution specifically provides for the suspension of habeas corpus when in "Cases of Rebellion or Invasion the public Safety may require it," but many scholars think that the president may not exercise this authority without congressional authorization.[118] Lincoln evidently disagreed, but the important point is that he thought he acted rightly even if he violated the Constitution. In his famous speech to Congress on July 4, 1861, he argued that the Framers intended to allow the executive to suspend the writ, at least when Congress was not in session. But he coupled this legal defense with the assertion that even if his constitutional argument was incorrect, he had nonetheless done the right thing.

> The whole of the laws which were required to be faithfully executed were being resisted and failing of execution in nearly one-third of the States. Must they be allowed to finally fail of execution, even had it been perfectly clear that by the use of the means necessary to their execution some single law, made in such extreme tenderness of the citizen's liberty that practically it relieves more of the guilty than of the innocent, should to a very limited extent be violated? To state the question more directly, are all the laws but one to go unexecuted and the Government itself go to pieces lest that one be violated? Even in such a case would not the official oath be broken if the Government should be overthrown, when it was believed that disregarding the single law would tend to preserve it?[119]

Suspension of habeas corpus was not the only constitutionally dubious action Lincoln took during the 1861 crisis. Like Jefferson before him, he spent unauthorized funds to raise troops, thereby violating not only the constitutional provision that prohibits expenditures except "in Consequence of Appropriations made by Law," but also the provision that gives Congress the seemingly exclusive power to raise and support armies.[120] In his July 4 speech, he did not even try to defend the legality of these expenditures. Instead, he insisted that this action, "whether strictly legal or not," was justified by "popular demand and a public necessity."[121]

Finally, in the immediate wake of the attack on Fort Sumter, he secretly ordered military officials to enter into private contracts for the supply of military equipment, in violation of appropriations measures and existing law. Lincoln did not discuss these expenditures in his July 4 speech, and they remained secret for months until Congress discovered them. At that point, Lincoln made no effort to defend the legality of what he had done. Instead, he confessed that his actions were "without any authority of law," and acknowledged that he was responsible for "whatever error, wrong, or fault was committed."[122]

Throughout the war, Lincoln authorized many other actions that were constitutionally dubious. For example, after former congressman Clement Vallandigham gave a speech attacking pursuit of the war, the congressman was arrested, tried, and incarcerated in seeming violation of his First Amendment rights. A public outcry ensued, and Lincoln, unwilling to turn Vallandigham into a martyr, responded by ordering his expulsion from the United States.[123] At least Vallandigham had a trial. Thousands of other citizens were placed in executive detention without the benefit of trial.[124]

Most commentators treat these incidents as at best constitutionally justified by the war but nonetheless regrettable, or at worst as constitutional lapses that are perhaps excusable.[125] The Emancipation Proclamation is very different. No one today apologizes for it or treats it as a source of regret. It is universally celebrated and widely thought to be among a handful of the greatest decisions ever made by an American president. Accordingly, if the Proclamation counts as an example of constitutional disobedience, it transforms the narrative of American constitutionalism.

Does it so count? Any fair treatment of the Proclamation must acknowledge its ambiguous straddling of the border between the conflicting traditions of constitutional fidelity and constitutional skepticism. Defenders of constitutional fidelity can point to the fact that Lincoln himself never admitted that the Proclamation was unconstitutional. On the contrary, he strongly defended it as an appropriate exercise of his commander-in-chief power and, to the consternation of some of his more radical allies, carefully cabined its geographical effect to locations where liberation advanced the war effort.[126]

Despite these facts, there is strong reason to count the Proclamation as an important—perhaps the most important—act of constitutional disobedience in our history. The skeptical account of the Proclamation begins with the sheer audacity of what Lincoln did. As historian Richard Slotkin has written:

At the stroke of the pen some $3.5 billion in property was legally annihilated—this at a time when national GDP was less than $4.5 billion and national wealth (the total value of all property) was about $16 billion. In purely economic terms, this was an expropriation of property on a scale approaching that of Henry VIII's seizures of church properties during the Reformation, exceeded only by the nationalization of factories and farms after the Bolshevik Revolution.[127]

Lincoln, together with many others in mid-nineteenth-century America, thought that these property rights were constitutionally protected, and he said so repeatedly. In his most extensive speech on slavery before his election, delivered in Peoria in 1854, Lincoln denounced it as a "monstrous injustice," but nonetheless acknowledged that the Constitution protected the rights of slaveholders. Northerners were obligated to adhere to the constitutional bargain "not grudgingly, but fully, and fairly." The rendition of escaped slaves was a "dirty, disagreeable job," but because of the fugitive slave clause, Lincoln voiced support for "any legislation, for the reclaiming of their fugitives, which should not, in its stringency, be . . . likely to carry a free man into slavery."[128]

Similarly, in his first inaugural address, Lincoln made clear that he lacked constitutional authority to interfere with slavery[129] and stated that he had no objection to the Corwin Amendment, which had already passed Congress and was awaiting state ratification (which, thankfully, never came). The amendment would have provided explicit constitutional protection for slavery and, to make matters still worse, proclaimed itself unamendable.[130] In his first inaugural address, Lincoln asserted that he had no objection to the amendment because it did no more than restate slaveholder rights already implicit in the Constitution.[131]

Even after the Civil War began, Lincoln demonstrated marked reluctance to interfere with slavery. As late as 1862 he stated that "emancipation was a subject exclusively under the control of the states."[132] He demonstrated little interest in enforcing the First

Confiscation Act,[133] which deprived slaveholders of their property right in slaves used to further the war effort.[134] When General John C. Frémont declared martial law in Missouri and ordered emancipation of all slaves in the state as a means of weakening the enemy, Lincoln countermanded the order and then removed Frémont from command.[135]

The strictly legal question, then, is whether military necessity and the president's commander-in-chief authority under Article II justified a massive, permanent, uncompensated destruction of private property and the negation of what Lincoln himself conceded would otherwise have been the constitutional rights of slaveholders. There are strong reasons to doubt that the military necessity argument can do this work. Indeed, Lincoln himself initially thought that it could not. In a letter to Senator Orville Browning after the Frémont episode, Lincoln wrote that Frémont's proclamation "is purely political, and not within the range of military law, or necessity. . . . Can it be pretended that it is any longer the government of the U.S.—any government of constitution and laws,—wherein a General, or a President, may make permanent rules of property by proclamation?"[136]

Of course, it is possible that changes in military circumstances made emancipation necessary when the Proclamation was issued even though it was not when Frémont acted. But in fact, events occurring after Lincoln wrote this letter further weakened the military necessity argument. If military necessity were really the reason for emancipation, one would have supposed that Lincoln would have ordered it when the North was losing the war. Instead, Lincoln self-consciously delayed emancipation until the North won its first major victory on the battlefield at Antietam.[137]

Moreover, as noted earlier, the First Confiscation Act provided a mechanism to liberate slaves who were used to aid the Confederate war effort. The Second Confiscation Act went further and provided such a mechanism for slaves owned by disloyal individuals whether or not the slaves were used to fight the war.[138] By the time of the Proclamation, then, the question had become whether there was a military necessity justifying the emancipation of slaves not already subject to manumission by the Confiscation Acts—that is, slaves not being used to fight the war and held by slaveholders who were loyal to the Union. It is hard to see how emancipation of these slaves served a significant military purpose.[139]

The fact that the emancipation was permanent poses another legal difficulty. The Preliminary Proclamation, which warned of impending emancipation if the South continued its revolt, declared that slaves would be "then, thenceforward, and forever free."[140] For reasons that remain mysterious, the final Proclamation left out the word "forever,"[141] but Lincoln made clear that he would not rescind the Proclamation even if southern states agreed to rejoin the union.[142] Yet, ironically, before he issued the Proclamation, Lincoln himself explained why permanent freedom could not be justified by military necessity. In the Browning letter quoted earlier, he stated:

> If a commanding general finds a necessity to seize the farm of a private owner . . . he has the right to do so, and to so hold it as long as the necessity lasts; and this is within military law, because within military necessity. But to say the farm shall no longer belong to the owner or his heirs forever; and this as well when the farm is not needed for military purposes as when it is, is purely political, without the savor of military law about it. And the same is true of slaves. If the General needs them, he can seize them, and use them; but when the need is past, it is not for him to fix their permanent future conditions.[143]

For these reasons, the legal argument supporting the Emancipation Proclamation is quite vulnerable. Of course, clever lawyers can make and have made arguments on the other side. But focusing exclusively on the legal argument misses the crucial point. For purposes of constructing a historical tradition, what matters most is not the technical legality of the Proclamation, but its cultural meaning.

That meaning is directly linked to the fact that emancipation was not merely a military necessity. To see this point, compare the Proclamation to General William Tecumseh Sherman's widespread destruction and seizure of civilian property during his infamous march through Georgia in 1864. Perhaps the actions of Sherman's troops were justified by military necessity, but no one today celebrates those actions as an iconic moment in American history.

The Emancipation Proclamation is celebrated precisely because people understood then and understand now that it was not merely a military tool, the use of which was necessary but nonetheless regrettable. Instead of advancing the North's war aims, the Proclamation changed those aims. A war that was initially fought to preserve the Constitution became a war to dismantle the constitutional structures that protected tyranny and oppression.

Both contemporary supporters and opponents of the Proclamation had no doubt that this was its true meaning. For example, the New York *Herald*, in an editorial opposing the Proclamation, warned that it would inaugurate a "social revolution."[144] The Springfield *Republican*, in an editorial supporting the Proclamation, came to a remarkably similar conclusion, declaring that "by the courage and prudence of the President, the greatest social and political revolution of the age will be triumphantly carried through in the midst of civil war."[145] In a letter home, a Union soldier wrote that "though the President carefully calls [the Proclamation] nothing but a war measure . . . it is the beginning of a great reform and the first blow struck at the real, original cause of the war."[146] Perhaps Karl Marx, then working as a newspaper correspondent, put it best when he described Lincoln as playing his part

hesitatively, reluctantly, and unwillingly, as though apologizing for being compelled by circumstances "to act the lion." The most redoubtable decrees—which will always remain remarkable historical documents—flung by him at the enemy all look like, and are intended to look like, routine summonses sent by a lawyer to party. . . . His latest proclamation, which is drafted in the same style, the manifesto abolishing slavery, is the most important document in American history since the establishment of the Union, tantamount to the tearing up of the old American Constitution.[147]

Indeed, Lincoln himself acknowledged as much. Before the Proclamation, in his first inaugural address, he made clear that he had "no purpose, directly or indirectly, to interfere with the institution of slavery in the States where it exists. I believe I have no lawful right to do so, and I have no inclination to do so." If there should be war, he declared, the war would be fought to support the proposition that "the laws of the Union be faithfully executed in all the States," as the Constitution commanded. He added that he had no objection to a constitutional amendment "to the effect that the Federal Government shall never interfere with the domestic institutions of the States, including that of persons held to service."[148]

After the Proclamation, things were different. The purpose of the war was not to ensure that the laws be "faithfully executed in all the States," but to show that a nation "conceived in liberty and dedicated to the proposition that all men are created equal" could "long endure." Instead of acquiescing to a constitutional amendment that guaranteed the rights of slaveholders, Lincoln promised "a new birth of freedom."[149] No longer content to merely stop the spread of slavery, he declared that

if God wills that [the war] continue until all the wealth piled by the bondsman's two hundred and fifty years of unrequited toil shall be sunk, and until every drop of blood drawn with the lash shall be paid by another drawn with the sword, as was said three thousand years ago, so still it must be said "the judgments of the Lord are true and righteous altogether."[150]

It is nonetheless true that Lincoln also supported formal, constitutional change in the form of the Thirteenth Amendment, which legalized, regularized, and extended the Proclamation. Yet even the struggle over the formal amendment process can be incorporated into the skeptical narrative. Opponents of the Thirteenth Amendment claimed that amendments contrary to the Framers' original intent were illegitimate.[151] Ultimately, proponents of the amendment overcame this opposition and, with it, the view that all major provisions in the Constitution were sacred and permanent.[152] Proponents successfully argued that the Constitution was flawed in important respects—a skeptical theme renewed by Justice Thurgood Marshall over a hundred years later when, writing on the bicentennial of the Constitution, he observed that he did not "find the wisdom, foresight, and sense of justice exhibited by the Framers particularly profound. To the contrary, the government they devised was defective from the start."[153]

More significantly, the Thirteenth Amendment itself would have been unthinkable but for the transformation in American political culture produced by the Civil War, the Proclamation, and the subsequent enlistment of 200,000 African American soldiers who fought gallantly on the Union side. African American chattel slavery is the greatest injustice in our nation's history. For three-quarters of a century, this injustice was protected by seemingly immutable constitutional text. When the injustice was finally rectified, the efficient cause of the change was not constitutional processes—which, on the contrary, made change seem impossible—but a bloody war that claimed over 700,000 lives.

One hundred years later, this understanding of the Civil War and of the Proclamation remains vibrant. Virtually no one today celebrates the Proclamation as an aberrant deviation from otherwise sacred constitutional rights, reluctantly embraced only out of military necessity. Instead, it symbolizes a constitutional transformation.

Can there be any doubt, then, that the story of emancipation should occupy a central place in the historical narrative of constitutional skepticism?

TEN

Ordaining and Establishing
This Constitution, Part 2

Skepticism in the Progressive Era

After the Civil War, the next important episode in the history of constitutional skepticism came with the rise of the progressive movement. Defenders of the movement associate it with the modernization and rationalization of government—including the protection of populations made vulnerable by industrialization, reform of the party system, and the beginnings of redistributive legislation.[1] Critics point to the racism of many progressives, their condescending attitudes toward ordinary Americans, and the fact that many progressive "reforms" shielded entrenched interests from the discipline of market competition.[2]

Modern students of progressivism on both sides of the debate are much less likely to emphasize the extent to which the movement offered a deep and biting challenge to American constitutionalism. Yet constitutional skepticism played a central role in progressive practice and theory. Progressive politicians rallied popular support by railing against supposed constitutional restraints on regulatory legislation, and progressive theorists over a range of disciplines developed important critiques of constitutionalism.[3]

Consider first progressive politics. With the possible exception of the original Antifederalists campaign, no political movement in American history attacked constitutionalism with as much gusto and persistence as the progressives. The high point of the attack came in 1912, when Theodore Roosevelt ran for president on his fabled Bull Moose ticket. Roosevelt's proposals for radical constitutional reform alienated longtime Republican supporters including Senator Henry Cabot Lodge and doomed Roosevelt's chance for the Republican nomination.[4] Undeterred, he ran as a third-party candidate on a party platform that declared that "the people are the masters of the Constitution" and demanded "such restrictions on the courts as shall leave to the people legitimate authority to determine fundamental questions of social welfare and public policy."[5]

Roosevelt himself was convinced that creating a modern government required the dismantling of separation of powers and constitutional protections for the states.[6] He proposed that "the people shall themselves have the right to say whether their representatives in the Legislature and the executive office were right, or whether their representatives on the Court were right."[7] In a speech delivered in Columbus, Ohio, he argued that the American people must be "the masters and not the servants of even the highest court in the land" and "the final interpreters of the Constitution." Without this final authority "ours is not a popular government."[8] And in a letter to fellow progressive Herbert Croly, he stated that "one way or the other, it will be absolutely necessary for the people themselves to take control of the interpretation of the constitution. Even in national matters this ought to be, and in my opinion will eventually be done."[9]

Roosevelt was hardly alone in attacking standard versions of constitutionalism. Woodrow Wilson, who ran successfully against Roosevelt in 1912, was much more restrained in his criticism, but Wilson had made his academic reputation years before with a book-length attack on the constitutional structure of the American government.[10] In 1908, he wrote that constitutional government "does not remain fixed in any unchanging form, but . . . is altered with the change of the nation's needs and purposes."[11] During the 1912 campaign, he joined Roosevelt in arguing that Article V of the Constitution should be revised so as to make amendment much easier.[12]

Robert La Follette, perhaps the most important progressive in Congress, called for the election and recall of judges. He referred to judges who issued antilabor decisions as "petty tyrants and arrogant despots" and argued that "we must put an ax to the root of this monstrous growth upon the body of our Government."[13] Jane Addams, the great social reformer, and Herbert Croly, the founding editor of the *New Republic* and the most widely read journalistic voice for progressivism, both insisted that social reform could be accomplished only by dismantling constitutional obstacles.[14] Croly was especially biting, repeatedly decrying "the monarchy of the law and the aristocracy of the robe" and arguing that "progressive democracy" should replace "worship of the Constitution."[15] On two occasions, the young Felix Frankfurter wrote in the pages of Croly's magazine that the due process clauses of the Fifth and Fourteenth Amendments should be repealed.[16] As legal scholar William Forbath has pointed out, leading progressives like John Dewey thought that constitutional rights "seemed destined to ossify into impediments to practical change" and were "exactly what the laissez-faire jurists insisted: a limit on democracy's capacity to reconstruct its social environment by redistributive means."[17]

No doubt, these attacks on judicial enforcement of the Constitution and on the Constitution itself were politically situated. Rightly or wrongly, progressives believed that conservative judges stood in the way of reforms they thought best for the country. They therefore had compelling instrumental reasons to delegitimize the basis of judicial power. Tellingly, when control over the judiciary shifted in the late 1930s, many progressives changed their views.

Still, political motivations should not obscure the important contributions that progressive intellectuals made to the ongoing debate about constitutionalism. These contributions included worked-out theories that served to undermine standard defenses of constitutionalism. The theories were as varied as the disciplines they came from. For example, progressive historians — most prominently Charles Beard — offered an account of the Constitution's drafting grounded in the narrow economic interests of the Framers.[18] As Beard himself later conceded,[19] some of his specific claims were hyperbolic, and most modern scholars think that a purely economic interpretation of the founding is far too simplistic. Nonetheless, Beard's more general thesis—that the Constitution was written at least in part to control and limit popular democracy that threatened important economic interests—has been widely accepted.[20]

Philosophical pragmatists such as William James, Charles Peirce, and John Dewey, many of whom were closely aligned with the progressive movement, offered important arguments that attacked constitutionalism's foundations.[21] Pragmatists held a radical theory of knowledge that rested on social understanding, rather than correspondence with external truths.[22] What we claimed to know about the world was always contingently held, experimentally derived, and, as William James famously insisted, subject to test for its "cash value."[23] This epistemological view was, to say the least, in deep tension with the view that a written constitution could or should entrench supposed political truths for all time.

The social orientation of pragmatists also led naturally to a deep skepticism about individual rights. As legal scholar David Rabban has written, progressives of this stripe "challenged the idea of natural, prepolitical rights held by autonomous individuals in isolation from society, associated law and constitutions with this erroneous conception, and rejected the related position that a laissez-faire government should do little more than protect individual rights."[24]

This critique was directed primarily against judicial protection for rights of property and contract, but importantly, leading pragmatists did not confine their argument to this sphere. For example, before and during World War I, John Dewey repeatedly equated all individual liberties with "privileges based on inequality."[25] At the height of the war, he caustically attacked not only antiwar activists, but also the civil libertarians who supported them for relying upon "early Victorian platitudes" about "the sanctity of individual rights and constitutional guarantees."[26]

Legal scholars associated with a jurisprudential movement called American legal realism were closely allied with the pragmatists and built on pragmatist insights to advance implicit, and occasionally explicit, attacks on constitutionalism. Realist scholars shared with pragmatists a deep skepticism about deriving definite results from general values such as liberty and equality. Even more specific legal rules and precedents could easily be manipulated to produce a wide variety of results in litigated cases. Judges were therefore inevitably pursuing contestable political or policy agendas when they decided cases. Realists insisted that these agendas should be discussed openly and not be obscured by claims that judges were mechanically following the Constitution.[27]

This rule skepticism, distrust of abstractions, and obsession with instrumental rationality translated easily into criticism of the main tools of constitutionalism. Most legal realists were convinced that judges who enforced supposed constitutional guarantees including freedom of contract or protection of private property were not acting out of constitutional compulsion, but out of a set of deeply contestable political views that they were foisting on the rest of the country. As Oliver Wendell Holmes wrote in his celebrated dissent in *Lochner v. New York*, courts should not decide cases based "upon an economic theory which a large part of the country does not entertain."[28]

In the same opinion, Holmes, who was deeply influenced by the pragmatists and a pioneer of legal realism, insisted that "[g]eneral propositions do not decide concrete cases[,]" because decisions "depend on a judgment or intuition more subtle than any articulate major premise." For Holmes, it followed that there should be a sharply constrained role for judges enforcing supposed constitutional commands. In particular, judges should be very reluctant to use the liberty protection of the Fourteenth Amendment "to prevent the natural outcome of a dominant opinion[.]"[29]

Progressive economists including John Commons, Thorstein

Veblen, Walton Hamilton, and Robert Hale, who pioneered an institutional approach, suggested still another line of attack on constitutionalism. Institutional economists insisted that the "laws" of economics were not autonomous.[30] Instead, market outcomes depended upon surrounding institutions. Although all the institutionalists criticized the laissez-faire assumptions that lay behind much of *Lochner*-era constitutionalism, Hale, a Harvard-trained economist who spent most of his career at Columbia Law School, offered a more far-reaching critique that held the potential to undermine any sort of constitutional guarantees.[31]

In a pathbreaking article, Hale brought into question core constitutional dichotomies such as the difference between coercion and freedom or that between public and private.[32] As he pointed out, constitutional law treated government action as presumptively coercive and therefore requiring restraint and private action as presumptively free and therefore requiring protection. In fact, though, virtually all market transactions could be characterized as coercive. A worker who accepted low wages and bad working conditions did so only because the employer was able to threaten him with starvation if he did not comply. Government nonintervention did not make this worker free; instead, it left him vulnerable to this private coercion, which the government could alleviate by restructuring the market. It did not follow, however, that this restructuring would create a world of perfect freedom. If the worker had more market power, then she could coerce the employer.

The upshot was that the link between constitutional rights and freedom was severed. Because coercion was everywhere, it was no longer a useful analytic category. One might still favor public policies based upon their efficacy or upon who was empowered by them, but the goal of achieving universal freedom, and with it the notion of constitutional rights as a protection for individual autonomy, dropped out of the picture.

Although Hale himself did not extend his argument, there was no obvious way to limit his analysis to market "freedoms." Just as "freedom" of contract permitted employers to coerce workers, so too "freedom" of speech, for example, allowed media owners to coerce people who wanted access to the means of effective communication. Of course, constitutions might still structure political outcomes, and people who favored certain outcomes would therefore favor the structures that produced them. But if one took Hale's ideas seriously, the historical conception of constitutional law as a neutral, apolitical protection for human liberty was no longer plausible.

I know of no evidence that Franklin Roosevelt was directly influenced by any of the progressive thinkers discussed previously. Unlike his cousin in 1912, the younger Roosevelt made no reference to constitutional reform in his election campaign of 1932. Unlike Lincoln and Jefferson, he never confessed to violating the Constitution. Nonetheless, his administration produced a constitutional revolution that shook the foundations of standard constitutionalism and provides important support for modern constitutional skepticism.

Although he attended Columbia Law School, the younger Roosevelt was not especially well versed in constitutional law and seems to have thought little about the subject.[33] Upon assuming office, however, he quickly became aware of the manner in which constitutional constraints might impede his effort to deal with the Depression. Roosevelt had little patience with abstractions or impediments to effective action and, so, little patience with these constraints. His efforts to overcome them so as to deal with the Depression and then with World War II led him to positions that deviated sharply from standard constitutional doctrine and, ultimately, to an understanding of how constitutionalism might be refashioned in a nonlegalistic manner.

The saga begins with Roosevelt's first inaugural address, famous for his declaration that "the only thing we have to fear is fear itself." Less famous, but more important to this narrative, was Roosevelt's elliptical but nonetheless unmistakable threat that if Congress did not act, he would assume extraordinary powers:

Our Constitution is so simple and practical that it is possible always to meet extraordinary needs by changes in emphasis and arrangement without loss of essential form. . . .

It is to be hoped that the normal balance of executive and legislative authority may be wholly adequate to meet the unprecedented task before us. But it may be that an unprecedented demand and need for undelayed action may call for temporary departure from that normal balance of public procedure.

I am prepared under my constitutional duty to recommend the measures that a stricken nation in the midst of a stricken world may require. These measures, or such other measures as the Congress may build out of its experience and wisdom, I shall seek, within my constitutional authority, to bring to speedy adoption.

But in the event that the Congress shall fail to take one of these two courses, and in the event that the national emergency is still critical, I shall not evade the clear course of duty that will then confront me. I shall ask the Congress for the one remaining instrument to meet the crisis—broad Executive power to wage a war against the emergency, as great as the power that would be given to me if we were in fact invaded by a foreign foe.[34]

This language is more important for the mindset that it revealed than for any immediate action that it presaged. In fact, with the possible exception of his arguably illegal executive order declaring a bank holiday, Roosevelt made no early attempts to upset the basic constitutional structure. A compliant Congress never put him to the test.[35] The passage nonetheless reveals two crucial aspects of Roosevelt's thought: his willingness to depart from widespread assumptions about constitutional limits when necessary to meet an emergency, and his ability to justify these departures by a rereading of the Constitution as a "simple and practical" document that did not impose rigid restraints.

Although Roosevelt did not establish the kind of dictatorship that some hoped for and others feared, there can be no doubt that the early New Deal upset standard conceptions of federalism and separation of powers. Many New Deal reforms had antecedents in earlier legislation. Still, when taken together, nothing in our constitutional experience rivaled them. Never before had the national government assumed such comprehensive power over the economy, and never before had Congress delegated so much authority and discretion to the executive branch.

Not surprisingly, these measures elicited constitutional challenge. In meeting that challenge, Roosevelt never expressly asserted his right to violate the Constitution. Indeed, he often asserted his reverence for the document. But that reverence was based on an idiosyncratic reading of it that combined an audacious insistence on his independent authority to interpret the Constitution with a substantive interpretation that eliminated virtually all occasions for violation.

Roosevelt's resistance to judicial interference was on display from the beginning to the end of his presidency. Early on, when it appeared that the Supreme Court might invalidate legislation that altered contracts providing for payment in gold, he made plans, never executed because the Court upheld the legislation, to utilize extraordinary measures that would circumvent the Court's decision.[36]

Later, when the Court did invalidate some important New Deal programs and threatened to invalidate more of them, Roosevelt considered and ultimately decided against the remedy of constitutional amendment. He seems to have rejected this course in part because he insisted on the correctness of his own interpretation of the Constitution, under which no amendment was necessary. Instead, he sought to discipline the Court by increasing its size. At first, he disingenuously argued for court-packing on the ground that it was necessary to relieve the workload of superannuated justices, but eventually he acknowledged what was obvious to everyone—that the legislation was designed to privilege his own constitutional interpretation over the views of the judiciary.[37]

Roosevelt's court-packing plan failed, but he ultimately managed to transform the Court through the power of appointment. And even after the Court was populated by justices he himself had appointed, Roosevelt continued to insist on his independent right to interpret the Constitution. When German saboteurs were caught on American territory during World War II, Roosevelt arranged for the men to be tried before a hastily convened military commission. He also made clear that he would adhere to these procedures no matter what a court said. As Attorney General Francis Biddle later recounted, Roosevelt announced, "I want one thing clearly understood, Francis. I won't give them up. . . . I won't hand them over to any United States marshal armed with a writ of habeas corpus. Understand?"[38] Faced with the prospect of being ignored, the Supreme Court caved. It announced a *per curiam* decision upholding Roosevelt's actions the day after oral argument, and did not get around to releasing its opinion in the case until after the men had been executed.[39]

Roosevelt's substantive view of the Constitution was unorthodox, to say the least. Broadly speaking, there were two branches to his thinking: a rejection of technical, constitutional limitations on government power, and an embrace of affirmative rights. These two branches, in turn, suggest a meaning of the Constitution that at once makes it "our law" but also advances an interpretation of "our law" at war with conventional accounts.

His first inaugural address briefly invoked the first view when he spoke of the Constitution as a "simple and practical" document. He argued for this position in more detail in his Constitution Day speech of 1937, one of the greatest yet least remembered major speeches of his presidency. The speech came in the immediate wake of the defeat of his court-packing plan and on the one hundred fiftieth anniversary of the Constitution. Speaking to a huge throng from the base of the Washington Monument,[40] Roosevelt declared that "[t]he men who wrote the Constitution were the men who fought the Revolution" and "had watched a weak emergency government almost lose the war." They created "a layman's document," he insisted, "not a lawyer's contract."[41] It "cannot be stressed too often," he claimed, that "Madison, most responsible for it, was not a lawyer; nor was Washington or Franklin, whose sense of the give-and-take of life had kept the Convention together." The Constitution, therefore was a "charter of general principles, completely different from the 'whereases' and the 'parties of the first part' and the fine print which lawyers put into leases and insurance policies and installment agreements."[42]

It naturally followed from this conception of the Constitution that the Supreme Court should not have the last word in enforcing it. "Contrary to the belief of many Americans, the Constitution says nothing about any power of the Court to declare legislation unconstitutional." Instead, "[a]gain and again the Convention voted down proposals to give the Justices of the Court a veto over legislation."[43] Roosevelt saw himself as participating in the latest skirmish in a 150-year-old battle between "those who would preserve this original broad concept of the Constitution as a layman's instrument of government" and the judges and lawyers "who would shrivel the Constitution into a lawyer's contract." Ultimately, he insisted, the American people would be victorious over "those who professionally or politically talk and think in purely legalistic phrases" and "cry 'unconstitutional' at every effort to better the conditions of our people."[44]

The Constitution as Roosevelt imagined it—a constitution that was not "legalistic," that contained only broad principles to structure discussion, and that was flexible enough to meet current needs (according to whom?)—might be thought to be no constitution at all, at least in the conventional sense. But Roosevelt's constitution fit seamlessly into the skeptical tradition. It was a constitution that enshrined attitudes and general goals, and promoted untrammeled political debate, not rigid rules or efforts to control politics with the dead hand of the past. Put differently, it was the skeptic's constitution.

Roosevelt linked this constitutional vision to a decentralized system of enforcement that deprived courts of final interpretive authority. His version of the Constitution was not grounded in the argument of lawyers. Instead it was a "layman's document" that provided a basis for good-faith contestation rather than haughty commands from elite judges.

If the Constitution were conceptualized in this way, Roosevelt thought, there was no contradiction between constitutional obligation on the one hand and revolutionizing American government on the other. His constitution was capacious enough to support not only pervasive national regulation of the American economy and the creation of the administrative state, but also, it must be admitted, the internment of Japanese Americans[45] and prosecution of dissenters against the war.[46]

The second branch of Roosevelt's theory of the Constitution flipped the historical association between constitutionalism and negative rights. Drawing on a generation of progressive thought, Roosevelt argued that the Constitution required the subordination of the private sphere to government regulation, rather than the protection of the private sphere from government overreaching.

Focus on Roosevelt's battle with the Supreme Court has tended to obscure this truly radical branch of New Deal jurisprudence. The argument over the constitutional validity of the New Deal turned on the extent of the political branches' discretionary power, and Roosevelt's ultimate victory loosened constitutional constraints. But Roosevelt was not satisfied with merely discretionary power. He argued that the Constitution compelled government intervention—the very thing that the Constitution was conventionally interpreted to prohibit.

There were hints of this position going back to his original 1932 campaign,[47] but Roosevelt spelled out his theory most clearly when he proposed a "second bill of rights" in a speech to Congress in early 1944.[48] In his view, the first Bill of Rights had "proved inadequate to assure us equality in the pursuit of happiness." This was so because "true individual freedom cannot exist without economic security and independence." Accordingly, the country needed a new bill of rights that included the right to "a useful and remunerative job," the right to "earn enough to provide adequate food and clothing and recreation," the right to "a decent home," the right to "a good education," and the right to "adequate medical care and the opportunity to achieve and enjoy good health."[49]

There is an obvious tension between these two branches of Roosevelt's constitutional jurisprudence. If the Constitution was not a legally enforceable document, how did it create a legal right to the positive goods that Roosevelt listed? The tension is lessened, although not completely resolved, by the fact that this second bill of rights was, apparently, to be implemented by legislation rather than judicial decree.[50] Put differently, the second bill of rights was part of the skeptic's constitution, not the standard constitution. By labeling it a "bill of rights," Roosevelt seemed to imply that Congress was under an obligation to enact the measures he proposed. But by remitting the question to the political sphere, he emphasized yet again that, for him, constitutional "rights" were a starting point for political negotiation, not fixed and inflexible legal commands.

The more serious tension, though, is between the second bill of rights and the standard tools of constitutional analysis. That analysis treated private markets as a baseline closely associated with individual liberty. On this view, speech was free so long as Congress made no laws, and the people were secure in their persons, houses, papers, and effects so long as the government conducted no unreasonable searches and seizures.

Roosevelt's second bill of rights dissolved this link. If true constitutional freedom required not just the protection *from* government but also the protection *of* government, then how were we to evaluate government coercion that increased the freedom of some by depriving others of freedom? On a view like this, the internment of Japanese Americans or suppression of wartime dissent might be not just constitutionally permissible, but actually constitutionally mandatory, if they were necessary to provide government protection for the majority.

Moreover, once the Constitution was seen to protect two different and sometimes conflicting sets of rights, enforcement of rights necessarily meant balancing some claims against others. Because the relative values of the rights to be protected *from* and *by* the government are not specified in the Constitution, the process of value assignment is inevitably political rather than legal.

Roosevelt succeeded in remaking the Supreme Court and opening the discretionary space for economic regulation, but the truly radical implications of his constitutional thought and, more broadly, the general progressive critique of constitutionalism never gained a firm foothold. By the time he spoke in 1944, progressive skepticism was already beginning to fall into disrepute. The rise of fascism in Europe gave a different cultural meaning to claims that law reflected no more than power, and the repopulation of the Supreme Court with Roosevelt-appointed judges made progressives themselves more at ease with judicial enforcement of constitutional norms. Moreover, the formation of a New Deal coalition that included racial, religious, and political minorities turned support for civil rights and civil liberties protections into a political necessity.

These political developments, in turn, led directly to the Warren Court, and to a different brand of constitutional skepticism in the modern period.

ELEVEN

Ordaining and Establishing This Constitution, Part 3

Modern Skepticism

In the fall of 1953, Chief Justice Fred Vinson suddenly succumbed to a heart attack. Vinson had been an ineffectual, mostly conservative leader who had been supportive of McCarthy-era prosecution of radicals and was an uncertain vote in *Brown v. Board of Education*, which was pending before the Court at the time of his death. In an uncharitable moment, his colleague Justice Felix Frankfurter is supposed to have remarked that Vinson's death was the first solid evidence he had seen of the existence of God.[1]

Pursuant to a deal he had made to secure the presidential nomination, President Eisenhower named Earl Warren as chief justice. Warren was a mild-mannered, moderate, but reform-minded Republican governor of California. He had strongly supported the internment of Japanese American citizens during World War II and had run for the vice presidency with Thomas Dewey in 1948.[2]

At the time of his selection, few anticipated the tumultuous events that occurred during his chief justiceship. Over the course of his first year in office, Warren painstakingly put together a unanimous Court to hold that segregated education was unconstitutional. In a series of landmark decisions that followed, the Court he headed revolutionized American criminal procedure, established the one-person-one-vote standard for reapportionment, and provided important support for free speech rights.

The country's experience during this period supports both standard constitutionalists and constitutional skeptics. Some commentators remain nostalgic for the Court that gave us Warren Court reforms and believe that its achievements demonstrate the unrealized possibilities of liberal constitutionalism.[3] But the more dominant modern view is that the Warren Court's obvious failures serve as a cautionary tale about the limits of judicially centered constitutional power.[4] On this view, the Court's long-term failures led to the modern period marked by what legal scholar Mark Tushnet has aptly called the chastening of constitutional aspiration.[5]

Consider first the civil rights revolution. The struggle over the Second Reconstruction offered a replay of the fusion of constitutional and anticonstitutional rhetoric that marked the antebellum period. Both sides used standard constitutional tools to advance their positions, but, when necessary, both sides also resorted to tactics and arguments that challenged constitutional norms. To the extent that both sides resorted to anticonstitutional tactics, their actions support the claim that constitutional skeptics make for the historical pedigree of their position.

The efforts of southern opponents of racial equality were less interesting because the theories were less original. Instead of developing new constitutional theories, they recycled old ones. Nullification, interposition, and states' rights made new appearances, and the theoretical musings of secessionists gained new popularity. Once again, these arguments were supplemented with extraconstitutional rhetoric and actions. While lawyers made legal arguments in court, thugs, in and out of uniform, coupled revolutionary rhetoric with violence in the streets.[6]

In contrast, opponents of racial segregation pioneered new legal and extralegal tactics,[7] but the division between constitutional and skeptical arguments, and the paradoxical conjunction of the two, was not new at all. The division is neatly if overly simply personified by the rivalry between Thurgood Marshall and Martin Luther King Jr. Marshall led the NAACP's legal campaign against Jim Crow by insisting on respect for the rule of law. Like Marshall, King grounded his arguments in constitutional rhetoric, but he deemphasized detailed legal argument before courts. Instead, he pursued a strategy of civil disobedience and direct action that effectively changed the meaning of the Constitution.[8]

Even a half century later, historians argue about which strategy was more successful. The ambiguity is symbolized by the Montgomery bus boycott. King's leadership of the boycott galvanized advocates of civil rights across the country, but the boycott came to a successful conclusion only after Marshall secured a holding from the Supreme Court that segregated public transportation was unconstitutional.[9]

Doubtless both Marshall's constitutional arguments and King's Constitution-changing social movement contributed to the shift in public attitudes that ultimately produced results on the ground. But even if one focuses only on judicial developments, actions of the Warren Court strongly support the skeptical tradition. It is true that Brown constitutes a remarkable reformulation of constitutional law to advance the cause of racial liberation. But there is strong evidence that at least some of the justices voted for the result in spite of, rather than because of, conventional constitutional argument. They cast their votes because of moral and political conviction—the kind of conviction that is at the heart of the skeptical constitution—rather than because they thought the result was legally required in the conventional sense.[10]

That fact is hardly surprising given the shaky support for the result in standard constitutional materials. Brown was almost certainly inconsistent with the original expected application of the Fourteenth Amendment and with decades of precedent.[11] Instead of utilizing the usual tools of constitutional analysis,[12] Chief Justice Warren relied upon social science evidence of dubious relevance and reliability.[13] Viewed from this perspective, Brown can be seen as analogous to President Lincoln's Emancipation

Proclamation—a courageous and crucial act of constitutional disobedience barely disguised by thin and unconvincing constitutional argument.

Moreover, even if *Brown* itself can be constitutionally justified, what came next fits easily within the skeptical tradition. After deciding that "separate but equal" was unconstitutional, the Court set the case for reargument on the question of remedy. According to conventional constitutionalism, a practice that violates the Constitution is legally void and cannot be enforced, but the Warren Court did not see things that way. The next year, the Court held that although jurisdictions had to make a reasonable start toward desegregation, they could utilize "all deliberate speed" in accomplishing this goal.[14] In the meantime, unconstitutional segregation could remain in place. Most students of *Brown* agree that this equivocation was the result of a political compromise dictated by the felt need to avoid violent resistance, rather than by conventional constitutional law.

On the same day that *Brown* was decided, the Court held that segregation in the District of Columbia violated the Fifth Amendment's due process clause despite the fact that the clause was ratified in 1791, long before enactment of the Thirteenth Amendment and at a time when it was reasonably clear that the Constitution protected slavery.[15] The Court made no serious effort to explain this result in conventional constitutional terms, asserting instead that it was simply "unthinkable" that the nation's capital should have segregated schools.

Brown had announced that school segregation was unconstitutional because of the special role of education and because of its effects on the hearts and minds of schoolchildren,[16] but, to the dismay of constitutionalists, without explanation the Court announced that the same rule applied in contexts that had nothing to do with children or education.[17] These decisions, too, support the view that Brown's legal arguments were for show and that the Court had actually embarked on an extraconstitutional social and political project.

The same point holds when, instead of extending *Brown*, the Court refused to recognize its obvious implications. Shortly after *Brown* was decided, an interracial couple sought to invalidate racist state statutes that prohibited miscegenation. The statutes were obviously unconstitutional, but now that the justices' private conference notes are available, we know that they were more worried about politics than law. Those notes reveal that, with some reason, they feared that striking down the statutes would intensify southern resistance and perhaps doom the entire desegregation effort. Instead of enforcing the principles that it had recently announced, the Court managed to dispose of the case without reaching the merits in a manner that most contemporary and modern commentators consider lawless.[18]

All of these decisions suggest that the justices saw their role as political rather than legal. Of course, when the Constitution served their purposes, they used constitutional rhetoric. It does not follow, though, that the justices were ultimately motivated by constitutional obedience. When constitutional obligation got in the way, they exhibited a remarkable readiness to override the piece of parchment in Washington.

In addition to its support for civil rights, the Warren Court revolutionized criminal procedure,[19] significantly expanded free speech protections,[20] provided important guarantees for voting rights,[21] and took tentative first steps toward providing constitutional protection for the poor.[22] If one includes the early years of the Burger Court in the historical reckoning, then the protection of reproductive rights and guarantees of gender equality should be added to the list of accomplishments. All of these decisions are widely celebrated by modern legal liberals. Unfortunately, though, the Warren Court too often mistook elite prejudices for eternal principles, and its efforts to constitutionalize criminal procedure underestimated the complexity of the problem. These difficulties, as well as the subsequent history of Warren Court reforms, support the claims of constitutional skeptics.

Writing in the immediate wake of the Warren years, law professor Alexander Bickel argued that the Court would ultimately
be judged by its ability to predict the future. He thought that the
Court had failed to do so,[23] and now that the future has arrived, it
seems that he was largely correct. The point is not so much that
Warren Court precedent has been overruled—although some of
it certainly has been[24]—as that it has become irrelevant. For example, the effort to end segregated schools was mostly undone
by neighborhood school policies superimposed upon residential
segregation.[25] Warren Court criminal procedure reforms failed
to prevent historically unprecedented increases in incarceration
rates[26] and a growing racial disproportion in those rates.[27] Some
commentators think that Warren Court decisions have actually
worsened these trends.[28] Similarly, the widespread implementa-
tion of political gerrymandering has made a mockery of the notion that one person, one vote could produce political fairness.[29]
The Court's hints that economic injustice might be subject to
constitutional attack were stillborn.[30]

On a more general level, the Warren Court had at best limited success in convincing the country that judicial power legitimated by constitutional text dictated broad-based social reforms.
Ultimately, the failure rested on a political miscalculation. The
justices thought that they could harness constitutional obligation
to produce meaningful social change. They seemed to think that
people would be motivated to do things that they would not otherwise do just because an elite institution told them that the Constitution required this action. It turned out, though, that the rhetoric
of obligation was insufficiently powerful to convince large numbers of people to accept change they did not want. Instead, as the
political winds shifted and the composition of the Court changed,
Warren Court interpretations were met with opposing interpretations that mandated different results that were more popular.
The upshot is an experience that strongly reinforces skeptical
doubts about whether constitutional law can effectively combat

the social, political, economic, and cultural forces that are the ultimate determinants of public policy.

Where does all this history leave us now? Today, no revered ex-president defends his own constitutional violations, raises questions about intergenerational obligation, or argues that Supreme Court decisions should be reversed by popular referendum. No one of consequence is burning the Constitution or calling it a pact with the devil. On the contrary, for many Americans, anxieties associated with the Trump administration have reinvigorated the argument for constitutional obedience. Both Trump and his rivals regularly invoke the Constitution. Even some legal academics associated with the left have embraced constitutional originalism. At least superficially, it seems that the skeptical tradition has run into a dead end.

But this conclusion is way too simple. True, skeptical arguments no longer receive the kind of overt and boisterous support they once did, but one does not have to look very far beneath the surface to see that constitutional skepticism is nonetheless alive and well.

Consider popular attitudes toward the Constitution. Many Americans profess unquestioning allegiance to the Constitution, and commentators regularly make constitutional arguments on all sides of public policy issues. Still, Trump's election in 2016 despite his failure to win the popular vote and his success in "stacking" the Supreme Court and lower federal courts have each raised nagging questions about whether our constitutionally ordained government structures are really serving our needs. Fears that the country is coming apart at the seams and that our supposedly common commitments are insufficient to sustain us as a nation are growing, if still nascent. If the current period is not quite the analogue to the 1850s, when civil war was just over the horizon, neither is it the analogue to the 1950s, when the American project seemed secure.

This unease is magnified by deep cynicism about the role that constitutional argument actually plays in our political culture. The cynicism finds clear expression in the media's regular identification of judges and justices with reference to the party of the president who appointed them. And it is on full display at judicial confirmation hearings, which have turned into undisguised political warfare.[31] According to polling data, most Americans believe that political considerations play at least some role in Supreme Court decision-making.[32] It escapes almost no one's attention that politicians regularly use constitutional arguments about, for example, healthcare, crime prevention, and voting rights to support conclusions that they would come to anyway.

This combination of outward devotion to the rhetoric and rituals of constitutionalism with inner doubt and despair is bound to be unstable. The situation is made only worse by the Supreme Court's own ambivalence. Consider, for example, two modern decisions exhibiting the two, rival forms of constitutional analysis currently in vogue. In the gun control case *District of Columbia v. Heller*,[33] both sides conspicuously deployed originalist methodology. Justice Scalia, writing for the Court, found that the original public meaning of the Second Amendment made the District's gun control statute unconstitutional. Justice Stevens, using the same techniques, found that the original public meaning of the amendment was consistent with the statute.[34] Both justices filled scores of pages of the *United States Reports* with detailed analysis of the linguistic structure, dictionary meanings, and popular contemporary understanding of the amendment. Remarkably, the upshot was a near standoff. Five justices thought that the statute was clearly inconsistent with the amendment, while four justices thought that it was clearly not.

Of course, all methods of analysis produce disagreement, but two additional facts about the Court's performance make the outcome in *Heller* especially troubling. First, the difference of opinion over supposedly apolitical matters such as semantics and dictionary meaning precisely tracked the ideological differences on the Court. Somehow, all five of the conservative justices read the amendment one way, while all four of the liberal justices read the same language the other way.

Second, virtually all of what the justices on both sides of the question wrote was deeply irrelevant to the important public policy question that ought to concern us. Gun control poses hard questions about which reasonable people can disagree. Does any sensible person suppose that these questions should be answered by determining what some people thought over two centuries ago in a society that was radically different in culture, technology, and geography?

Many people who think that this is not a sensible way to decide questions like this adhere to the "living constitution" theory of interpretation. On this view, judges should not be limited by the original understanding of constitutional language, but instead should strive to give it modern meaning. Although Justice Kennedy did not identify it as such, he used this approach in *Obergefell v. Hodges*,[35] the case creating a constitutional right to same-sex marriage. Justice Kennedy's opinion made no effort to uncover the original meaning of constitutional text or the specific intent of its Framers. Indeed, he barely identified the text he relied upon. Instead, his opinion consisted of an extended sermon on the virtues of marriage and respect for individual rights.

In angry dissenting opinions, the conservative justices correctly pointed out that Kennedy's opinion rested on an implicit, nonconstitutional moral premise—that gay sex and marriage were at worst morally neutral and at best an important means of human expression. One might suppose from this attack that the conservatives stood for principled neutrality in what Justice Scalia has referred to as our "culture war."[36] Unfortunately for them, however, their own votes and opinions in racial affirmative action cases rest on a similarly contestable moral premise. Like Kennedy's opinion in *Obergefell*, the opinions written by conservatives in cases about so-called racial preferences never investigate original public meaning. Instead, they rest exclusively on moral and sociological judgments about the supposed evil of racial categorization.[37]

Hypocrisy of this sort is too obvious to miss. Nor does it require deep analysis to discover that the votes in *Obergefell* and in affirmative action cases once again precisely track the Court's political divisions. Given these facts, it is not surprising that so many members of the general public have difficulty taking the Court's constitutional pretensions seriously.

Perhaps more importantly, though, a surprisingly large number of Americans think that it is a good thing when the Court does not decide cases based solely upon the Constitution. For example, a CBS News poll conducted in 2013 asked respondents whether the Supreme Court, when deciding an important constitutional case, should consider only the legal issue or also "what a majority of the public thinks about that subject." Forty-seven percent of respondents thought that the justices should confine themselves to the legal issue, but 45 percent thought that they should also consider public opinion.[38] According to another poll, over a quarter of Americans disagree with the statement "The United States Constitution is an enduring document that remains relevant today" and agreed instead with the view "The United States Constitution is an outdated document that needs to be modernized."[39]

The public's ambivalent attitude toward the Constitution is mirrored in the academy. To be sure, virtually all modern scholars of constitutional law begin with some kind of commitment to constitutional fidelity. Only a tiny handful of legal academics overtly raise questions about constitutional obligation. Despite this fact, constitutional skepticism plays a central role in contemporary constitutional scholarship.

Sometimes it shows up in quite surprising places. Consider, for example, the "Constitution in exile" movement. Some conservative judges and scholars have argued that much of modern government, including the entire apparatus of the administrative state, violates the Constitution.[40] Of course, their fervent complaints about this state of affairs are grounded in constitutional fidelity. If one looks beneath the surface, however, their argument also supports the skeptical position. After all, if it is really true that for years broad swaths of legal doctrine have been infected by blatant constitutional violation, then it cannot also be true that constitutional obedience plays a central role in maintaining the stability of our government and culture. In a backhanded way, the claims of the "Constitution in exile" proponents support the skeptical argument that the standard Constitution is unnecessary to hold the country together.

Moreover, if the "Constitution in exile" proponents are correct, we are faced with the daunting question of what to do about it. A return to original constitutional understandings might, among other things, permit the revival of overt gender discrimination[41] and allow states to outlaw interracial marriage.[42] A few diehards are prepared to accept this and more, but even most originalists find these outcomes too much to swallow. Accordingly, they avoid these results with transparent dodges like reliance on precedent or dependence on the same sort of tendentious, result-driven arguments that they (rightly) accuse their opponents of using. In obvious ways, the use of both techniques supports the skeptical position.

Other conservative judges and academics are much more straightforward in endorsing aspects of constitutional skepticism. For example, conservative natural-law advocates including law professor Adrian Vermeule reject the proposition that we should rely on the Constitution if it is not supported by sound moral principles.[43] Richard Posner, until his retirement perhaps the best-known lower federal court judge in the country and once the darling of conservatives, maintains that the United States Supreme Court is political in its orientation and denies that constitutional law, at least as conventionally understood, explains or justifies what judges do.[44] J. Harvie Wilkinson, another distinguished conservative jurist, purports to disagree with Posner but apparently shares his view that no theory of constitutional law is satisfactory.[45]

Scholars on the left are, if anything, even more receptive to skeptical positions. For example, academics associated with the critical legal studies school, including Mark Tushnet,[46] Duncan Kennedy,[47] and Peter Gabel,[48] have attacked the very concept of constitutional rights. More recently, Tushnet,[49] together with law professor Larry Kramer[50] and legal philosopher Jeremy Waldron,[51] argued against the assumption that judges should enforce the Constitution. Tushnet has coupled this attack with an endorsement of a "thin"[52] — some would say anorexic[53] — Constitution, limited to the ideals expressed in the Preamble and the Bill of Rights.

In two important books, law professor Sanford Levinson has written in detail about the Constitution's many deficiencies and called for a new constitutional convention to correct them.[54] Other distinguished law professors have expressed similar skeptical doubts. For example, Yale law professor Bruce Ackerman[55] and his colleague Akhil Amar[56] have both argued that the Constitution can be and has been changed outside the formal amendment process. Maryland law professor Mark Graber[57] and Yale law professor Jack Balkin[58] have written more generally about the problem of "constitutional evil." Georgetown law professor Girardeau Spann has argued that constitutional judicial review systematically harms racial minorities,[59] and his colleague Gary Peller has attacked the standard integrationist view, which dominates constitutional treatments of race.[60] Another Georgetown colleague, Robin West, has maintained that constitutionalism, especially when associated with judicial review, stunts moral imagination.[61]

In short, reports of the death of constitutional skepticism are greatly exaggerated. Of course, every generation refashions skeptical arguments to suit its own needs, just as every generation has its own version of constitutionalism. The skepticism of early twenty-first-century America is not the same as the skepticism of the Founders, or of the antebellum period, or of the Progressives. Yet amid all of the celebration of the American Constitution and

denigration of its critics, something identifiable as a skeptical tradition, connected to crucial political events throughout our history, continues to survive and flourish.

All political entities have to tell a coherent story about themselves
over time. We need to believe that the United States is not just
a collection of people who happen to inhabit the same physical
space. We are a nation—a people—and not just a random collection of people.

To be a people, we need a common history. Defenders of
constitutionalism claim that the Constitution is at the center of
our history—that it is "our law." We need not deny that there is
some truth to this story, but the skeptical argument begins with
the observation there are also others we could tell. Our history is
not something that just exists. It is constructed and reconstructed
through political struggle. There is a version of our history that
emphasizes constitutional obedience, but there is also a version,
more than adequately supported by the historical record, that emphasizes continual struggle against constitutional authority. We
have a choice as to which version to embrace.

Once one understands that there really is a choice, in some
sense the choice has already been made. The argument for constitutional obedience ultimately rests on a perception of powerless-
ness. The Constitution is just there; we are stuck with it, whether
we like it or not, because it is our law, it is embedded in our history, and our law and history define who we are. Once one sees
that we in fact have power to define for ourselves who we are, this
argument collapses.

All that remains, then, is to summon the courage to use the
power that we have always already had.

TWELVE

Bending Toward Justice?

Both Martin Luther King Jr. and Barack Obama liked to quote the nineteenth-century transcendentalist Theodore Parker: "The arc of the universe is long, but it bends toward justice."[1] By now, the quotation has been repeated so often that it has become little more than a vaguely comforting cliché. Suppose, though, that one took the assertion seriously. How could one know that it is true, and what does it even mean?

At the beginning of Tom Stoppard's great play *Rosencrantz and Guildenstern Are Dead*, the two title characters are betting on coin flips. Rosencrantz has flipped heads ninety-two times in a row. At that moment, the arc of the universe was definitely bending toward heads. A statistician would tell you, though, that those ninety-two heads tell us nothing about the ninety-third flip— unless the fix is in because, for example, the coin is weighted.

King probably thought that the fix was in. He had faith in a God that bent the arc of the universe. Was he right? Perhaps, but many constitutional skeptics doubt it. They suspect that the universe is neither good nor bad. Instead, it is cold, dark, and empty. Its arc is infinite, random, unknowable, and meaningless. It might bend one way for a million years, but then bend another way for a million years. There is no overall "bend," and even if there were, we could not know what it was because the full pattern would be visible only at the end of time, and time has no end.

This doubt about the bend of the universe creates a difficulty for the constitutional skeptic: skepticism about cosmic justice tends to undermine skepticism about constitutions. If the universe is random and meaningless, then on what ground does the constitutional skeptic stand when she criticizes constitutionalism? If cosmic justice is a myth, then the American Constitution is neither just nor unjust. And if commitment to the Constitution is morally neutral, then why go to the trouble of trying to undo the commitment?

For many constitutional skeptics, the answer lies in recognition of the inevitability of choice and responsibility. Whether or not there is cosmic justice, we face unavoidable decisions about how to construct our country. Doing nothing is itself a decision, and not an admirable one.

A constitutional skeptic looks to neither the standard Constitution nor to the universe to avoid this responsibility. Constitutions cannot tell us what to do, and the universe has no arc. When things go wrong, we cannot blame the Founders, the constitutional text, the law, or the universe. We have the responsibility to make meaning, and we have only ourselves to blame if we make a mess of the job.

Understanding this responsibility can turn people into constitutional skeptics. But what of the skeptic's constitution? The skeptic's constitution must recognize human agency and reasonable disagreement on the one hand but avoid anarchic chaos on the other. Conventional constitutionalism tries to solve the problem by sacrificing agency to avoid anarchy. On this view, people must be made to see that the Supreme Court, American tradition, the law writ large, uncontroversial premises derived from rationality and neutrality, foundational conceptions of rights, and the arc of the universe all command particular outcomes. A skeptic knows that none of this will work.

In fact, the constitutional skeptic knows that in the long run, not even brute force will work. Even the most vicious tyrant does not himself wield enough power to make others comply. The

seemingly fearsome East German regime turned out to be powerless when guards at its borders refused to shoot people determined
to leave. To exercise power, even a tyrant must convince the people with guns to use them, and their choice, too, implicates human agency.

For the constitutional skeptic, it follows from these foundational facts that neither constitutional law nor force can hold a
society together. What is required instead is individual free and
consensual acts. That necessity, in turn, forces confrontation with
the other side of the dilemma. If we recognize individual agency,
how do we avoid anarchy?

The beginning of an answer involves recognizing the difference between constitutional and ordinary law. Much of what is
necessary to avoid anarchy rests on statutes and judicial decisions
in nonconstitutional cases. If this ordinary lawmaking is authorized by a constitution, and if that constitution is itself justified,
then it follows that the ordinary law is justified. In most cases,
then, the obligation to obey ordinary law based on a just constitution will ward off anarchy.

That is only the beginning of an answer, though, because we
are still left with the large problem of justifying a constitution
that authorizes ordinary law. For the constitutional skeptic, this
requires imagining a different kind of constitution. Constitutional
skeptics are not nihilists; they have strong commitments and values. For just that reason, constitutional skeptics resist the commands of others. And for just *that* reason, they recognize the right
of *others* to resist commands. Constitutional skeptics therefore
have no desire to reach permanent outcomes or cut off debate.
Instead, they value dialogue among people who disagree. The
only admission ticket to the dialogue is a shared commitment to
make the country the best it can be. Because participants disagree
on the implications of that commitment, the dialogue can have
no foreordained outcome and it will never end. Precisely because
the universe has no arc, it is up to us to agree on the temporary

direction in which we will travel, always recognizing that we might at any moment change direction.

The skeptic's constitution is not easily reduced to writing. It is an attitude, a way of living, not a set of rules. It is exemplified by the way we treat our fellow citizens—how we negotiate our differences, how we listen to others, how we compromise rather than insist on using all the power we have. Supreme Court decisions, based on conventional constitutionalism, supposedly settle disputes by declaring a winner and a loser. The winner gloats, and the loser's anger builds. The skeptic's constitution declares no permanent winners and losers. Instead, it builds community by ruling no outcomes out of bounds and encouraging unending argument.

Although no document can fully capture this way of living, in our culture the Constitution's Preamble comes close enough to embodying it. The Framers invoked "We the People" and promised to "form a more perfect Union, establish Justice, insure domestic Tranquility, provide for the common defence and promote the general Welfare, and secure the Blessings of Liberty." Because they dictate no final outcomes, these words work well enough as an invitation to the dialogue on which skeptical constitutionalism rests.

No doubt, many readers will find this description of the skeptic's constitution fanciful. How could such a constitution possibly function at the ground level? How will we know when to hold presidential elections, when a mere proposal becomes a law, when state coercion is justified? What will prevent the government from persecuting racial and religious minorities, closing down newspapers, or ending reproductive freedom? Doesn't a requirement of universal consent ultimately end in anarchy?

These are legitimate questions, but there are good answers to them. All of the answers ultimately rest on a single assertion: we don't have to guess whether the skeptic's constitution will work because, in important respects, it is the Constitution we already have, and—at least until recently—it has worked well enough.

To see how this is true, suppose that we ask a different set of questions. Why has Congress never refused to appropriate money paying the salary of the president's press secretary or reduced the size of the Supreme Court to two justices? Why has the president never threatened to veto every bill that Congress enacts unless he gets his way? Why do Supreme Court justices refrain from openly campaigning for political candidates? None of these things is prohibited by our written constitution. At least until recently, though, all of them were unthinkable. The reason they were unthinkable was that they violate long-standing traditions and accommodations that are widely recognized as necessary to keep our country together. Put differently, these things don't happen because, if they did, they would violate the skeptic's constitution.

Is it really true that a written document, safely behind glass in the National Archives Building, prevents the president from extending his term for two extra years? Is it really the mighty wrath of the long-dead authors of the Fourteenth Amendment that prevents us from taking citizenship away from African Americans? Do we have to consult Article I of the Constitution to know that commands that I write down on a piece of paper are not the laws of the United States? Of course not.

The point seems so obvious that I am embarrassed to make it, but perhaps it is necessary to say that words on a piece of paper command no armies and compel no outcomes. What ultimately prevents these outcomes is also the skeptic's constitution. An effort to change the president's term of office, for example, would violate years of tradition and produce chaos and violence. It is precisely because Americans know that anarchy is worse than temporary political loss—just because they hold their own principles of political justice while also recognizing that some fellow citizens hold different conceptions—that they would resist this effort.

It does not follow, though, that the skeptic's constitution produces outcomes identical to those of conventional constitutionalism. The skeptic's constitution recognizes the force of tradition, custom, reciprocal restraint, and inertia. Under normal circumstances, those forces are sufficient to prevent devolution into a war of all against all. But constitutional skeptics are also pragmatists who favor all-things-considered judgments. There are times and places when tradition, custom, reciprocal restraint, and inertia must give way, and in all times and places the argument that they should give way is at least on the table.

The experience of the United Kingdom, which lacks an integrated written constitution, provides an example for us. By statute and long custom, parliamentary sessions last no more than five years.[2] In theory, Parliament could repeal this provision tomorrow, but the country does not devolve into chaos or civil war whenever the five-year period ends. Under normal circumstances, forces of mutual restraint prevent serious consideration of change. But when circumstances are not normal, the matter is at least up for debate. In fact, twice in the last century or so—during the crises produced by both world wars—the United Kingdom temporarily suspended elections.[3]

Suppose someone were to propose suspending elections in the United States. How should one respond? The conventional constitutionalist would dismiss the argument without providing reasons for the dismissal: "You just can't do that; it is unconstitutional!" But that gets us nowhere. The advocate of the suspension would respond: "Oh yes I can. Here is a (creative) interpretation of the Constitution that permits this outcome" or, perhaps more honestly, "To hell with the Constitution."

The skeptic's response is different: "Well, what are your reasons for doing this? Do they really outweigh the fraying of our political commitments to each other that would surely ensue?" If reasons are then offered and an argument made, the skeptic must listen and offer counterarguments.

Constitutional skeptics believe that we have the freedom and responsibility to make rules for our own time and our own country. That responsibility should not be delegated to people who are long dead, to a piece of parchment slowly turning to dust under glass, to judges shielded from public responsibility, or to the impersonal arc of the universe. Being a citizen in a free republic entails an obligation on the part of all of us to assume that responsibility for ourselves.

A final question looms large and ominous: what if these habits of restraint, tolerance, compromise, and dialogue are not in place? There is growing evidence that the habits are eroding and may soon completely give way. "Constitutional hardball"—the practice of violating long-standing norms in ways that don't directly countermand constitutional text—has become much more common.[4] We are treated to the spectacle of presidents and Congress threatening to default on the national debt if they do not get their way, blocking even measures with which they agree so as to disadvantage the opposing party, threatening to sue the press when it criticizes official actions, systematically refusing to confirm judges and other officials on strictly partisan grounds, and resisting the outcome of a free and fair election.

If these events and fears portend the complete collapse of restraint, tolerance, compromise, and dialogue, then the skeptic's constitution is doomed. Constitutional skeptics believe that, most of the time, we can avoid explosive and unresolvable foundational disputes, and that the promise of a more perfect union—the prospect of a better life for our children, some measure of material prosperity, safety, and stability, some tolerance for difference, some empathy for others, and some respect for our history and tradition—is enough to keep us together.

But not all the time. There are occasions when one simply cannot ignore foundational disagreement, when things come apart at the seams. Importantly, though, if we are now in such a time, conventional constitutionalism will not save us either. Ultimately, if a people decides that they no longer want to live together as fellow citizens and political equals, there is no constitution—no words on a piece of paper and no way of living—that will save us. Like a married couple that discovers they have irreconcilable differences, we will then have to find a method by which we can go our separate ways.

The prospects of such an outcome are now more immediate than they have been at any time since the Civil War. No political arrangement is permanent. Everything eventually ends and, for better or worse, gives way to new beginnings. No sensible person should dismiss the possibility that we are now at such a point.

If so, we will have to live with the consequences. No one should suppose, though, that a divorce would be friendly and costless. Even with all of our differences, we will be much better off if we can somehow work things out. At this point, it remains at least possible that the "mystic chords of memory," which Lincoln invoked at an earlier moment when rupture seemed imminent, might yet motivate us to postpone the inevitable. If we still retain the will, then the skeptic's constitution provides the means by which we might ward off entropy and meaninglessness for a little while longer.

ACKNOWLEDGMENTS

Being a skeptic means changing your mind quite a bit, and over the years, I have changed my mind about much of what I write in this book. I owe my new (and no doubt temporary) enlightenment to two very old friends who have guided me through this process: Mark Tushnet and Michael Klarman. I would like to say that they convinced me of their positions through the sheer potency of their arguments, and, in fact, that is part of what happened. But coming to views about law and life cannot be reduced to an intellectual process. If I am to be honest, I have to say that Mark and Michael persuaded me not just because of what they thought, but because of who they are. I have come to see that I would like to live my life the way that they have lived theirs. Because their understandings of constitutional law are part of who they are, it is now part of who I am.

Aside from Mark and Mike, the person most responsible for the form this book has taken is Diane Wachtell, my editor at The New Press. With just the right combination of flattery and criticism, patience and persistence, she persuaded me to eliminate page after page of dense, sometimes otherworldly prose. More significantly, she guided me toward a structure and presentation that made my sometimes ill-formed ideas more accessible and perspicacious. At The New Press, I would also like to thank Rachel Vega-DeCesario and Emily Albarillo for their help in bringing this book into the world.

Many research assistants helped me with this project, but I am especially grateful to two of them: Casey Chalbeck and Caiti Ver-Brugge. Calling Casey a "research assistant" doesn't really capture her role. Over the course of working on this project, she has become a colleague, a trusted advisor, and a friend. Caiti combines three traits not often joined in nature: a capacity for extraordinarily hard work, an insistence on meeting the highest standards of competence and persistence, and unremitting cheerfulness in the face of pressing deadlines and unreasonable demands.

I've singled out Casey and Caiti because they worked on the entire manuscript, but other research assistants made important contributions to individual chapters. I am especially grateful to Noah Barron, Hannah Kohler, Melissa Stewart, Morgan Stoddard, Katie Wrede, and the staff of the Georgetown University Law Center Library for their help in gathering sources for Chapters 9, 10, and 11.

Lisa Goldfluss has been my friend for almost forty years. I owe her for so much, but somewhere on the list is her willingness to read and critique several chapters of this book and to come up with its title.

So many colleagues and friends gave generously of their time to read and comment on all or portions of the book. Among those whose contributions were most important: Jack Balkin, M. Gregge Bloche, Adam Cox, Michael Diamond, Peter Edelman, Daniel Ernst, Aziz Huq, Vicki Jackson, Jerry Kang, Michael Kazin, Betsy Kuhn, Genevieve Lakier, Martin Lederman, Daryl Levinson, Deborah Malamud, Allegra McLeod, Carrie Menkel-Meadow, Gary Peller, Daria Rothmyer, Adam Samaha, James Sleeper, Girardeau Spann, Laura Weinrib, Russell Stevenson, Robin West, Brian Wolfman, and Raef Zreik.

Portions of this book originally appeared in somewhat different form in articles published by the *Columbia Law Review*, the *University of Connecticut Law Review*, and the *University of Pennsylvania Journal of Constitutional Law*. I am grateful to the publishers of these journals for permission to use this material.

This book is intended as a provocation, but, for me at least, provoking the outside world requires inner peace. I am so grateful to my family for proving the stability and love that make creativity possible: my children, Andrew Seidman and Jessica Seidman; Andrew's partner, Stacy Carmichael; my brothers, Bob Seidman and Peter Seidman; their partners, Maureen O'Connor and Julie Minter; my granddaughter, Lyra Seidman; and most of all, my wife, Judy Mazo.

NOTES

Introduction

1. The winners in 1992 (Clinton), 1996 (Clinton), 2000 (Bush), and 2016 (Trump) received less than half of the popular vote. *See* List of United States Presidential Elections by Popular Vote Margin, en.wikipedia.org/wiki/List_of _United_States_presidential_elections_by_popular_vote_margin (last visited 1/7/21).

2. Al Gore received more votes than George W. Bush in 2000, and Hillary Clinton received more votes than Donald Trump in 2016. *See* id.

3. *See* Philip Bump, *By 2040, Two-thirds of Americans Will Be Represented by 30 Percent of the Senate*, WASH. POST, Nov. 28, 2017.

4. *See* Supreme Court of the United States, Justices 1789 to Present, supreme court.gov/about/members_text.aspx (last visited 1/7/21).

5. *See* List of United States Presidential Elections by Popular Vote Margin, en.wikipedia.org/wiki/List_of_United_States_presidential_elections_by_popular _vote_margin (last visited 1/7/21).

6. *See* United States v. Stevens, 559 U.S. 460 (2010).

7. For the leading contemporary accounts of the framing detailing these facts, see MICHAEL J. KLARMAN, THE FRAMER'S COUP: THE MAKING OF THE UNITED STATES CONSTITUTION (2016). *See also* PAULINE MAIER, RATIFICATION: THE PEOPLE DEBATE THE CONSTITUTION, 1787–1788 (2010); WOODY HOLTON, UNRULY AMERICANS AND THE ORIGINS OF THE CONSTITUTION (2007).

One. We the People, Part 1: The Problem of Democracy and Representation

1. *See* Gallup, Confidence in Institutions, news.gallup.com/poll/1597/con fidence-institutions.aspx (last visited 1/6/21).

2. *See* id.

3. *See* David Kent, The Countries Where People Are Most Dissatisfied with How Democracy Is Working (2019), www.pewresearch.org/fact-tank/2019/05/31 /the-countries-where-people-are-most-dissatisfied-with-how-democracy-is-working (last visited 2/5/21).

4. *See* Pew Social & Demographic Trends Poll Database, www.pew
socialtrends.org/question-search/?qid=1927255&pid=56&ccid=56#top (last visited 2/5/21).

5. *See* id.

6. *See* Peter Moore, Could a Coup Really Happen in the United States?, today
.yougov.com/topics/politics/articles-reports/2015/09/09/could-coup-happen-in
-united-states (last visited 1/6/21).

7. *See* Gallup, Confidence in Institutions, news.gallup.com/poll/1597/con
fidence-institutions.aspx (last visited 1/6/21).

8. *See* id.

9. *See* Bush v. Gore, 531 U.S. 98 (2000).

10. *See* Obergefell v. Hodges, 576 U.S. 644 (2015).

11. For a detailed account, see MICHAEL J. KLARMAN, THE FRAMER'S COUP:
THE MAKING OF THE UNITED STATES CONSTITUTION 257–97 (2016).

12. Madison himself strongly supported a population-based formula for representation in the Senate, *see* id. at 184, but small state delegates "threatened to
abandon the convention—and, if necessary, the union—rather than relinquish
their position." Id. at 192.

13. *See* WOODY HOLTON, UNRULY AMERICANS AND THE ORIGINS OF THE CON-
STITUTION 5 (2007).

14. *Federalist No. 10* in THE FEDERALIST 61 (Jacob E. Cooke ed., 1961).

15. Id. at 57.

16. Id. at 62 (arguing that in a republic, decisions would be made by a "body
of citizens, whose wisdom may best discern the true interest of their country, and
whose patriotism and love of justice, will be least likely to sacrifice it to temporary
or partial considerations").

17. Id. at 63.

18. Id.

19. Id. at 57.

20. Id. at 60.

21. Id. at 349.

22. Id. at 351.

23. Id. at 349.

24. *Federalist No. 10* in id. at 60.

25. According to the Pew Research Center, only 56 percent of voting-age
Americans cast ballots in the 2016 election. That puts the United States seventh
from the bottom of countries in the Organization for Economic Cooperation
and Development and compares with 87.2 percent turnout rates in Belgium and
82.6 percent turnout rates in Sweden. Only Luxemburg, Slovenia, Poland, Chile,
Latvia, and Switzerland have lower participation rates. *See* Drew Desilva, In Past
Elections, U.S. Trailed Most Developed Countries in Voter Turnout, www.pew
research.org/fact-tank/2018/05/21/u-s-voter-turnout-trails-most-developed-countries
(last visited 1/11/21).

26. *See* ALEXIS DE TOCQUEVILLE, DEMOCRACY IN AMERICA 395–98 (Eduardo
Nolla ed., 2012).

27. *See* ROBERT D. PUTNAM, BOWLING ALONE: THE COLLAPSE AND REVIVAL OF AMERICAN COMMUNITY (2000).

28. John Adams, *Thoughts on Government*, in I AMERICAN POLITICAL WRITING DURING THE FOUNDING ERA 1760–1805 at 408–9 (Charles S. Hyneman & Donald S. Lutz eds., 1983).

29. Marbury v. Madison, 5 U.S. (1 Cranch) 137, 176 (1803).

30. Thomas Jefferson to James Madison, September 6, 1789, with Copies and Fragment, in VI THE WORKS OF THOMAS JEFFERSON 3 (Paul Leicester Ford ed., 1904).

Two. We the People, Part 2: Some Modest Proposals

1. At least one study has found that making election day a national holiday would have a significant effect on voter turnout. *See* Caitlyn Bradfield & Paul Johnson, *The Effect of Making Election Day a Holiday: An Original Survey and a Case Study of French Presidential Elections Applies to the U.S. Voting System*, 34 SIGMA: J. POL. & INT. STUD. 19, 30 (2017). Similarly, there is good reason to think that automatic registration would significantly increase voter turnout. *See* David W. Nickerson, *Do Voter Registration Drives Increase Participation? For Whom and When?*, 77 J. POL. 88, 99 (2015).

2. Many studies show that voting by mail increases voter turnout and, despite many claims made during the 2020 electoral cycle, has no effect on the balance of voters between the two parties. *See generally* Lee Drutman, *There Is No Evidence That Voting by Mail Gives One Party an Advantage*, FIVETHIRTYEIGHT (May 12, 2020), https://fivethirtyeight.com/features/there-is-no-evidence-that-voting-by-mail-gives-one-party-an-advantage/; Daniel M. Thompson, Jennifer Wu, et al., The Neutral Partisan Effects of Vote-by-Mail: Evidence from County-Level Roll-Outs, Working Paper No. 20-015 (Apr. 2020), https://siepr.stanford.edu/sites/default/files/publications/20-015.pdf; Adam J. Berinsky et al., *Who Votes by Mail? A Dynamic Model of the Individual-Level Consequences of Voting-by-Mail Systems*, 65 PUB. OPIN. QUART. 178 (2001).

3. For one such proposal, see Richard L. Hasen, *Clipping Coupons for Democracy: An Egalitarian/Public Choice Defense of Campaign Finance Vouchers*, 84 CALIF. L. REV. 1, 5 (1996).

4. *See* Rucho v. Common Cause, 139 S. Ct. 2484 (2019).

5. *See* Planned Parenthood of Southeastern Pennsylvania v. Casey, 505 U.S. 833, 874 (1992) (opinion of O'Connor, Kennedy, & Souter, JJ).

6. *See, e.g.*, Fisher v. University of Texas, 570 U.S. 297, 309 (2013).

7. *See* Miller v. Johnson, 515 U.S. 900, 916 (1995).

8. For some evidence on the mixed record of redistricting commissions, see DOUGLAS J. AMY, REAL CHOICES/NEW VOICES: HOW PROPORTIONAL REPRESENTATION ELECTIONS COULD REVITALIZE AMERICAN DEMOCRACY 64 (2002).

9. For a proposal along these lines, see Lani Guinier, *The Representation of Minority Interests: The Question of Single-Member Districts*, 14 CARDOZO L. REV. 1135, 1136 (1992).

10. *See* Richard H. Pildes & Kristen A. Donoghue, *Cumulative Voting in the United States*, 1995 U. CHICAGO LEGAL FORUM 241.

11. For a book-length account of this history, see ALEXANDER KEYSSAR, WHY DO WE STILL HAVE THE ELECTORAL COLLEGE? (2020).

12. *See, e.g.*, Richard A. Posner, *In Defense of the Electoral College*, SLATE (Jan. 23, 2014), http://austinclemens.com/blog/data/electoral_college.pdf.

13. *See* Philip Bump, *By 2040, Two-thirds of Americans Will Be Represented by 30 Percent of the Senate*, WASH. POST, Nov. 28, 2017.

14. For a summary of contemporary literature arguing for and against sortition, see Peter Stone, *Sortition, Voting and Democratic Equality*, 19 CRIT. REV. INT'L. SOC. & POL. PHIL. 339, 348 (2016). For a description of modern experiments with sortition, see Dimitri Courant, Thinking Sortition: Modern Selection, Deliberative Frameworks, and Democratic Principles, www.psa .ac.uk/sites/default/files/conference/papers/2017/Courant%20Dimitri%2C%20 Thinking%20Sortition%2C%20version%20PSA%2C%2011%20A5%2C%20201 7.03_0.pdf (last visited 1/12/21).

15. For an account, *see* A.H.M. JONES, ATHENIAN DEMOCRACY 100–107 (1969).

16. *See* ROBERT FINLAY, POLITICS IN RENAISSANCE VENICE 141–42 (1980).

17. For a description of the experiment, see Silvia Suteo, *Constitutional Conventions in the Digital Era: Lessons from Iceland and Ireland*, 38 B.C. INT. & COMP. L. REV. 251, 261 (2015).

18. *See* ROBERT DAHL, AFTER THE REVOLUTION: AUTHORITY IN A GOOD SOCIETY (1990). *See also* JOHN BURNHEIM, IS DEMOCRACY POSSIBLE? THE ALTERNATIVE TO ELECTORAL POLITICS (1985); BENJAMIN BARBER, STRONG DEMOCRACY: PARTICIPATORY POLITICS FOR A NEW AGE (1984). For a proposal that combines election with random selection, see Akhil Amar, *Choosing Representatives by Lottery Voting*, 93 YALE L. J. 1283 (1984).

19. *See* Jeremy Stahl, *This Team Thinks They Can Fix the Electoral College by 2024*, SLATE (Dec. 14, 2020), https://slate.com/news-and-politics/2020/12 /electoral-college-trump-popular-vote-compact.html (last visited 1/12/21).

20. *Note: Packing the Union: A Proposal to Admit New States for the Purpose of Amending the Constitution to Ensure Equal Representation*, 133 HARV. L. REV. 1049 (2020).

Three. Establishing Justice: The Problem of the Supreme Court

1. Henry M. Hart Jr., *Foreword: Time Chart of the Justices*, 73 HARV. L. REV. 84 (1959).

2. *See The Statistics*, 134 HARV. L. REV. 610 (Table A) (2020).

3. *See The Statistics*, 133 HARV. L. REV. 412 (2019).

4. For example, during the 1975 term, the Court decided 156 cases. *See The Statistics*, 90 HARV. L. REV. 276 (Table A) (1976).

5. *See The Statistics*, 134 HARV. L. REV. 610 (Table A) (2020).

6. *See The Statistics*, 134 HARV. L. REV. 610 (Table F) (2020).

7. *See* William W. Van Alstyne, *A Critical Guide to Marbury v. Madison*, 1969 Duke L. J. 1, 3–5.

8. *See* David J. Garrow, *Mental Decrepitude on the U.S. Supreme Court: The Historical Case for a 28th Amendment*, 67 U. Chi. L. Rev. 995, 1001–2 (2000).

9. Carl Brent Swisher, Stephen J. Field: Craftsman of the Law 442 (1930).

10. *See* David J. Garrow, *Mental Decrepitude on the U.S. Supreme Court: The Historical Case for a 28th Amendment*, 67 U. Chi. L. Rev. 995, 1002–7 (2000).

11. *See* John M. Cormack, *The Legal Tender Cases: A Drama of American Legal and Financial History*, 16 Va. L. Rev. 132, 140–44 (1929).

12. *See, e.g.*, Paul Finkelman, *You Can't Always Get What You Want . . . : Presidential Elections and Supreme Court Appointments*, 35 Tulsa L. J. 473, 480–81 (2000).

13. *See* Alpheus Mason, William Howard Taft: Chief Justice 216–17 (1964).

14. *See* A. Leon Higgenbotham Jr. & William C. Smith, *The Hughes Court and the Beginning of the End of the "Separate but Equal" Doctrine*, 76 Minn. L. Rev. 1099, 1110 (1992).

15. *See* Mark Tushnet, *Willis Van Devanter: The Person*, 45 J. S. Ct. Hist. 308, https://onlinelibrary.wiley.com/doi/abs/10.1111/jsch.12249?af=R (last visited 1/13/21).

16. *See* William O. Douglas, The Court Years: 1939–1975, at 173–74 (1980).

17. *See* David J. Garrow, *Mental Decrepitude on the U.S. Supreme Court: The Historical Case for a 28th Amendment*, 67 U. Chi. L. Rev. 995, 1045–50 (2000).

18. *See id.* at 1027–29.

19. For an account of Black's nomination and the controversy that followed, *see* Howard Ball, Hugo L. Black: Cold Steel Warrior 89–106 (1996).

20. *See* Laura Kalman, Abe Fortas: A Biography 323–78 (1990).

21. *See* Adam Liptak, *New Look at Old Memo Casts More Doubt on Rehnquist*, N.Y. Times, Mar. 19, 2012.

22. The statement is based on a data search of all patent cases that came before Marshall, the results of which are on file with the author.

23. *See* Bernard Wolfman, Jonathan L.F. Silver, & Marjorie A. Silver, *Behavior of Justice Douglas in Federal Tax Cases*, 122 U. Pa. L. Rev 235, 289, 325 (1973).

24. *See* Gillian Thomas, *When a Chief Justice Declared That Women Make Better Secretaries*, The Atlantic, Dec. 9, 2015.

25. *See* Bob Woodward & Scott Armstrong, The Brethren: Inside the Supreme Court 283–84 (1979).

26. Obergefell v. Hodges, 135 S. Ct. 2584, 2629 (2015) (Scalia, J., dissenting).

27. Id. at 2630.

28. Id. at 2629.

29. Id. at 2628.

30. Id. at 2630 n. 22.

31. Id.

32. Romer v. Evans, 517 U.S. 620, 636 (1996) (Scalia, J., dissenting).

33. *See* JANE MAYER & JILL ABRAMSON, STRANGE JUSTICE: THE SELLING OF CLARENCE THOMAS (1994).

34. *See* Neil A. Lewis, *At the Bar: The Press Is Caught in a Misrepresentation of Clarence Thomas' Words, or Is It*, N.Y. TIMES, Dec. 20, 1991.

35. *See* Haley Britzky, *How We Got Here: The Kavanaugh Timeline*, AXIOS, Oct. 2, 2018, https://www.axios.com/brett-kavanaugh-timeline-allegations-vote -412d33d6-e5dd-43eb-9322-fd2a3867be9b.html (last visited 1/13/21).

36. *See* Emma Brown, *A California Professor, Writer, of Confidential Brett Kavanaugh Letter, Speaks Out About Allegations of Sexual Assault*, WASH. POST, Sept. 16, 2018.

37. *See* Anthony Zurcher, *Christine Blasey Ford and Brett Kavanaugh Hearings, What We Learned*, BBC NEWS, https://www.bbc.com/news/world-us-can ada-45660297 (last visited 1/13/21).

38. A mostly failed politician, Minton gained appointment to the Supreme Court because of his close friendship with Harry Truman. For years, Supreme Court law clerks awarded a "Shermie" to the worst opinion of the year.

39. Duvall, who served on the Court between 1811 and 1835, has been the subject of a vigorous, if tongue-firmly-in-cheek, scholarly debate about whether he was the "most insignificant" justice in the Court's history. University of Chicago law professor David Currie insisted that "impartial examination of Duvall's performance reveals to even the uninitiated observer that he achieved an enviable standard of insignificance against which all other justices must be measured." David P. Currie, *The Most Insignificant Justice: A Preliminary Inquiry*, 50 U. CHI. L. REV. 466, 466 (1983). His colleague Frank Easterbrook, then a law professor and now a judge, responded that Currie had failed to give "serious consideration [to] candidates so shrouded in obscurity that they escaped proper attention even in a contest of insignificance." After careful research, Easterbrook concluded that Justice Thomas Todd was even more insignificant than Duvall. Frank Easterbrook, *The Most Insignificant Justice: Further Evidence*, 50 U. CHI. L. REV. 482, 482 (1983).

40. Cheney v. United States District Court, 541 U.S. 913, 917 (2004) (memorandum of Scalia, J.).

41. The facts that follow are drawn from the Supreme Court of the United States, Justices: Current Members, https://www.supremecourt.gov/about/bio graphies.aspx (last visited 1/13/21).

42 *See, e.g.*, Trump v. New York, 141 S. Ct. 530 (2020).

43. *See, e.g.*, Trump v. Vance, 140 S. Ct. 2412 (2020) (opinion of Roberts, C.J., rejecting President Trump's legal objections to subpoena); National Federation of Independent Businesses v. Sebelius, 567 U.S. 519 (2012) (opinion of Roberts, C.J., upholding Affordable Care Act).

44. Adam Liptak, *Chief Justice Defends Judicial Independence After Trump Attacks "Obama Judge*," N.Y. TIMES, Nov. 21, 2018.

45. *See, e.g.*, GEOFFREY R. STONE, PERILOUS TIMES: FREE SPEECH IN WARTIME 29–73 (2004); JOHN MORTON SMITH, FREEDOM'S FETTERS: THE ALIEN AND

SEDITION LAWS AND AMERICAN CIVIL LIBERTIES (1956); Kevin R.C. Gutzman, *The Jeffersonian Republicans vs. the Federalist Court*, 14 U. ST. THOMAS L. J. 56 (2018).

46. 42 U.S. (16 Pet.) 539 (1842).

47. Dred Scott v. Sandford, 60 U.S. (19 How.) 393 (1857).

48. *See* CHARLES LANE, THE DAY FREEDOM DIED: THE COLFAX MASSACRE, THE SUPREME COURT, AND THE BETRAYAL OF RECONSTRUCTION (2008).

49. United States v. Cruikshank, 92 U.S. 542 (1875).

50. *See* The Civil Rights Cases, 109 U.S. 3 (1883).

51. *See* United States v. Reese, 92 U.S. 214 (1875).

52. 163 U.S. 537 (1896).

53. Id. at 544.

54. Id. at 551.

55. Cumming v. Board of Education, 175 U.S. 528 (1899).

56. Giles v. Harris, 189 U.S. 475 (1903).

57. Id. at 486.

58. *See, e.g.*, DAVID M. RABBAN, FREE SPEECH IN ITS FORGOTTEN YEARS 130–31 (1997).

59. Buck v. Bell, 274 U.S. 200 (1927).

60. Id. at 207.

61. *See* GEOFFREY R. STONE, PERILOUS TIMES: FREE SPEECH IN WARTIME 192–98 (2004); Michael J. Klarman, *Rethinking the Civil Rights and Civil Liberties Revolution*, 82 VA. L. REV. 1, 11–12 (1996).

62. *See* Debs v. United States, 249 U.S. 11 (1919).

63. 157 U.S. 429 (1895).

64. 198 U.S. 45 (1905).

65. Id. at 64.

66. Id.

67. 156 U.S. 1 (1895).

68. 268 U.S. 295 (1925).

69. *See* Hammer v. Dagenhart, 247 U.S. 251 (1918).

70. *See* Champion v. Ames, 188 U.S. 321 (1903).

71. *See* William Leuchtenburg, *The Origins of Franklin D. Roosevelt's "Court-Packing" Plan*, 1966 SUP. CT. REV. 347.

72. *See, e.g.*, Adler v. Bd. of Educ., 342 U.S. 485, 495 (1952) (upholding a statute prohibiting the employment of teachers who belonged to listed organizations); Garner v. Bd. of Pub. Works, 341 U.S. 716, 723–24 (1951) (upholding an oath required of government employees, as a condition of employment, swearing that they did not belong to an organization advocating forceful overthrow of the government).

73. *See* Korematsu v. United States, 3232 U.S. 214 (1944).

74. Id. at 223.

75. Ex parte Quirin, 317 U.S. 1 (1942).

76. *See* note 71, *supra.*

77. *See* Dennis v. United States, 341 U.S. 494, 516–17 (1951).

78. *See, e.g.*, Brown v. Board of Education, 347 U.S. 483 (1954).

79. *See, e.g.,* Miranda v. Arizona, 384 U.S. 466 (1966).

80. *See, e.g.,* Reynolds v. Sims, 377 U.S. 533 (1964).

81. *See, e.g.,* Shapiro v. Thompson, 394 U.S. 618 (1969).

82. *See, e.g.,* Roe v. Wade, 410 U.S. 113 (1973).

83. *See, e.g.,* Craig v. Boren, 429 U.S. 190 (1976).

84. *See, e.g.,* GERALD N. ROSENBERG, THE HOLLOW HOPE: CAN COURTS BRING ABOUT SOCIAL CHANGE? (2008).

85. *See* Pierson v. Ray, 386 U.S. 547 (1967).

86. 392 U.S. 1 (1968).

87. *See* RICHARD J. LAZARUS, THE RULE OF FIVE: MAKING CLIMATE HISTORY AT THE SUPREME COURT 170–71, 223, 233 (2020).

88. Lisa Heinzerling, *The Rule of Five Guys*, 119 MICH. L. REV. ___, ___ (2021) (forthcoming).

89. *See* Bush v. Gore, 531 U.S. 98 (2000).

90. Id. at 109.

91. *See, e.g.,* Miller v. Johnson, 515 U.S. 900 (1995).

92. *See* Rucho v. Common Cause, 139 S. Ct. 2484 (2019).

93. *See* Crawford v. Marion County Elec. Bd., 553 U.S. 181 (2008).

94. *See, e.g.,* Citizens United v. FEC, 558 U.S. 310 (2010).

95. *See* Shelby County v. Holder, 133 S. Ct. 2612 (2013).

96. *See* National Federation of Independent Business v. Sebelius, 567 U.S. 519 (2012).

97. *See, e.g.,* Adarand Constructors, Inc. v. Pena, 515 U.S. 200 (1995).

98. *See* Parents Involved in Community Schools v. Seattle School Dist. No. 1, 551 U.S. 701 (2007).

99. *See* District of Columbia v. Heller, 554 U.S. 570 (2008).

100. *See* John Kruzel, *Dozens of Legal Experts Throw Weight Behind Supreme Court Term Limit Bill*, THE HILL, Oct. 23, 2020, https://thehill.com/regulation/court-battles/522447-dozens-of-legal-experts-throw-weight-behind-supreme-court-term-limit (last visited 1/14/21).

101. *See* David A. Graham, *The Democrats Discover the Supreme Court*, THE ATLANTIC, June 4, 2019.

102. *See* Daniel Epps & Ganesh Sitaraman, *How to Save the Supreme Court*, 129 YALE L. J. 148 (2019).

103. 135 S. Ct. 2584 (2015).

104. James B. Thayer, *The Origin and Scope of the American Doctrine of Constitutional Law*, 7 HARV. L. REV. 129, 144 (1893).

Four. Promoting the General Welfare: The Problem of Economic Distribution

1. RONALD DWORKIN, TAKING RIGHTS SERIOUSLY 272–73 (1978).

2. *See* United States v. Verdugo-Urquidez, 494 U.S. 259 (1990).

3. Toomer v. Witsell, 334 U.S. 385, 395 (1948).

4. *See, e.g.,* City of Philadelphia v. New Jersey, 437 U.S. 617 (1978).

5. *See, e.g.,* Saenz v. Roe, 526 U.S. 489 (1999).

6. *See* Troxel v. Granville, 530 U.S. 57 (2000).

7. *See* William Raspberry, *Mrs. Luce: An Awful Interview*, WASH. POST, Sept. 15, 1982.

8. *See* A.L.A. Schechter Poultry Corp. v. United States, 295 U.S. 495 (1935).

9. *See* United States v. Butler, 297 U.S. 1 (1936).

10. For an account, see William Leuchtenberg, *The Origins of Franklin D. Roosevelt's "Court-Packing" Plan*, 1966 SUP. CT. REV. 347.

11. *See generally* HOWARD GILMAN, THE CONSTITUTION BESIEGED. *Cf.* Barry Cushman, *Some Varieties and Vicissitudes in Lochnerism*, 85 B. U. L. REV. 881 (2005).

12. Ferguson v. Scrupa, 372 U.S. 726, 730 (1963).

13. *See, e.g.*, DAVID TRUMAN, THE GOVERNMENTAL PROCESS (1963); ROBERT DAHL, A PREFACE TO DEMOCRATIC THEORY (1956).

14. *See* United States v. Carolene Products, 304 U.S. 144, 153 n. 4 (1938).

15. *See* United States v. Eichman, 496 U.S. 310 (1990); Texas v. Johnson, 491 U.S. 397 (1989).

16. *See id.* at n. 8 (1989) ("nothing in our opinion should be taken to suggest that one is free to steal a flag so long as one later uses it to communicate an idea").

17. *See* A Bill: To grant the United States a copyright to the flag of the United States and to impose criminal penalties for the destruction of a copyrighted flag, HR 3883, 104th Cong, 2d Sess. (July 23, 1996).

18. *See* Lamont v. Postmaster General, 381 U.S. 301 (1965).

19. United States Postal Service v. Council of Greenburgh Civic Assns., 453 U.S. 14 (1981).

20. *See id.* at 128–34.

21. *See* Citizens United v. FEC, 558 U.S. 310, 342–43 (2010) (holding that corporations have a constitutional right to expend money in conjunction with political campaigns); Buckley v. Valeo, 424 U.S. 1, 45 (1976) (invalidating expenditure limits for political campaigns).

22. *See, e.g.*, Lorillard Tobacco C. v. Reilly, 533 U.S. 525 (2001) (invalidating regulations on cigarette advertising).

23. *See* Janus v. Am. Fed'n. of State, Cty., & Mun. Emps., Council 31, 138 S. Ct. 2448, 2471 (2018) (holding that compelled contributions to unions by government employees violate freedom of speech).

24. *See* Cent. Hudson Gas & Elec. v. Pub. Serv. Comm'n., 447 U.S. 557, 571 (1980) (holding that a prohibition on promotional advertising by an electric utility violates the First Amendment).

25. A.J. Liebling, *The Wayward Press: Do You Belong in Journalism?*, NEW YORKER, May 14, 1960, at 109.

26. 558 U.S. 310 (2010).

27. *See* Goldberg v. Kelly, 397 U.S. 254 (1970).

28. *See, e.g.*, Cleveland Board of Education v. Loudermill, 470 U.S. 532 (1985).

29. *See* Perry v. Sindermann, 408 U.S. 593 (1972).

30. *See* Board of Regents of State Colleges v. Roth, 408 U.S. 564 (1972).

31. 414 U.S. 70 (1973).

32. *See* United States v. Rylander, 460 U.S. 752, 758 (1983).

33. 536 U.S. 24 (2002).

Five. Securing the Blessings of Liberty, Part 1: The Problem of Civil Liberties and Cultural Power

1. For a detailed account of the trial, see EDWARD J. LARSON, SUMMER FOR THE GODS: THE SCOPES TRIAL AND AMERICA'S CONTINUING DEBATE OVER SCIENCE AND RELIGION 87–146 (2006).

2. *See* id.

3. Id. at 173–74.

4. *See* MICHAEL KAZIN, A GODLY HERO: THE LIFE OF WILLIAM JENNINGS BRYAN 76–77, 107–8, 164, 215–242 (2006).

5. Id. at 271–77.

6. On Darrow's defense of labor, see ANDREW EDMUND KERSTEN, CLARENCE DARROW: AMERICAN ICONOCLAST 107–51 (2011). On his religious skepticism, see id. at 221–22. On his material determinism, see id. at 197.

7. *See* EDWARD J. LARSON, SUMMER FOR THE GODS: THE SCOPES TRIAL AND AMERICA'S CONTINUING DEBATE OVER SCIENCE AND RELIGION 177–83 (2006).

8. 274 U.S. 200 (1927).

9. EDWARD J. LARSON, SUMMER FOR THE GODS: THE SCOPES TRIAL AND AMERICA'S CONTINUING DEBATE OVER SCIENCE AND RELIGION 200–201 (2006).

10. Id. at 244.

11. The Tennessee Supreme Court reversed the judgment on the ground that "a jury alone can impose the penalty this act requires" that "the trial judge exceeded his jurisdiction in levying this fine," and that the Court was "without power to correct his error." Scopes v. State, 154 Tenn. 105, 121, 289 S.W. 363, 367 (1927).

12. *See* id. ("We see nothing to be gained by prolonging the life of this bizarre case. On the contrary, we think the peace and dignity of the state, which all criminal prosecutions are brought to redress, will be the better conserved by the entry of a nolle prosequi herein. Such a course is suggested to the Attorney General").

13. *See* EDWARD J. LARSON, SUMMER FOR THE GODS: THE SCOPES TRIAL AND AMERICA'S CONTINUING DEBATE OVER SCIENCE AND RELIGION 221 (2006).

14. In Dayton, Bryan proclaimed that "[t]he real issue is not *what* can be taught in public schools, but *who* shall control the education system." EDWARD J. LARSON, SUMMER FOR THE GODS: THE SCOPES TRIAL AND AMERICA'S CONTINUING DEBATE OVER SCIENCE AND RELIGION 104 (2006). *See also* William Jennings Bryan, *Speech to Legislature*, in ORTHODOX CHRISTIANITY VERSUS MODERNISM 45–46 (1923) ("[Teachers in public schools] have no right to demand pay for teaching that which the parents and the taxpayers do not want taught. The hand that writes the paycheck rules the school"). For discussion, see Edward J. Larson, *The Scopes Trial and the Evolving Concept of Freedom*, 85 VA. L. REV. 503, 510–11 (1999).

15. In a contemporaneous explanation of the stakes of the Scopes trial, the ACLU envisioned it as presenting a "clear legal test of the right of a majority acting through the legislature to determine what shall or shall not be taught in public school" and of the "tyranny over minority and unpopular views." LAURA WEINRIB, THE TAMING OF FREE SPEECH: AMERICA'S CIVIL LIBERTIES COMPROMISE 157–58 (2016). On the ACLU's more general embrace of academic freedom as a means of protecting radical speech, see id. 151–57 (2016).

16. For a compilation of the dispatches, see H.L. Mencken, "The Monkey Trial": A Reporter's Account, University of Missouri–Kansas School of Law, available at http://law2.umkc.edu/fculty/projects/ftrials/menk.htm.

17. FREDERICK LEWIS ALLEN, ONLY YESTERDAY: AN INFORMAL HISTORY OF THE 1920s, 99–106 (1931).

18. For a transcript, see The Clarence Darrow Digital Collection: The Scopes Trial 284–304, available at http://moses.law.umn.edu/darrow/documents /Scopes%206th%20&%207th%20days.pdf.

19. See The Many Faces of Evolution in Europe, c. 1860–1914 xi (Patric Dassen & Mary Keperink eds., 2005) (noting that "[a]round 1900 the theory of natural selection was so unpopular that Darwin's opponents believed that it would never recover" and that "[i]t was only in the late 1930s . . . that natural selection was accepted as the main mechanism of evolution").

20. For example, the neo-Lamarckian Robert Chambers thought that "living beings, including man and society, [were] the products of a gradual and progressive development. Higher forms came into being because of a small change in a species which was 'lower' in the evolutionary chain. This process, guided by God, was directed at a fixed goal, namely man." Id. at xi.

21. See J.S. WEINER, THE PILTDOWN FORGERY 1–16 (2003).

22. See Charles Dawson & Arthur Smith Woodward, On the Discovery of Paleolithic Human Skull and Mandible, QUARTERLY JOURNAL OF THE GEOLOGICAL SOCIETY OF LONDON 69, 149 (1913) (quoting Dawkins).

23. See Man Had Reason Before He Spoke, N.Y. TIMES, Dec. 20, 1912 (quoting Woodward)

24. See EDWARD J. LARSON, SUMMER FOR THE GODS: THE SCOPES TRIAL AND AMERICA'S CONTINUING DEBATE OVER SCIENCE AND RELIGION 26 (2006).

25. See The Clarence Darrow Digital Collection: The Scopes Trial 284–304, available at http://moses.law.umn.edu/darrow/documents/Scopes%206th%20 &%207th%20days.pdf. 237 (statement of Dr. Fay-Cooper Cole); id. at 278 (statement of Prof. Horatio Hackett Newman).

26. For an account of the unraveling of the hoax, see J.S. WEINER, THE PILTDOWN FORGERY 37–49 (2003).

27. See, e.g., The Clarence Darrow Digital Collection: The Scopes Trial 284–304, available at http://moses.law.umn.edu/darrow/documents/Scopes%20 6th%20&%207th%20days.pdf. 285 ("It is hard to believe for you, but easy for me. A miracle is a thing performed beyond what a man can perform. When you get beyond what man can do, you get within the realm of miracles; and it is just as easy to believe the miracle of Jonah as any other miracle in the Bible").

28. Id. at 286. Later in the examination, when queried about whether God had created the earth in six days, Bryan acknowledged that "days" did not mean literal, twenty-four-hour days. Id. at 302.

29. *See, e.g.,* id. at 292–93.

30. For a sympathetic account of Bryan that strongly emphasizes these points, see MICHAEL KAZIN, A GODLY HERO: THE LIFE OF WILLIAM JENNINGS BRYAN 262–65 (2006).

31. The Clarence Darrow Digital Collection: The Scopes Trial 284–304, available at http://moses.law.umn.edu/darrow/documents/Scopes%206th%20&%207th%20days.pdf. At 288–89.

32. For accounts, see ADAM COHEN, IMBECILES: THE SUPREME COURT, AMERICAN EUGENICS, AND THE STERILIZATION OF CARRIE BUCK 93–97 (2016); PAUL A. LOMBARDO, THREE GENERATIONS, NO IMBECILES x–xi (2010).

33. *See* ADAM COHEN, IMBECILES: THE SUPREME COURT, AMERICAN EUGENICS, AND THE STERILIZATION OF CARRIE BUCK 98–99 (2016).

34. Buck v. Bell, 274 U.S. 200 (1927).

35. *See* THOMAS C. LEONARD, ILLIBERAL REFORMERS: RACE, EUGENICS & AMERICAN ECONOMICS IN THE PROGRESSIVE ERA 108–28 (2016); ADAM COHEN, IMBECILES: THE SUPREME COURT, AMERICAN EUGENICS, AND THE STERILIZATION OF CARRIE BUCK 55–71 (2016).

36. Virginia Foundation for the Humanities, Primary Resource: Chapter 46B of the Code of Virginia § 1095h-m (1924), Encyclopedia Va., available at http://www.encyclopediavirginia.org/Chapter_46B_of_the_Code_of_Virginia_.

37. *See* ADAM COHEN, IMBECILES: THE SUPREME COURT, AMERICAN EUGENICS, AND THE STERILIZATION OF CARRIE BUCK 108 (2016).

38. Id. at 23–24.

39. Id. at 21, 24.

40. Id. at 27.

41. Apparently, Buck was chosen because of the previous finding of feeble-mindedness, the fact that her mother had been declared a "moron," the fact that she was an unwed mother, and the fact that she was young. *See* id. at 91–92.

42. For a description of the surgery, see PAUL A. LOMBARDO, THREE GENERATIONS, NO IMBECILES 185 (2010).

43. *See* id. at 284.

44. *See* ADAM COHEN, IMBECILES: THE SUPREME COURT, AMERICAN EUGENICS, AND THE STERILIZATION OF CARRIE BUCK 284 (2016).

45. CHARLES DARWIN, THE DESCENT OF MAN 134 (1871).

46. FRANCIS GALTON, INQUIRIES INTO HUMAN FACULTY AND ITS DEVELOPMENT 17 n. 1 (electronic ed., 2001).

47. *See* THE EUGENICS EDUCATION SOCIETY, PRESIDENTIAL ADDRESS BY MAJOR LEONARD DARWIN (1911).

48. *See* RONALD A. FISHER, THE GENETICAL THEORY OF NATURAL SELECTION (1930).

49. Darrow characterized eugenics as a "gaudy little plan" designed to impose a "caste system." VICTORIA F. NOURSE, IN RECKLESS HANDS: *SKINNER V.*

OKLAHOMA AND THE NEAR TRIUMPH OF AMERICAN EUGENICS 15 (2008). *See also* THOMAS C. LEONARD, ILLIBERAL REFORMERS 111 n. 17 (1990).

50. *See* EDWARD J. LARSON, SUMMER FOR THE GODS: THE SCOPES TRIAL AND AMERICA'S CONTINUING DEBATE OVER SCIENCE AND RELIGION 135 (2006).

51. *See* GEORGE WILLIAM HUNTER, A CIVIC BIOLOGY: PRESENTED IN PROBLEMS 194–96 (1914) (endorsing evolution and noting that evolution had culminated in "the highest type of all, the Caucasians, represented by the civilized white inhabitants of Europe and America"); id. at 261–65 (noting that "[h]undreds of [families with mental and moral defects] exist to-day, spreading disease, immorality, and crime to all parts of this country" and that "we . . . have the remedy of separating the sexes in asylums or other places and in various ways preventing intermarriage and the possibilities of perpetuating such a low and degenerate race").

52. *See* THOMAS C. LEONARD, ILLIBERAL REFORMERS 111 (1990).

53. EDWARD J. LARSON, SUMMER FOR THE GODS: THE SCOPES TRIAL AND AMERICA'S CONTINUING DEBATE OVER SCIENCE AND RELIGION 115 (2006).

54. *See* ADAM COHEN, IMBECILES: THE SUPREME COURT, AMERICAN EUGENICS, AND THE STERILIZATION OF CARRIE BUCK 122 (2016).

55. *See* id. at 66.

56. *See* MICHAEL KAZIN, A GODLY HERO: THE LIFE OF WILLIAM JENNINGS BRYAN 263 (2006).

57. *See* EDWARD J. LARSON, SUMMER FOR THE GODS: THE SCOPES TRIAL AND AMERICA'S CONTINUING DEBATE OVER SCIENCE AND RELIGION 101 (2006).

58. Id. at 28.

59. ADAM COHEN, IMBECILES: THE SUPREME COURT, AMERICAN EUGENICS, AND THE STERILIZATION OF CARRIE BUCK 55 (2006) (linking eugenics to progressive reformers); THOMAS C. LEONARD, ILLIBERAL REFORMERS 117–19 (1990) (same); DONALD K. PICKENS, EUGENICS AND THE PROGRESSIVES (1968) (same).

60. Victoria Brignell, *When America Believed in Eugenics*, THE NEW STATESMAN 4–5 Dec. 10, 2010.

61. PAUL A. LOMBARDO, THREE GENERATIONS, NO IMBECILES 26 (2010).

62. *See* Oliver Wendell Holmes Jr., *Ideals and Doubts*, 10 ILL. L. REV. 1, 3 (1915) ("I believe that the wholesale social regeneration which so many now seem to expect, if it can be helped by conscious, co-ordinated human effort, cannot be affected appreciably by tinkering with the institution of property, but only by taking in hand life and trying to build a race. That would be my starting point for an ideal for the law"); Yosul Rogat, *Mr. Justice Holmes: A Dissenting Opinion*, 15 STAN. L. REV. 254, 282 (1963) ("It is difficult to overestimate the importance of eugenicism in Holmes's social thought").

63. *See* G. EDWARD WHITE, OLIVER WENDELL HOLMES JR. 94–96 (2006) (explaining how a "group of progressive intellectuals" claimed Holmes as a hero).

64. *See* MELVIN I. UROFSKY, LOUIS D. BRANDEIS: A LIFE 206–22 (2009) (describing Brandeis's association with the progressive movement).

65. *See* ALPHEUS THOMAS MASON, HARLAN FISKE STONE: PILLAR OF THE LAW 252–54 (1956) (describing Stone's contemporaneous movement toward Brandeis and Holmes in their "battle against formalistic jurisprudence").

66. *See* DAVID W. SOUTHERN, THE PROGRESSIVE ERA AND RACE: REACTION AND REFORM, 1900–1917, at 50 (2005) ("Eugenics appealed to tough-minded progressives because it was reformist, involved the use of government, and was, seemingly, based on cutting-edge science"); David E. Bernstein & Thomas C. Leonard, *Excluding Unfit Workers: Social Control Versus Social Justice in the Age of Economic Reform*, 72 LAW & CONTEMP. PROBS. 177, 179 (2009) (associating progressive elitism with belief in social control through judgments of hereditary fitness).

67. *See generally* EDWARD J. LARSON, SEX, RACE, AND SCIENCE: EUGENICS IN THE DEEP SOUTH (1995). But *cf.* THOMAS C. LEONARD, ILLIBERAL REFORMERS: RACE, EUGENICS & AMERICAN ECONOMICS IN THE PROGRESSIVE ERA 115 (2016) (noting that the appeal of genetics crossed ideological boundaries).

68. 250 U.S. 616 (1919).

69. Id. at 630 (Holmes, J., dissenting).

70. ADAM COHEN, IMBECILES: THE SUPREME COURT, AMERICAN EUGENICS, AND THE STERILIZATION OF CARRIE BUCK 252–54 (2016) (detailing growing opposition to eugenics at time when *Buck* was decided).

71. 250 U.S., at 630 (Holmes, J., dissenting).

72. 198 U.S. 45 (1905).

73. Id. at 75 (Holmes, J., dissenting).

74. Buck v. Bell, 274 U.S. 200, 207 (1927) ("In view of the general declarations of the Legislature and the specific findings of the Court obviously we cannot say as matter of law that the grounds do not exist, and if they exist they justify the result").

75. Id.

76. *Cf.* Tennessee v. Lane, 541 U.S. 509, 534 (2004) (Souter, J., concurring) (noting that Buck v. Bell "was not grudging in sustaining the constitutionality of the once-pervasive practice of involuntarily sterilizing those with mental disabilities").

77. See Bleeker Van Wagenen, Eugenics Education Society, Preliminary Report of the Committee of the Eugenic Section of the American Breeders' Association to Study and to Report on the Best Practical Means for Cutting Off the Defective Germ-Plasm in the Human Population 464 (1912), available at https://readingroom .law.gsu.edu/cgi/viewcontent.cgi?referer=&httpsredir=1&article=1073&context =buckvbell.

78. *See* ADAM COHEN, IMBECILES: THE SUPREME COURT, AMERICAN EUGEN-ICS, AND THE STERILIZATION OF CARRIE BUCK 118 (2016).

79. Id. at 33–34.

80. Id. at 34.

81. Id. at 110.

Six. Securing the Blessings of Liberty, Part 2: Civil Liberties and Cultural Power Today

1. *See* Board of Trustees v. Garrett, 531 U.S. 356, 369 n. 6 (2001) (noting that eugenics-based laws were "upheld against constitutional attack 70 years ago in

Buck v. Bell"); Regents of the University of California v. Bakke, 438 U.S. 265, 336 (1973) (opinion of Brennan, White, Marshall, and Blackmun, concurring in the judgment in part and dissenting in part) (noting Justice Holmes's remark that the equal protection clause was the "last resort of constitutional arguments"); Roe v. Wade 410 U.S. 113, 154 (1973) (citing *Buck* for the proposition that the Court has "refused to recognize an unlimited" scope for the right of privacy).

2. *See* PAUL A. LOMBARDO, THREE GENERATIONS, NO IMBECILES 227 (2010). In contrast, only 70 percent favored distribution of birth control information, and 65 percent favored the death penalty for murder. More than half the respondents favored "mercy deaths" for "hopeless invalids." Id.

3. Relf v. Weinberger, 372 F. Supp. 1196, 1199 (D.D.C. 1974).

4. *See* Laura I. Appleman, *Deviancy, Dependency, and Disability: The Forgotten History of Eugenics and Mass Incarceration*, 68 DUKE L. J. 417, 461 (2018). For efforts to trace modern hyperincarceration to roots in the eugenics movement, see id.; James C. Oleson, *The New Eugenics: Black Hyper-Incarceration and Human Abatement*, 5 SOC. SCI. 1 (2016).

5. There is evidence that the Nazis used the American genetics program as a model, and Nazis on trial in Nuremberg cited Buck v. Bell in defense of their actions. *See* ADAM COHEN, IMBECILES: THE SUPREME COURT, AMERICAN EUGENICS, AND THE STERILIZATION OF CARRIE BUCK 10–11 (2016). By the late 1930s, however, the German regime had begun to characterize America as populated by weaker white "races," thereby helping to discredit "scientific" racism and, with it, the eugenics project. *See* VICTORIA A. NOURSE, IN RECKLESS HANDS: *SKINNER V. OKLAHOMA* AND THE NEAR TRIUMPH OF AMERICAN EUGENICS 15 (2008).

6. 316 U.S. 535 (1942).

7. *See* id. at 538–44.

8. Id. at 537.

9. The paragraph appeared "[i]n a large, cloud-shaped bubble at the top of [Douglas's] penciled draft." VICTORIA A. NOURSE, IN RECKLESS HANDS: *SKINNER V. OKLAHOMA* AND THE NEAR TRIUMPH OF AMERICAN EUGENICS 151 (2008).

10. Skinner v. Oklahoma, 316 U.S. 535, 536 (1942).

11. *See* VICTORIA A. NOURSE, IN RECKLESS HANDS: *SKINNER V. OKLAHOMA* AND THE NEAR TRIUMPH OF AMERICAN EUGENICS 146 (2008).

12. *See* ADAM COHEN, IMBECILES: THE SUPREME COURT, AMERICAN EUGENICS, AND THE STERILIZATION OF CARRIE BUCK 309 (2016).

13. See Herbert Hovenkamp, *The Progressives: Racism and Public Law*, 59 ARIZ. L. REV. 947, 972 (2017).

14. *See* VICTORIA A. NOURSE, IN RECKLESS HANDS: *SKINNER V. OKLAHOMA* AND THE NEAR TRIUMPH OF AMERICAN EUGENICS 146 (2008).

15. *See* id.

16. Skinner v. Oklahoma, 316 U.S. 535, 538 (1942).

17. Id. at 545 n. 1.

18. Id. at 539.

19. Id. at 546 (Jackson, J., concurring).

20. Id. at 544 (Stone, C.J., concurring).

21. *Cf.* Herbert Hovenkamp, *The Progressives: Racism and Public Law*, 59

Ariz. L. Rev. 947, 956 (2017) ("One characteristic of progressive policy ever since its inception was its tendency to follow prevailing science, changing its political views when dominant scientific views changed").

22. Skinner v. Oklahoma, 319 U.S. 624 (1943).

23. 319 U.S. 624 (1943).

24. 310 U.S. 546 (1940).

25. Skinner v. Oklahoma, 319 U.S. 624, 638 (1943).

26. Id. at 642.

27. Id. at 639.

28. Id. at 640.

29. Minersville School Dist. v. Gobitis, 310 U.S. 546, 599 (1940).

30. Cf. Wisconsin v. Yoder, 406 U.S. 205, 242 (1972) (Douglas, J., dissenting) ("[N]o analysis of religious liberty claims can take place in a vacuum. If the parents in this case are allowed a religious exemption, the inevitable effect is to impose the parents' notions of religious duty upon their children").

31. This point was made prominently in the Court's famous opinion in Brown v. Board of Education, 347 U.S. 483 (1954), where it argued that education was "the very foundation of good citizenship. . . . [It] is the principal instrument in awakening the child to cultural values, in preparing him for later professional training, and in helping him to adjust normally to his environment." Id. at 493.

32. West Virginia Board of Education v. Barnette, 319 U.S. 624, 637 (1943).

33. Vincent Blasi & Seana V. Shiffrin, The Story of West Virginia Board of Education v. Barnette: The Pledge of Allegiance and Freedom of Thought, in Constitutional Law Stories 420 (2d ed., 2009). For a comprehensive account of the state and private persecution of Witnesses during this period, see Shawn Francis Peters, Judging Jehovah's Witnesses: Religious Persecution and the Dawn of the Rights Revolution 96–152 (2000).

34. Vincent Blasi & Seana V. Shiffrin, The Story of West Virginia Board of Education v. Barnette: The Pledge of Allegiance and Freedom of Thought, in Constitutional Law Stories 420, 421 (2d ed., 2009).

35. Id.

36. Id. at 422.

37. See Shawn Francis Peters, Judging Jehovah's Witnesses: Religious Persecution and the Dawn of the Rights Revolution 251 (2000).

38. West Virginia Board of Education v. Barnette, 319 U.S. 624, 641–42 (1943).

39. Id.

40. Id. at 640.

41. Id. at 641–42.

42. Id. at 646 (Frankfurter, J. dissenting).

43. Id. at 646–47 (Frankfurter, J., dissenting).

44. Id. at 648 (Frankfurter, J., dissenting).

45. Id. at 655 (Frankfurter, J., dissenting).

46. Id. (Frankfurter, J., dissenting).

47. Id. at 637.

48. Id. at 638.

49. *See, e.g.,* Loving v. Virginia, 388 U.S. 1 (1967) (racial classifications); Harper v. Virginia State Bd. of Elections, 383 U.S. 663 (1966) (voting as fundamental right); Shapiro v. Thompson, 394 U.S. 618 (1969) (travel as fundamental right).

50. *See* Griswold v. Connecticut, 379 U.S. 826 (1965).

51. 410 U.S. 113 (1973).

52. *See* School Dist. of Abington v. Schempp, 374 U.S. 203 (1963); Engel v. Vitale, 370 U.S. 421 (1962).

53. *See* Board of Ed. of Central Sch. Dist. No. 1 v. Allen, 392 U.S. 236, 242 (1968) (permitting the use of public funds for the purchase of secular textbooks, but endorsing the view that "the Establishment Clause bars . . . any 'tax in any amount, large or small . . . levied to support any religious activities or institutions, whatever they may be called, or whatever form they may adopt to teach or practice religion.'") (quoting Everson v. Bd. of Educ., 330 U.S. 1, 15–16 (1947)).

54. *See* Epperson v. Arkansas, 393 U.S. 97 (1968).

55. *See* Brown v. Bd. of Educ., 347 U.S. 483 (1954).

56. *See generally* ROBERT M. LICHTMAN, THE SUPREME COURT AND THE McCARTHY-ERA REPRESSION: ONE HUNDRED DECISIONS (2012).

57. *See* Keyishian v. Bd. of Regents, 385 U.S. 589 (1967); Sweezy v. New Hampshire, 354 U.S. 234 (1957).

58. *See, e.g.,* Roth v. United States, 354 U.S. 476 (1957); Redrup v. New York, 386 U.S. 767 (1967).

59. LUCAS A. POWE JR., THE WARREN COURT AND AMERICAN POLITICS (2000).

60. Id. at 489–94.

61. Id. at 215.

62. *See, e.g.,* Reynolds v. Sims, 377 U.S. 533 (1964).

63. Lucas v. Forty-fourth General Assembly of State of Colo., 377 U.S. 713, 736–37 (1964).

64. *See, e.g.,* Jesse Choper, *Consequences of Supreme Court Decisions Upholding Individual Rights,* 83 MICH. L. REV. 1, 91 & n. 624 (1984).

65. In his separate opinion in Keyes v. School Dist., No. 1, 413 U.S. 189 (1973), Justice Powell, then the only southern justice on the Court, attacked the "merely regional application" of *Brown* and argued that southern de jure and northern de facto segregation should be held to the same legal standard. Id. at 219. Although the Court never endorsed Justice Powell's position, for a short period it did appear poised to attack at least some forms of de facto segregation. *See* Swann v. Charlotte-Mecklenburg Board of Educ., 402 U.S. 1 (1971) (upholding use of busing to overcome segregation resulting from residential segregation in system that had been segregated on de jure basis); Keyes v. School Dist. No. 1, 413 U.S. 189 (1973) (upholding judicially mandated desegregation plan in northern context). However, when northern opposition to desegregation intensified, the Court quickly retreated. *See* Milliken v. Bradley, 418 U.S. 717 (1974) (limiting availability of interdistrict relief in northern context); Missouri v. Jenkins, 515 U.S. 70 (1995) (limiting judicial remedies for school segregation in Kansas City, Missouri); Pasadena Board of Educ. v. Spangler, 427 U.S. 424 (1976) (disapproving judicial remedies to prevent resegregation in northern context). Ultimately,

the Court invalidated even voluntary, race-conscious remedies for de facto segregation. *See* Parents Involved in Community Schools v. Seattle School Dist. No. 1, 551 U.S. 701 (2001).

66. *See, e.g.*, Lucas A. Powe Jr., The Warren Court and American Politics 198, 492 (2000); Burt Neuborne, *The Gravitational Pull of Race on the Warren Court*, 2010 Sup. Ct. Rev. 59, 84–87.

67. *See* id. at 199.

68. New York Times v. Sullivan, 376 U.S. 643 (1961).

69. *See* Gideon v. Wainwright, 372 U.S. 335 (1963) (holding that the Sixth Amendment, as incorporated by the Fourteenth Amendment, guaranteed indigent criminal defendants the right to appointed counsel).

70. *See* Williams v. Illinois, 399 U.S. 235 (1970) (holding that the equal protection clause prohibited the imprisonment of an indigent defendant for failure to pay a fine).

71. *See* Harper v. Virginia State Bd. of Elections, 383 U.S. 663 (1966) (holding that the poll tax unconstitutionally infringed on the right to vote).

72. *See* Goldberg v. Kelly, 397 U.S. 254 (1970) (holding that the due process clause prohibited the termination of welfare benefits prior to a hearing); Shapiro v. Thompson, 394 U.S. 618 (1969) (holding that states could not impose durational residency requirements on welfare recipients).

73. *See, e.g.*, Michael Tigar, *The Supreme Court, 1969 Term—Foreword: Waiver of Constitutional Rights: Disquiet in the Citadel*, 84 Harv. L. Rev. 1 (1970); Albert Alschuler, *Plea Bargaining and Its History*, 79 Colum. L. Rev. 1 (1979).

74. Box v. Planned Parenthood of Indiana and Kentucky, 139 S. Ct. 1780, 1784–94 (2019) (Thomas, J., concurring).

75. *See* Adam Cohen, *Clarence Thomas Knows Nothing of My Work*, The Atlantic, May 29, 2019, available at https://www.theatlantic.com/ideas/ar chive/2019/05/clarence-thomas-used-my-book-argue-against-abortion/590455/?f bclid=IwAR3fOv3gn3FzzMn7dFAVQWLZ-EFVi-53zYNA8WK5fYmtFmneD UxTbsv1SvU ("Between eugenic sterilization and abortion lie two crucial differences: who is making the decision, and why they are making it. In eugenic sterilization, the state decides who may not reproduce, and acts with the goal of 'improving' the population. In abortion, a woman decides not to reproduce, for personal reasons related to a specific pregnancy").

76. *See, e.g.*, Masterpiece Cakeshop Ltd. v. Colorado Civil Rights Commn., 138 S. Ct. 1719 (2018) (reversing on constitutional grounds a state decision that merchant had violated the state's discrimination act by refusing to prepare cake to celebrate the wedding of gay couple).

77. In keeping with the conservative co-optation of populism, the decisions echo Bryan's concern about the denigration of religious values, but not Bryan's association between Christianity and social justice.

78. *See* Town of Greece v. Galloway, 572 U.S. 565 (2014) (upholding practice of beginning town board meetings with prayers almost always delivered by Christian clergy against establishment clause attack).

79. *See, e.g.*, Espinoza v. Montana Dept. of Revenue, 140 S. Ct. 2246 (2020).

80. *See* American Legion v. American Humanist Assn., 588 U.S. ___ (2019) (upholding placement on public land of roman cross as part of World War I memorial); Van Orden v. Perry, 545 U.S. 677 (2005) (holding that placement of a six-foot-high monolith inscribed with the Ten Commandments on state capitol grounds did not violate establishment clause); Pleasant Grove City, Utah v. Summum, 555 U.S. 460 (2009) (holding that a privately donated Ten Commandments memorial in a public park was "government speech," and, therefore, did not create a public forum where there was a right to engage in competing speech).

81. *See* Masterpiece Cakeshop, Ltd. v. Colorado Civil Rights Comm'n., 138 S. Ct. 1719 (2018) (invalidating on narrow grounds state civil rights commission decision to issue a cease and desist order against merchant who refused to sell wedding cake to a same-sex couple); Burwell v. Hobby Lobby, 573 U.S. 682 (2014) (holding that Religious Freedom Restoration Act gave corporations with religious objections to birth control the right to an exemption from a mandate that these services be provided to employees).

82. *See* Gratz v. Bollinger, 539 U.S. 244 (2003) (invalidating University of Michigan affirmative action program). *Cf.* Parents Involved in Community Schools v. Seattle School Dist. No. 1, 127 S. Ct. 2738 (2007) (invalidating race-conscious voluntary desegregation plan). *But cf.* Grutter v. Bollinger, 339 U.S. 306 (2003) (utilizing strict scrutiny, but upholding affirmative action program); Fisher v. University of Texas, 136 S. Ct. 2198 (2016) (same).

83. *See, e.g.*, Adarand Constructors, Inc. v. Pena, 515 U.S. 200, 240–41 (1995) ("There can be no doubt that the paternalism that appears to lie at the heart of this [affirmative action] program is at war with the principle of inherent equality that underlies and infuses our Constitution"); Grutter v. Bollinger, 539 U.S. 306, 367 (2003) (Thomas, J., concurring in part and dissenting in part) (attacking "legacy preferences" in "elite institutions" as part of argument against affirmative action); id. at 368 (asserting that "there is nothing ancient, honorable, or constitutionally protected about 'selective' admissions").

84. Obergefell v. Hodges, 135 S. Ct., at 2629 (Scalia, J., dissenting).
    For similar rhetoric, see Roemer v. Evans, 570 U.S. 620, 636, 652 (1996) (Scalia, J., dissenting):

> This Court has no business imposing upon all Americans the resolution favored by the elite class from which the Members of this institution are selected. . . .

> When the Court takes sides in the culture wars, it tends to be with the knights rather than the villeins—and more specifically with the Templars, reflecting the views and values of the lawyer class from which the Court's Members are drawn. How that class feels about homosexuality will be evident to anyone who wishes to interview job applicants at virtually any of the Nation's law schools. The interviewer may refuse to offer a job because the applicant is a Republican; because he is an adulterer; because he went to the wrong prep school or belongs to the wrong country club; because he eats snails; because he is a womanizer; because she wears real-animal fur; or even because he hates the Chicago Cubs. But if the interviewer should wish

not to be an associate or partner of an applicant because he disapproves of the applicant's homosexuality, *then* he will have violated the pledge which the Association of American Law Schools requires all its members. This law-school view of what "prejudices" must be stamped out may be contrasted with the more plebeian attitudes that apparently still prevail in the United States Congress, which has been unresponsive to repeated attempts to extend to homosexuals the protections of federal civil rights laws . . . , and which took the pains to exclude them specifically from the Americans with Disabilities Act of 1990. . . .

85. Grutter v. Bollinger, 529 U.S., at 362 (Thomas, J., concurring in part and dissenting in part).

86. *See* IRA KATZNELSON, FEAR ITSELF: THE NEW DEAL AND THE ORIGINS OF OUR TIME 151, 159–60 (2013) (describing New Deal's accommodation of southern racists).

87. *See, e.g.,* WILLIAM E. LEUCHTENBURG, FRANKLIN D. ROOSEVELT AND THE NEW DEAL 268 (1963) (Roosevelt experienced "a humiliating drubbing"). For a more nuanced account that nonetheless reaches the same conclusion, see generally Charles M. Price & Joseph Boskin, *The Roosevelt "Purge": A Reappraisal,* 28 THE J. OF POLITICS 660 (1966).

88. *See* W.H. Lawrence, *Truman, Barkley Named by Democrats; South Loses on Civil Rights, 35 Walk Out; President Will Recall Congress July 26,* N.Y. TIMES (July 15, 1948), available at https://archive.nytimes.com/www.nytimes.com /library/politics/camp/480715convention-dem-ra.html.

89. *See* TAYLOR BRANCH, PILLAR OF FIRE 404 (1998) (quoting Johnson as saying that his civil rights policies had lost the South to the Democratic Party "for your lifetime and mine").

90. *See* Sidney M. Milkis, *Lyndon Johnson, the Great Society, and the "Twilight" of the Modern Presidency,* in THE GREAT SOCIETY AND THE HIGH TIDE OF LIBERALISM 19–21 (Sidney M. Milkis & Jerome M. Mileur eds., 2005).

91. *See* Martin Carcasson, *Ending Welfare as We Know It: President Clinton and the Rhetorical Transformation of the Anti-Welfare Culture,* 9 RHET. & PUB. AFF. 655 (2006) (arguing that the Clinton repeal of the welfare mandate was motivated by a desire to help the "working poor").

92. *See* Timothy A. Canova, *The Legacy of the Clinton Bubble,* DISSENT (summer 2008), available at https://www.dissentmagazine.org/article/the-legacy-of -the-clinton-bubble (detailing deregulatory efforts by the Clinton administration).

93. *See* James McBride & Mohammed Aly Sergie, NAFTA's Economic Impact (Oct. 2, 2018), available at https://www.cfr.org/backgrounder/naftas -economic-impact (assessing economic effects, including effects on labor markets, of the North American Free Trade Agreement).

94. Patient Protection and Affordable Care Act, Pub. L. No. 111-148, 124 Stat. 119 (2010).

95. Dodd-Frank Wall Street Reform and Consumer Protection Act, Pub. L. No. 111-203, 124 Stat. 1376 (2010).

96. Bipartisan Campaign Reform Act of 2002, Pub. L. No. 107-155m 116 Stat. 81 (2002).

97. Utility Air Regulatory Group v. EPA, 573 U.S. 302, 343 (2014) (Breyer, J., concurring in part and dissenting in part).

98. *See* Daubert v. Merrill Dow Pharmaceuticals, Inc., 509 U.S. 579, 594–95 (1993).

99. *See, e.g.,* Webster v. Reproductive Health Services, 495 U.S. 490, 565 (1989) (Stevens, J., concurring in part and dissenting in part) ("I am persuaded that the absence of any secular purpose for the legislative declarations that life begins at conception and that conception occurs at fertilization makes the relevant portion of the preamble invalid under the Establishment Clause of the First Amendment to the Federal Constitution").

Seven. Establishing a More Perfect Union: The Problem of Rights and Rhetoric

1. Robert P. George & Gerard V. Bradley, *Marriage and the Liberal Imagination,* 84 Geo. L. J. 301 (1995).

2. Id. at 306.

3. Id. at 307.

4. William Shakespeare, The Merchant of Venice, Act III, scene 1.

5. The argument in the next several paragraphs tracks an argument first articulated in Peter Westen, *The Empty Idea of Equality,* 95 Harv. L. Rev. 537 (1982). *See also* Christopher J. Peters, *Equality Reconsidered,* 110 Harv. L. Rev. 1210 (1997); Derek Parfit, *Equality or Priority,* in The Idea of Equality 111 (Matthew Clayton & Andrew Williams eds., 2002).

6. *See, e.g.,* Welsh v. United States, 398 U.S. 333, 362 (1970) (Harlan, J., concurring) (where a statute is defective because of underinclusion "a court may declare it a nullity and order that the benefits not extend to the class that the legislature intended to benefit, or it may extend the coverage of the statute to include those who are aggrieved by exclusion").

7. *See* Cumming v. Board of Education, 175 U.S. 528 (1899).

8. 137 S. Ct. 1678 (2017).

9. *See, e.g.,* Thomas J. Miceli & Kathleen Segerson, *Defining Efficient Care: The Role of Income Distribution,* 24 J. Leg. Stud. 189, 191–96 (1995) (defining Pareto efficiency and the Pareto criterion).

10. *See, e.g.,* Richard H. McAdams, *Relative Preferences,* 102 Yale L. J. 1 (1992) (offering detailed evidence that people have a preference for a position relative to others).

11. *But cf.* Martha C. Nussbaum, *A Right to Marry?,* 98 Cal. L. Rev. 667, 694 (2010) (asking whether "government [should] continue to marry people at all").

12. *See* John Rawls, A Theory of Justice (1971).

13. *See* John Finnis, Natural Law and Natural Rights (2011).

14. *See* Martha Nussbaum, Women and Human Development: The Capabilities Approach (2000).

15. *See* Amartya Sen, Development as Freedom (1999).

16. *See* John Stuart Mill, On Liberty (1859).

17. *See* Lujan v. Defenders of Wildlife, 504 U.S. 555 (1992).

18. *See* Allen v. Wright, 468 U.S. 737, 756 (1984).

19. *See* Regents of the University of California v. Bakke, 438 U.S. 265, 281 n. 14 (1978).

20. *See* Thomas Kaplan, *Elizabeth Warren Has Quick Comeback to Gay Marriage Question*, N.Y. TIMES, Oct. 10, 2019.

21. RONALD DWORKIN, TAKING RIGHTS SERIOUSLY xi (1977).

22. 489 U.S. 189 (1989).

23. *See* Barbara E. Armacost, *Affirmative Duties, Systemic Harms, and the Due Process Clause*, 94 MICH. L. REV. 982 (1996).

24. *See, e.g.,* United States v. Johnson, 333 U.S. 10 (1948).

25. *See* Eyal Benvenisti, *Margin of Appreciation, Consensus, and Universal Standards*, 31 N.Y.U. J. INT'L L. & POL. 843 (1999).

26. *See* Calvin R. Massey, *The Locus of Sovereignty: Judicial Review, Legislative Supremacy, and Federalism in the Constitutional Traditions of Canada and the United States*, 1990 DUKE L. J. 1229, 1231–32.

27. *See* RANDY E. BARNETT, RESTORING THE LOST CONSTITUTION: THE PRESUMPTION OF LIBERTY (2004).

28. *See* PATRICIA J. WILLIAMS, THE ALCHEMY OF RACE AND RIGHTS: A DIARY OF A LAW PROFESSOR (1991).

Eight. Insuring Domestic Tranquility: The Problem of Violence

1. THOMAS HOBBES, LEVIATHAN 89 (Richard Tuck ed., 1996).

2. Id.

3. United States Constitution, Art. II, § 3.

4. Id. at Art II, § 2.

5. Id. at Art. IV, § 3, cl. 2.

6. Mark Murray, *Poll: 80 Percent of Voters Say Things Are Out of Control in U.S.*, NBC NEWS, https://www.nbcnews.com/politics/meet-the-press/poll-80-percent-voters-say-things-are-out-control-u-n1226276 (last visited 1/16/21).

7. *See* NationMaster, Crime Levels: Countries Compared, www.nationmaster.com/country-info/stats/Crime/Crime-levels (last visited 1/16/21).

8. *See* NationMaster, Rape: Countries Compared, www.nationmaster.com/country-info/stats/Crime/Rape-rate (last visited 1/16/21).

9. *See* NationMaster, Robberies: Countries Compared, www.nationmaster.com/country-info/stats/Crime/Robberies (last visited 1/16/21).

10. *See* Heather C. West, *Prison Inmates at Midyear 2009 — Statistical Tables*, BUREAU OF JUSTICE STATISTICS STATISTICAL TABLES 2 (June 2010) (reporting 2,297,400 inmates in state and federal prisons, local jails, and under physical guardianship).

11. *See* Roy Walmsley, World Prison Population List 2009 (8th ed.), available at http://www.kcl.ac.uk/depsta/law/research/icps/downloads/wppl-8th 41.pdf (reporting that the United States has the highest prison population rate in the world with 756 incarcerated individuals per 100,000 in population, followed by Russia (629), Rwanda (604), St. Kitts &Nevis (588), and Cuba (about 531).

12. Violent and property crime rates, including the rate of every type of violent and property crime measured by the National Crime Victimization Survey, declined between 1999 and 2008. By 2008, crime rates were at or near their lowest levels in over three decades. *See* Michael R. Rand, *Criminal Victimization, 2008*, BUREAU OF JUSTICE STATISTICS BULLETIN 1 (2009), available at http://bjs. ojp.usdoj.gov/content/pub/pdf/cv08.pdf.

13. *See* Heather C. West, *Prison Inmates at Midyear 2009—Statistical Tables*, BUREAU OF JUSTICE STATISTICS STATISTICAL TABLES 2 (June 2010) at 2.

14. *See* Becky Pettit & Bruce Western, *Mass Imprisonment and Life Course: Race and Class Inequality in U.S. Incarceration*, 69 AMER. SOC. REV. 151 (2004).

15. *See By the Numbers: US Police Kill in Days More than Other Countries Do in Years*, THE GUARDIAN, www.theguardian.com/us-news/2015/jun/09/the-counted-police-killings-us-vs-other-countries (last visited 2/16/21).

16. *See* National Intimate Partner and Sexual Violence Survey, www.cdc.gov /violenceprevention/pdf/nisvs_report2010-a.pdf (last visited 1/16/21).

17. *See* Aaron Carp, Estimating Global Civilian-Held Firearms by Numbers, http://www.smallarmssurvey.org/fileadmin/docs/T-Briefing-Papers/SAS-BP -Civilian-Firearms-Numbers.pdf (last visited 1/16/21).

18. *See* Edith M. Lederer, *Americans Own 46% of the World's 1 Billion Guns, Says U.N. Report*, TIME, June 8, 2018.

19. *See* Joseph Palazzolo & Alexis Flynn, *U.S. Leads World in Mass Shootings*, WALL STREET JOURNAL, Oct. 3, 2015.

20. *See* District of Columbia v. Heller, 554 U.S. 570 (2008).

21. *See, e.g.*, Maryland v. Pringle, 540 U.S. 366 (2003); Navarette v. California, 134 S. Ct. 1683 (2014).

22. *Compare, e.g.*, Allen v. Wright, 468 U.S. 737 (1984) (parents of African American students lack standing to complain about IRS policy that failed to deny tax exempt status to private segregated schools) *with* Northeastern Florida Chapter of Associated General Contractors v. Jacksonville, 508 U.S. 656 1993) (nonminority contractor has standing to complain about affirmative action policy even though the plaintiff would not have received the contract if the policy were not in place).

23. *See* District of Columbia v. Heller, 554 U.S. 570 (2008).

24. *See* United States v. Morrison, 529 U.S. 598 (2000).

25. *See* United States v. Lopez, 514 U.S. 549 (1995).

26. *See, e.g.*, Immigration and Naturalization Service v. Delgado, 466 U.S. 210 (1984); United States v. Drayton, 536 U.S. 194 (2002).

27. *See* Wilson v. Arkansas, 514 U.S. 927 (1995); Hudson v. Michigan, 547 U.S. 586 (2006).

28. *See, e.g.*, California v. Greenwood, 486 U.S. 35 (1988); Florida v. Riley, 488 U.S. 445 (1989).

29. *See, e.g.*, New York v. Quarles, 467 U.S. 649 (1984); Berghuis v. Thompkins, 560 U.S. 370 (2010).

30. *See, e.g.*, Shinn v. Kayer, 141 S. Ct. 517 (22021); Woods v. Donald, 135 S. Ct. 1372 (2017).

31. *See* Antiterrorism and Effective Death Penalty Act of 1996, Pub. L. No. 104-132, 110 Stat. 214, 219.

32. *See, e.g.,* Teague v. Lane, 489 U.S. 288 (1989); Butler v. McKellar, 494 U.S. 407 (1990).

33. *See* Whren v. United States, 517 U.S. 806 (1996).

34. *See* United States v. Armstrong, 517 U.S. 456 (1996).

35. *See* McCleskey v. Kemp, 481 U.S. 279 (1987).

36. *See* United States v. Martinez-Fuerte, 428 U.S. 543, 563 (1976).

37. *See* United States v. Leon, 468 U.S. 897 (1984).

38. *See* Illinois v. Krull, 480 U.S. 340 (1987).

39. *See* Herring v. United States, 555 U.S. 135 (2009).

40. *See* Davis v. United States, 564 U.S. 229 (2011).

41. *See* Walder v. United States, 347 U.S. 62 (1954).

42. *See* Immigration and Naturalization Service v. Lopez-Mendoza, 468 U.S. 1032 (1984).

43. *See* United States v. Janis, 428 U.S. 433 (1976).

44. *See* Hudson v. Michigan, 547 U.S. 586 (2006).

45. *See* Murray v. United States, 487 U.S. 533 (1988).

46. *See* Nix v. Williams, 467 U.S. 431 (1984).

47. *See* Wong Sun v. United States, 371 U.S. 471 (1963).

48. *See* Hudson v. United States, 547 U.S. 586, 597–99 (2006).

49. *See, e.g.,* City of Escondido v. Emmons, 139 S. Ct. 500 (2019); Kisela v. Hughes, 138 S. Ct. 1148 (2018); Anderson v. Creighton, 483 U.S. 635 (1987).

50. *See, e.g.,* Lujan v. Defenders of Wildlife, 504 U.S. 555 (1992).

51. *See* City of Los Angeles v. Lyons, 461 U.S. 95 (1983).

52. *See* District of Columbia v. Heller, 554 U.S. 570, 626–28 (2008).

53. *See, e.g.,* DeShaney v. Winnebago County Dept. of Social Services, 489 U.S. 189 (1989) (holding that the Constitution does not require the government to protect individuals from private violence).

54. *See, e.g.,* Mapp v. Ohio, 367 U.S. 643 (1961).

55. *See* Miranda v. Arizona, 384 U.S. 436 (1966).

56. 5 U.S. (1 Cranch) 137 (1803).

57. 384 U.S. 436 (1966).

58. *See, e.g.,* Spano v. New York, 360 U.S. 315 (1959).

59. *See, e.g.,* Betts v. Brady, 316 U.S. 455 (1942).

60. *See* Gideon v. Wainwright, 372 U.S. 335 (1963).

61. *See* Rochin v. California, 342 U.S. 165 (1952).

62. *See* Mapp v. Ohio, 367 U.S. 643 (1961).

63. *See, e.g.,* United States v. Rabinowitz, 339 U.S. 56 (1950).

64. *See, e.g.,* Chimel v. California, 395 U.S. 752 (1969).

65. *See, e.g.,* Warden v. Hayden, 387 U.S. 294 (1967).

66. *See, e.g.,* California v. Acevedo, 500 U.S. 565 (1991).

67. *See, e.g.,* Schneckloth v. Bustamonte, 412 U.S. 281 (1973).

68. *See, e.g.,* Vernonia School District 47J v. Acton, 515 U.S. 646 (1995).

69. *See, e.g.,* New York v. Burger, 482 U.S. 691 (1987).

Nine. Ordaining and Establishing This Constitution, Part 1: Early American
Skepticism

1. *See, e.g.,* GORDON S. WOOD, THE CREATION OF THE AMERICAN REPUBLIC,
1776–1787, at 259–62 (1991).
2. LARRY KRAMER, THE PEOPLE THEMSELVES 30 (2004).
3. *See* JACK RAKOVE, ORIGINAL MEANINGS: POLITICS AND IDEAS IN THE MAK-
ING OF THE CONSTITUTION 97 (1996). *See also* LARRY KRAMER, THE PEOPLE
THEMSELVES 57 (2004).
4. Both Jefferson and John Adams apparently took this view. *See* id.
5. *See, e.g.,* id. at 59.
6. For a general discussion of the problem, see Bruce Ackerman, *Storrs Lectures: Discovering the Constitution,* 93 YALE L. J. 1013, 1019–20 (1984).
7. Calder v. Bull, 3 U.S. 386, 398 (1798) (Iredell, J., concurring).
8. It is collected in THE COMPLETE ANTI-FEDERALIST (Herbert J. Storing ed.,
1981).
9. *See* PAULINE MAIER, RATIFICATION: THE PEOPLE DEBATE THE CONSTITU-
TION, 1787–88 at 115–16 (2010) (recounting contemporary view that ratification
was "a lost cause").
10. *See* id. at 7 (1981) (noting that the Antifederalists "often objected even
to entering into debate on the Constitution because of legal irregularities in the
Proceedings of the Philadelphia Convention").
11. *See* Bruce Ackerman, *Storrs Lectures: Discovering the Constitution,* 93 YALE
L. J. 1013, 1039 (1984) (celebrating occasions when the American people "after
sustained debate and struggle hammer out new principles to guide public life").
12. *See, e.g.,* GORDON S. WOOD, THE CREATION OF THE AMERICAN REPUB-
LIC, 1776–1787, at 139–43 (1969) ; GORDON S. WOOD, THE RADICALISM OF THE
AMERICAN REVOLUTION 187–89 (1991).
13. *See* GORDON WOOD, THE CREATION OF THE AMERICAN REPUBLIC, 1776–
1789, at 53–70 (1969).
14. *See Federalist No. 48* (Madison) in THE FEDERALIST 256 (arguing against
"parchment barriers"); *Federalist No. 73* (Hamilton) in THE FEDERALIST 380
(pointing to insufficiency of "a mere parchment delineation").
15. *Federalist No. 84* in THE FEDERALIST 446.
16. Letter from James Madison to Thomas Jefferson (Oct. 17, 1788), in 11
THE PAPERS OF JAMES MADISON 295, 297 (Charles F. Hobson & Robert A. Rutland eds., 1977).
17. *Federalist No. 51* in THE FEDERALIST 267–272.
18. *See generally* Daryl Levinson, *Parchment and Politics: The Positive Puzzle
of Constitutional Commitment,* 124 HARV. L. REV. 657 (2011).
19. *Federalist No. 78* in THE FEDERALIST 401–8.
20. Id. at 40.
21. II THE COMPLETE ANTI-FEDERALIST 442 (Herbert J. Storing ed., 1981)
(emphasis in original). *See generally* Shlomo Slonim, *Federalist No. 78 and Brutus' Neglected Thesis on Judicial Supremacy,* 23 CONST. COMM. 7 (2006).

22. *Federalist No. 78* in THE FEDERALIST 402.

23. Madison might be read as rejecting an independent judiciary as a solution to the problem when he writes that "creating a will in the community independent of the majority, that is, of the society itself . . . is but a precarious security; because a power independent of the society may as well espouse the unjust views of the major, as the rightful interests of the minor party, and may possibly be turned against both parties." *Federalist No. 51* in id. at 270.

24. Id. at 268.

25. *Federalist No. 48* in id. at 256.

26. Id.

27. See *Federalist Nos. 48–50* in id. at 256–64.

28. *Federalist No. 51* in id. at 267.

29. See, e.g., David S. Law & Milsa Bersteeg, *The Declining Influence of the United States Constitution*, 87 N.Y.U. L. REV. 762 (2012); Mark Tushnet, *State Action, Social Welfare Rights, and the Judicial Role: Some Comparative Observations*, 3 CHI. J. INT. L. 435 (2002).

30. See, e.g., Michael Klarman, *Rethinking the Civil Rights and Civil Liberties Revolutions*, 82 U. VA. L. REV. 1 (1996); GERALD N. ROSENBERG, THE HOLLOW HOPE: CAN COURTS BRING ABOUT SOCIAL CHANGE? (1991). Cf. GEOFFREY R. STONE, PERILOUS TIMES: FREE SPEECH IN WARTIME FROM THE SEDITION ACT OF 1789 TO THE WAR ON TERRORISM (2004).

31. See WOODY HOLTON, UNRULY AMERICANS AND THE ORIGINS OF THE CONSTITUTION 253 (2007).

32. See, e.g., Kurt T. Lash, *The Original Meaning of an Omission: The Tenth Amendment, Popular Sovereignty, and "Expressly" Delegated Power*, 83 NOTRE DAME L. REV. 1889, 1915–18 (2008); Akhil Amar, *The Bill of Rights and the Fourteenth Amendment*, 101 YALE L. J. 1193, 1202 (1992). The point is most obvious with regard to the establishment clause of the First Amendment which, far from guaranteeing religious freedom, was understood to protect state establishments against federal interference. See, e.g., Kurt T. Lash, *The Second Adoption of the Establishment Clause*, 27 ARIZ. ST. L. J. 1085, 1091–92 (1995). Cf. School Dist. of Abington Tp. v. Schempp, 374 U.S. 203, 255 (1963) (Brennan, J., concurring).

33. See RICHARD LABUNSKI, MADISON AND THE STRUGGLE FOR THE BILL OF RIGHTS 159 (2006); ROBERT ALLEN RUTLAND, THE BIRTH OF THE BILL OF RIGHTS, 1776–1791, at 171–73 (1955).

34. See PAULINE MAIER, RATIFICATION: THE PEOPLE DEBATE THE CONSTITUTION, 1787–1788, 446 (2010) (quoting Madison's letter to Jefferson just before start of first Congress stating that he favored bill of rights "to extinguish opposition [to the Constitution] or at least break the force of it, by detaching the deluded opponents from their designing leaders"). Cf. WOODY HOLTON, UNRULY AMERICANS AND THE ORIGINS OF THE CONSTITUTION 257 (2007) (noting that Madison "probably could not have been reelected" had he reneged on his promise to introduce a bill of rights, but that the energy he "brought to the fight for the Bill of Rights indicated that he had developed a deep personal commitment to the cause").

35. Letter from James Madison to Thomas Jefferson (Oct. 17, 1788), in 11

THE PAPERS OF JAMES MADISON 295, 297 (Charles F. Hobson & Robert A. Rutland eds., 1977). In the letter, Madison claimed that he had "always been in favor of a bill of rights" but had "never thought the omission a material defect, nor been anxious to supply it even by *subsequent* amendment, for any other reason than that it is anxiously desired by others." Id. (emphasis in original).

36. Many federalist congressmen, including Jackson, Sherman, White, Vining, Goodhue, and Livermore, objected to even discussion of a bill of rights until Congress has accomplished what they thought of as more important tasks. See I ANNALS OF CONGRESS 439–65 (Joseph Gales ed., 1834); THE AMERICAN REPUBLIC: PRIMARY SOURCES 446–51 (Bruce Frohnen ed., 2002).

37. For example, Representative Burke claimed that rather than "those solid and substantial amendments which the people expect," the proposals were "whip-syllabub" (a dessert that was "frothy and full of wind, formed only to please the palate") or "like a tub thrown out to a whale" (which sailors used to divert the whale from attacking a ship). Quoted in PAULINE MAIER, RATIFICATION: THE PEOPLE DEBATE THE CONSTITUTION, 1787–1788, 452 (2010).

38. See Keith E. Whittington, *Judicial Review of Congress Before the Civil War*, 97 GEO. L. J. 1257 (2009); Mark Graber, *Naked Land Transfers and American Constitutional Development*, 53 VAND. L. REV. 73, 75 (2000).

39. Dred Scott v. Sandford, 60 U.S. (19 How.) 393 (1857).

40. See Acts of Congress Held Unconstitutional in Whole or in Part by the Supreme Court of the United States, www.gpo.gov/fdsys/pkg/GPO-CONAN-2002/pdf/GPO-CONAN-2002-10.pdf. The first case was Lamont v. Postmaster General, 381 U.S. 301 (1965). As early as 1943, the Court narrowly construed a federal statute so as to avoid free speech difficulties. See Schneiderman v. United States, 320 U.S. 118, 133 (1943) ("because of our firmly rooted tradition of freedom of belief, we certainly will not presume in construing the naturalization and denaturalization acts that Congress meant to circumscribe liberty of political thought by general phrases in those statutes").

41. See, e.g., *Federalist No. 84* (Hamilton) in THE FEDERALIST 445–46.

42. I ANNALS OF CONGRESS at 456.

43. Compare, e.g., Randy E. Barnett, *Reconceiving the Ninth Amendment*, 74 CORNELL L. REV. 1 (1988) (individual rights view) with Kurt T. Lash, *The Lost Original Meaning of the Ninth Amendment*, 83 TEX. L. REV. 331 (2004) (federalism view). For my own view, see Louis Michael Seidman, *Our Unsettled Ninth Amendment*, 98 CAL. L. REV. 2129 (2010).

44. See II DUMAS MALONE, JEFFERSON AND THE RIGHTS OF MAN 162 (1951).

45. VIII THE WRITINGS OF THOMAS JEFFERSON 247 (Paul Leicester Ford ed., 1892–97).

46. II DUMAS MALONE, JEFFERSON AND THE RIGHTS OF MAN 342–43 (1951).

47. See ADRIENNE KOCH, JEFFERSON AND MADISON: THE GREAT COLLABORATION 185–87 (1950).

48. See DAVID N. MAYER, THE CONSTITUTIONAL THOUGHT OF THOMAS JEFFERSON 211 (1994).

49. See, e.g., LEONARD W. LEVY, JEFFERSON & CIVIL LIBERTIES: THE DARKER

SIDE 14–15 (1973) (observing that although Jefferson's ideas were "not always libertarian," with regard to religious liberty, "[a]lthough it exposed him to abusive criticism he carried on his fight for separation of church and state, and for the free exercise of religion, throughout his long public career without significant contradiction").

50. JOSEPH J. ELLIS, AMERICAN SPHINX: THE CHARACTER OF THOMAS JEF-FERSON 10 (1996).

51. Thomas Jefferson to James Madison, September 6, 1789, with Copies and Fragment, in VI THE WORKS OF THOMAS JEFFERSON 3 (Paul Leicester Ford ed., 1904).

52. Id.

53. Id.

54. Id.

55. X THE WRITINGS OF THOMAS JEFFERSON 37(Andrew A. Lipscomb ed., 1903).

56. XVI THE WRITINGS OF THOMAS JEFFERSON 48 (Andrew A. Lipscomb ed., 1903).

57. 5 U.S. (1 Cranch) 137 (1803).

58. See, e.g., DAVID N. MAYER, THE CONSTITUTIONAL THOUGHT OF THOMAS JEFFERSON 267 (1994).

59. Id. at 257.

60. "Letter to Thomas Ritchie," in X THE WRITINGS OF THOMAS JEFFERSON 169, 170 (Andrew A. Lipscomb ed., 1903).

61. Id. at 171.

62. See DAVID N. MAYER, THE CONSTITUTIONAL THOUGHT OF THOMAS JEF-FERSON 205 (1994).

63. See ADRIENNE KOCH, JEFFERSON AND MADISON: THE GREAT COLLABORA-TION 185–87 (1950).

64. See VII THE WRITINGS OF THOMAS JEFFERSON 301 (Andrew A. Lipscomb ed., 1903).

65. See DAVID N. MAYER, THE CONSTITUTIONAL THOUGHT OF THOMAS JEF-FERSON 207 (1994).

66. For a discussion of changes in the language of the Virginia Resolutions making them less radical, see ADRIENNE KOCH, JEFFERSON AND MADISON: THE GREAT COLLABORATION 190–91 (1950).

67. Jefferson's letter to Madison advocating this course of action is reproduced in id. at 196–97.

68. Letter from Thomas Jefferson to John B. Colvin (Sept. 20, 1810), in IX THE WRITINGS OF THOMAS JEFFERSON, 1807–1815, at 279, 280 (Paul Leicester Ford ed., 1898).

69. Id.

70. See Jefferson H. Powell, The Political Grammar of Early Constitutional Law, 71 N.C. L. REV. 949, 994 (1993) (noting Federalists' constitutional objections to the embargo).

71. See VIII THE WRITINGS OF THOMAS JEFFERSON 241 n. 1 (Andrew A. Lipscomb ed., 1903).

72. Id.

73. Id. at 247.

74. *See* David N. Mayer, The Constitutional Thought of Thomas Jefferson 250 (1994).

75. Id.

76. *See* id. at 254.

77. Id.

78. XII The Writings of Thomas Jefferson 419–20 (Andrew A. Lipscomb ed., 1903).

79. *See* II William W. Freehling, The Road to Disunion: Secessionists Triumphant, 1854–1861, at 346 (2007) (discussing secessionists' reliance on constitutional argument). For a sympathetic recounting of the various constitutional arguments supporting secession, see Jesse T. Carpenter, The South as a Conscious Minority 1789–1861: A Study in Political Thought 200–220 (1930).

80. *Remarks on the Special Message on Affairs in South Carolina. Jan. 10, 1861*, in Southern Pamphlets on Secession, November 1860–April 1861 at 118 (Jon L. Wakelyn ed., 1996).

81. Shearer Davis Bowman, At the Precipice: Americans North and South During the Secession Crisis 47 (2010) (quoting Davis).

82. Id. at 39 (quoting Davis).

83. Id.

84. As Jefferson Davis put it in his inaugural address as president of the Confederacy, "[I]t is not unreasonable to expect that States from which we have recently parted may seek to unite their fortunes to ours under the Government which we have instituted." Confederate States of America—Inaugural Address of the President of the Provisional Government, February 18, 1861, http://avalon.law.yale.edu/19th_century/csa_csainau.asp. *See also* Shearer Davis Bowman, At the Precipice: Americans North and South During the Secession Crisis 151 (2010) (many southerners hoped for "a compromise and a reconciliation").

85. *See Remarks on the Special Message on Affairs in South Carolina*, in Southern Pamphlets on Secession, November 1860–April 1861 at 135 (Jon L. Wakelyn ed., 1996).

86. Id. at 132.

87. Id. at 103.

88. Id. at 107.

89. On constitutional law's canon and anticanon, see Jamel Greene, *The Anticanon*, 125 Harv. L. Rev. 379 (2011); J.M. Balkin & Sanford Levinson, *The Canons of Constitutional Law*, 111 Harv. L. Rev. 963 (1998); Richard A. Primus, *Canon, Anti-Canon, and Judicial Dissent*, 48 Duke L. J. 243 (1998).

90. *See* Margaret L. Coit, John C. Calhoun 28 (1950).

91. *See* Kevin M. Gannon, *Escaping "Mr. Jefferson's Plan of Destruction": New England Federalists and the Idea of a Northern Confederacy, 1804–1804*, 21 J. of the Early Republic 413 (2001); Dumas Malone, Jefferson the President: First Term, 1801–1805, at 403–7 (1970).

For example, Timothy Pickering, who had served as postmaster general, secretary of war, and secretary of state in the Washington and Adams administrations, wrote that secession

> would be welcomed in Connecticut, and could we doubt of New Hampshire? But New York must be associated; and how is her concurrence to be obtained? She must be made the center of the confederacy. Vermont and New Jersey would follow of course, and Rhode Island of necessity.

Quoted in EDWARD PAYSON POWELL, NULLIFICATION AND SECESSION IN THE UNITED STATES: A HISTORY OF SIX ATTEMPTS DURING THE FIRST CENTURY OF THE REPUBLIC 128–29 (2002).

92. *See* JAMES M. BANNER JR., TO THE HARTFORD CONVENTION: THE FEDERALISTS AND THE ORIGINS OF PARTY POLITICS IN MASSACHUSETTS 1780–1815 at 328–29 (1970).

93. *See generally* id.

94. *See* id. at 338–39.

95. EDWARD PAYSON POWELL, NULLIFICATION AND SECESSION IN THE UNITED STATES: A HISTORY OF SIX ATTEMPTS DURING THE FIRST CENTURY OF THE REPUBLIC 238 (2002).

96. *See* HENRY MAYER, ALL ON FIRE: WILLIAM LLOYD GARRISON AND THE ABOLITION OF SLAVERY 445 (1998).

97. For an account of his original beliefs and his reasons for changing them, see FREDERICK DOUGLASS, MY BONDAGE AND MY FREEDOM 396 (1855). During the secession crisis of 1861, Douglass at least conditionally reembraced disunionism. *See* ERIC FONER, THE FIERY TRIAL: ABRAHAM LINCOLN AND AMERICAN SLAVERY 146 (2010) ("If the Union can only be maintained by new concessions to the slaveholders, let the Union perish").

98. Quoted in EDWARD PAYSON POWELL, NULLIFICATION AND SECESSION IN THE UNITED STATES: A HISTORY OF SIX ATTEMPTS DURING THE FIRST CENTURY OF THE REPUBLIC 208 (2002).

99. *See* Speech by William H. Seward on Freedom in the New Territories, U.S. Congress, Senate, Congressional Record, 31st Cong., 1st sess., appendix, 264. Immediately after making this statement, Seward made clear that he believed it was only hypothetical. "But I deny that the Constitution recognizes property in man. I submit, on the other hand, most respectfully that the Constitution not merely does not affirm that principle, but, on the contrary, altogether excludes it. Id. *But cf.* id. at 263 ("I know that there are laws of various sorts which regulate the conduct of men. There are constitutions and statutes . . . but when we are legislating for States . . . all these laws must be brought to the standard of the laws of God and must be tried by that standard and must stand or fall by it").

100. Quoted in EDWARD PAYSON POWELL, NULLIFICATION AND SECESSION IN THE UNITED STATES: A HISTORY OF SIX ATTEMPTS DURING THE FIRST CENTURY OF THE REPUBLIC 208 (2002).

101. *See* DAVID M. POTTER, THE IMPENDING CRISIS, 1848–1861, at 133–35 (1976).

102. Quoted in ERIC FONER, THE FIERY TRIAL: ABRAHAM LINCOLN AND AMERICAN SLAVERY 134 (2010).

103. *See* ERIC FONER, FREE SOIL, FREE LABOR, FREE MEN: THE IDEOLOGY OF THE REPUBLICAN PARTY BEFORE THE CIVIL WAR 292–29 (1995).

104. *See* JAMES BREWER STEWART, HOLY WARRIORS: THE ABOLITIONISTS AND AMERICAN SLAVERY 169 (1997).

105. ERIC FONER, THE FIERY TRIAL: ABRAHAM LINCOLN AND AMERICAN SLAVERY xviii, 57–584 (2010).

106. Even after signing the preliminary Emancipation Proclamation, Lincoln told African American leaders that

[y]ou and we are different races. We have between us a broader difference than exists between almost any other two races. . . . [T]his physical difference is a great disadvantage to us both, as I think your race suffers very greatly . . . by living among us, while ours suffer from your presence. . . . [O]n this broad continent, not a single man of your race is made equal of a single man of ours. . . . It is better for us both, therefore to be separated.

V THE COLLECTED WORKS OF ABRAHAM LINCOLN 371–72 (Roy P. Basler ed., 1953). On Lincoln's change of heart toward the end of his life, see ERIC FONER, THE FIERY TRIAL: ABRAHAM LINCOLN AND AMERICAN SLAVERY 259–63 (2010).

107. The Lyceum address is reproduced at http://www.abrahamlincoln online.org/lincoln/speeches/lyceum.htm.

108. *See* THE ADDRESS OF THE HON. ABRAHAM LINCOLN, IN INDICATION OF THE POLICY OF THE FRAMERS OF THE CONSTITUTION AND THE PRINCIPLES OF THE REPUBLICAN PARTY (1860).

109. For example, Lincoln wrote to Samuel Chase, his secretary of the treasury, that "[t]he original proclamation has no Constitutional or legal justification, except as a military measure. The exemptions were made because the military necessity did not apply to the exempted localities. . . . If I take the step [of repealing the exemptions] must I not do so, without the argument of military necessity, and so, without any argument except the one that I think the measure politically expedient and morally right? Would I not thus give up all footing upon the Constitution and law?" LOUIS P. MASUR, LINCOLN'S HUNDRED DAYS: THE EMANCIPATION PROCLAMATION AND THE WAR FOR THE UNION 244 (2012). It must be noted, though, that here, as elsewhere, Lincoln's actual motives were ambiguous and complex. Immediately after the passage just quoted, he suggested, perhaps paradoxically, that the desire to appear to be acting out of constitutional obligation rather than political expediency was, itself, politically expedient. "Can this pass unnoticed, or unresisted? . . . Would not many of our own friends shrink away appalled? Would it not lose us elections, and with them, the very cause we seek to advance?" Id.

110. *See* THE ADDRESS OF THE HON. ABRAHAM LINCOLN, IN INDICATION OF THE POLICY OF THE FRAMERS OF THE CONSTITUTION AND THE PRINCIPLES OF THE REPUBLICAN PARTY 5 (1860).

111. *See* id. at 6–18.

112. Id. at 31.

113. Id. at 32.

114. For the first order, see Abraham Lincoln, *Executive Order to the Commanding General of the Army of the United States* (Apr. 27, 1861), in VI A COMPILATION OF THE MESSAGES AND PAPERS OF THE PRESIDENTS 1789–1897 at 18 (James D. Richardson ed., 1897). For a discussion and citations to other orders, see David Barron & Martin Lederman, *The Commander in Chief at the Lowest Ebb—A Constitutional History*, 121 HARV. L. REV. 941, 998–1000 & n. 210 (2008). *See also* DANIEL FARBER, LINCOLN'S CONSTITUTION 117–41 (2003); J.G. RANDALL, CONSTITUTIONAL PROBLEMS UNDER LINCOLN 118–39 (1951).

115. STEPHEN C. NEFF, JUSTICE IN BLUE AND GRAY: A LEGAL HISTORY OF THE CIVIL WAR 35 (2010).

116. *See* Ex parte Merriman, 17 F. Cas. 144 (C.C.D. Md. 1861).

117. *See* J.C. RANDALL, CONSTITUTIONAL PROBLEMS UNDER LINCOLN 161–62 (1951).

118. *See, e.g.,* Amanda L. Tyler, *Suspension as an Emergency Power*, 118 YALE L. J. 600, 689 (2009); III JOSEPH STORY, COMMENTARIES ON THE CONSTITUTION OF THE UNITED STATES 483 (Ronald D. Rotunda & John E. Nowack eds., 1987). For judicial authority, see Ex parte Bollman, 4 Cranch 75, 101, (1807); Hamdi v. Rumsfeld, 542 U.S. 507, 561–63 (2004) (Scalia, J., dissenting).

119. Abraham Lincoln, *Special Session Message* (July 4, 1861), in VI A COMPILATION OF THE MESSAGES AND PAPERS OF THE PRESIDENTS, 1789–1897, at 25 (James D. Richardson ed., 1897).

120. For an account, see David Barron & Martin Lederman, *The Commander in Chief at the Lowest Ebb—A Constitutional History*, 121 HARV. L. REV. 941, 1001 (2008).

121. Abraham Lincoln, *Special Session Message* (July 4, 1861), in VI A COMPILATION OF THE MESSAGES AND PAPERS OF THE PRESIDENTS, 1789–1897, at 25 (James D. Richardson ed., 1897).

122. Cong. Globe, 37th Cong., 2d Sess. At 2383 (message from the president to the Senate and House).

123. For an account, see GEOFFREY R. STONE, PERILOUS TIMES: FREE SPEECH IN WARTIME FROM THE SEDITION ACT OF 1789 TO THE WAR ON TERRORISM 98–120 (2004).

124. *See* STEPHEN C. NEFF, JUSTICE IN BLUE AND GRAY: A LEGAL HISTORY OF THE CIVIL WAR 156–58 (2010).

125. For generally sympathetic accounts, see J.C. RANDALL, CONSTITUTIONAL PROBLEMS UNDER LINCOLN 161–62 (1951); DANIEL FARBER, LINCOLN'S CONSTITUTION (2003); Dennis J. Hutchinson, *Lincoln the Dictator*, 55 S.D. L. REV. 284 (2010).

126. *See* LOUIS P. MASUR, LINCOLN'S HUNDRED DAYS 244 (201).

127. RICHARD SLOTKIN, THE LONG ROAD TO ANTIETAM: HOW THE CIVIL WAR BECAME A REVOLUTION 365 (2012).

128. *See* Peoria Speech, October 16, 1854, www.nps.gov/liho/historyculture/peoriaspeech.html.

129. Lincoln quoted from a previous speech where he had said that "I have no purpose, directly or indirectly, to interfere with the institution of slavery in the States where it exists. I believe I have no lawful right to do so, and I have no

inclination to do so." Abraham Lincoln, First Inaugural Address, March 4, 1861, www.bartleby.com/124/pres31.html.
130. The amendment provided:

> No amendment shall be made to the Constitution which will authorize or give to Congress the power to abolish or interfere, within any State, with the domestic institutions thereof, including that of persons held to labor or service by the laws of said State.

The Failed Amendments, available at http://www.usconstitution.net/con stamfail.html.
131.

> I understand a proposed amendment to the Constitution—which amendment, however, I have not seen—has passed Congress, to the effect that the Federal Government shall never interfere with the domestic institutions of the States, including that of persons held to service. To avoid misconstruction of what I have said, I depart from my purpose not to speak of particular amendments so far as to say that, holding such a provision to now be implied constitutional law, I have no objection to its being made express and irrevocable.

Abraham Lincoln, First Inaugural Address, March 4, 1861, www.bartleby .com/124/pres31.html.
132. Quoted in Louis P. Masur, Lincoln's Hundred Days: The Emancipation Proclamation and the War for the Union 43 (2012).
133. Act of Aug. 6, 1861, ch. 60, 12 Stat. 3.
134. See Silvana R. Siddali, From Property to Person: Slavery and the Confiscation Acts, 1861–1862, at 19 (2005).
135. See Eric Foner, The Fiery Trial: Abraham Lincoln and American Slavery 176–77 (2010).
136. Quoted in Stephen C. Neff, Justice in Blue and Gray: A Legal History of the Civil War 138 (2010).
137. See Richard Slotkin, The Long Road to Antietam: How the Civil War Became a Revolution 89 (2012).
138. See Act of July 17, 1862, ch. 195, 12 Stat. 589.
139. This is not to say that the Confiscation Acts were effective in freeing slaves. As the leading student of the acts has written, they were "of dubious efficacy." Silvana R. Siddali, From Property to Person: Slavery and the Confiscation Acts, 1861–1862, at 6 (2005). But the Emancipation Proclamation was similarly ineffective when first promulgated. The ultimate emancipation of African American slaves depended on the advance of Union armies, which neither the acts nor the Proclamation could bring about.
140. See Preliminary Emancipation Proclamation, September 22, 1862, www.archives.gov/exhibits/american_originals_iv/sections/transcript_preliminary _emancipation.html.
141. See The Emancipation Proclamation, January 1, 1863, available at http://www.archives.gov/exhibits/featured_documents/emancipation_proclama tion/transcript.html.

142. *See* Eric Foner, The Fiery Trial: Abraham Lincoln and American Slavery 271–72, 302–7 (2010).

143. Quoted in Stephen C. Neff, Justice in Blue and Gray: A Legal History of the Civil War 138 (2010).

144. Quoted in Louis P. Masur, Lincoln's Hundred Days 106 (2012).

145. Id. at 115.

146. Id. at 130.

147. Id. at 114.

148. Abraham Lincoln, First Inaugural Address, March 4, 1861, www.bartleby.com/124/pres31.html.

149. *See* Gettysburg Address, www.avalon.law.yale.edu/19th_century/gettyb.asp.

150. *See* Second Inaugural Address of Abraham Lincoln, www.avalon.law.yale.edu/19th_century/lincoln2.asp.

151. *See* Michael Vorenberg, Final Freedom: The Civil War, The Abolition of Slavery, and the Thirteenth Amendment 107–12 (2001).

152. Id.

153. Thurgood Marshall, *Reflections on the Bicentennial of the United States Constitution*, 101 Harv. L. Rev. 1, 2 (1987).

Ten. Ordaining and Establishing This Constitution, Part 2: Skepticism in the Progressive Era

1. *See, e.g.*, Richard Hofstadter, The Age of Reform: From Bryan to FDR (1955).

2. *See, e.g.*, Richard A. Epstein, How Progressives Rewrote the Constitution (2006).

3. *See, e.g.*, William E. Forbath, *Popular Constitutionalism in the Twentieth Century: Reflections on the Dark Side, the Progressive Constitutional Imagination, and the Enduring Role of Judicial Finality in Popular Understanding of Popular Self-Rule*, 81 Chi.-Kent L. Rev. 967, 974, 976 (2006) (arguing that "[p]rogressives set out to rethink and remake the Constitution root and branch"); William G. Ross, A Muted Fury: Populists, Progressives, and Labor Unions Confront the Courts, 1890–1937 at 49 (1994) (noting progressive "impatience with all constitutional orthodoxies, including the Constitution itself").

4. *See* id. at 138; William E. Forbath, *Popular Constitutionalism in the Twentieth Century: Reflections on the Dark Side, the Progressive Constitutional Imagination, and the Enduring Role of Judicial Finality in Popular Understanding of Popular Self-Rule*, 81 Chi.-Kent L. Rev. 967, 780 (2006).

5. Quoted in Larry Kramer, The People Themselves 215 (2004).

6. William E. Forbath, *Popular Constitutionalism in the Twentieth Century: Reflections on the Dark Side, the Progressive Constitutional Imagination, and the Enduring Role of Judicial Finality in Popular Understanding of Popular Self-Rule*, 81 Chi.-Kent L. Rev. 967, 977 (2006).

7. "Roosevelt Answers Cry of Revolution," N.Y. Times, Feb. 27, 1912, at 1, 3, quoted in Victoria Nourse, *A Tale of Two Lochners: The Untold History of*

Substantive Due Process and the Idea of Fundamental Rights, 97 CAL. L. REV. 751, 774 (2009).

8. "A Charter of Democracy," in THEODORE ROOSEVELT, SOCIAL JUSTICE AND POPULAR RULE: ESSAYS, ADDRESSES, AND PUBLIC STATEMENTS RELATING TO THE PROGRESSIVE MOVEMENT (1910–1916) at 141–42 (1925).

9. WILLIAM G. ROSS, A MUTED FURY: POPULISTS, PROGRESSIVES, AND LABOR UNIONS CONFRONT THE COURTS, 1890–1937, at 144 & n. 6 (1994).

10. WOODROW WILSON, CONGRESSIONAL GOVERNMENT: A STUDY IN AMERICAN POLITICS (1885).

11. WOODROW WILSON, CONSTITUTIONAL GOVERNMENT IN THE UNITED STATES 22 (1908).

12. See William Forbath, *Popular Constitutionalism in the Twentieth Century: Reflections on the Dark Side, the Progressive Constitutional Imagination, and the Enduring Role of Judicial Finality in Popular Understanding of Popular Self-Rule*, 81 CHI.-KENT L. REV. 967 (2006). Louis Brandeis, then the leading public interest lawyer in the United States, made a similar plea. Id.

13. See WALTER F. MURPHY, CONGRESS AND THE COURT 50 (1962).

14. See William E. Forbath, *Reflections on the Dark Side, the Progressive Constitutional Imagination, and the Enduring Role of Judicial Finality in Popular Understanding of Popular Self-Rule*, 81 CHI.-KENT LAW REV. 967, 980–81 (2006).

15. HERBERT CROLY, PROGRESSIVE DEMOCRACY 215 (1914).

16. See Felix Frankfurter, *The Due Process Clause Ought to Go*, THE NEW REPUBLIC, vol. 40, at 113 (1924); Felix Frankfurter, *The Supreme Court as Legislature*, THE NEW REPUBLIC, vol. 46, at 158 (1926), *reprinted in* FELIX FRANKFURTER ON THE SUPREME COURT: EXTRAJUDICIAL ESSAYS ON THE COURT AND THE CONSTITUTION 158–67, 181–85 (Philip B. Kurland ed., 1970).

17. See William E. Forbath, *Reflections on the Dark Side, the Progressive Constitutional Imagination, and the Enduring Role of Judicial Finality in Popular Understanding of Popular Self-Rule*, 81 CHI.-KENT LAW REV. 967, 985–86 (2006).

18. CHARLES A. BEARD, AN ECONOMIC INTERPRETATION OF THE CONSTITUTION OF THE UNITED STATES (1935). For examples of the apoplectic criticism Beard's work produced, see PETER NOVICK, THAT NOBLE DREAM: THE "OBJECTIVITY QUESTION" AND THE AMERICAN HISTORICAL PROFESSION 96–97 (1988).

19. Beard wrote to Max Farrand that he had been "more belligerent than was necessary and overemphasized a number of matters in order to get a hearing that might not have been accorded to a milder statement." Quoted in id. at 97.

20. See id. (noting that "many other scholars" agreed that "the propertied classes had seen the Constitution as a bulwark against popular democracy").

21. See David M. Rabban, *Free Speech in Progressive Social Thought*, 74 TEX. L. REV. 951 (1996). On Dewey, James, Peirce and their relationship with the progressive movement, see generally LOUIS MENAND, THE METAPHYSICAL CLUB (2001).

22. See, e.g., JAMES T. KLOPPENBERG, UNCERTAIN VICTORY: SOCIAL DEMOCRACY AND PROGRESSIVISM IN EUROPEAN AND AMERICAN THOUGHT 1870–1920 at 64–65 (1986).

23. WILLIAM JAMES, PRAGMATISM 95–113 (1975).

24. David M. Rabban, *Free Speech in Progressive Social Thought*, 74 TEX. L. REV. 95, 958 (1996).

25. Id. at 966.

26. Id. at 956. After the war ended, Dewey changed his mind and became an active civil libertarian. Id. at 957.

27. *See generally* MORTON J. HORWITZ, THE TRANSFORMATION OF AMERICAN LAW, 1870–1960: THE CRISIS OF LEGAL ORTHODOXY (1992); WILFRED E. RUMBLE, AMERICAN LEGAL REALISM: SKEPTICISM, REFORM, AND THE JUDICIAL PROCESS (1968). For a collection of realist texts, see AMERICAN LEGAL REALISM (William W. Fisher III, Morton J. Horwitz & Thomas Reed eds., 1993). For a revisionist account, see BRIAN Z. TAMANAHA, BEYOND THE FORMALIST-REALIST DIVIDE: THE ROLE OF POLITICS IN JUDGING (2010).

28. Lochner v. New York, 198 U.S. 45, 75 (1905) (Holmes, J., dissenting).

29. Id.

30. *See generally* KAP K. WILLIAM, THE FOUNDATIONS OF INSTITUTIONAL ECONOMICS (2011); GEOFFREY MARTIN HODGSON, THE EVOLUTION OF INSTITUTIONAL ECONOMICS: AGENCY, STRUCTURE, AND DARWINISM IN AMERICAN INSTITUTIONALISM (2004).

31. For a good account of Hale's life and thought, see BARBARA FRIED, THE PROGRESSIVE ASSAULT ON LAISSEZ FAIRE: ROBERT HALE AND THE FIRST LAW AND ECONOMICS MOVEMENT (1998).

32. *See* Robert L. Hale, *Coercion and Distribution in a Supposedly Non-Coercive State*, 38 POL. SCI. Q. 470 (1923).

33. *See* FRANK FREIDEL, FRANKLIN D. ROOSEVELT: A RENDEZVOUS WITH DESTINY 14–15 (1990).

34. Id.

35. *See* JEFF SHESOL, SUPREME POWER: FRANKLIN ROOSEVELT VS. THE SUPREME COURT 22 (2010).

36. Id. at 95–100.

37. For a full account, see id.

38. FRANCIS BIDDLE, IN BRIEF AUTHORITY 331 (1962).

39. *See* Ex parte Quirin, 317 U.S. 1 (1942).

40. For a description of the setting for the speech, see JEFF SHESOL, SUPREME POWER: FRANKLIN ROOSEVELT VS. THE SUPREME COURT (2010).

41. *See* Franklin D. Roosevelt, Address on Constitution Day, September 17, 1937, www.presidency.ucsb.edu/ws/?pid=15459.

42. Id.

43. Id.

44. Id.

45. *See* Korematsu v. United States, 323 U.S. 214. For an account, see PETER H. IRONS, JUSTICE AT WAR: THE STORY OF THE JAPANESE-AMERICAN INTERNMENT CASES (1983).

46. For an account of Roosevelt's persistent interest in jailing critics of the war, see GEOFFREY R. STONE, PERILOUS TIMES: FREE SPEECH IN WARTIME FROM THE SEDITION ACT OF 1789 TO THE WAR ON TERRORISM 255–58 (2004).

47. In his Commonwealth Club address, for example, he argued that "the exercise of . . . property rights might so interfere with the rights of the individual that the Government, without whose assistance the property rights could not exist, must intervene, not to destroy individualism, but to protect it." Franklin D. Roosevelt, Campaign Address on Progressive Government at the Commonwealth Club (Sept. 23, 1932), in I THE PUBLIC PAPERS AND ADDRESSES OF FRANKLIN D. ROOSEVELT 746 (Samuel I. Rosenman ed., 1938).

48. See State of the Union Message to Congress, January 11, 1944, http://www.fdrlibrary.marist.edu/archives/address_text.html. For a discussion of the speech and its influence, see Cass R. Sunstein, *Constitutionalism After the New Deal*, 101 HARV. L. REV. 421, 423 (1987). For an illuminating debate about the speech, see Cass R. Sunstein & Randy Barnett, *Constitutive Commitments and Roosevelt's Second Bill of Rights*, 53 DRAKE L. REV. 205 (2005).

49. See State of the Union Message to Congress, January 11, 1944, http://www.fdrlibrary.marist.edu/archives/address_text.html.

50. Roosevelt did not call for a formal constitutional amendment or for judicial decisions implementing the Second Bill of Rights. Instead he "ask[ed] the Congress to explore the means for implementing this economic bill of rights— for it is definitely the responsibility of the Congress so to do." Id.

Eleven. Ordaining and Establishing This Constitution, Part 3: Modern Skepticism

1. See BERNARD SCHWARTZ, SUPER CHIEF: EARL WARREN AND HIS SUPREME COURT—A JUDICIAL BIOGRAPHY 72 (1983).

2. See id.

3. See, e.g., GEOFFREY R. STONE & DAVID A. STRAUSS, DEMOCRACY AND EQUALITY: THE ENDURING CONSTITUTIONAL VISION OF THE WARREN COURT (2020); Morton J. Horwitz, *The Warren Court and the Pursuit of Justice*, 50 WASH & LEE L. REV. 5 (1993).

4. See, e.g., LUCAS A. POWE, THE WARREN COURT AND AMERICAN POLITICS (2000); FRED P. GRAHAM, THE SELF-INFLICTED WOUND (1970).

5. See Mark Tushnet, *Foreword: The New Constitutional Order and the Chastening of Constitutional Aspiration*, 113 HARV. L. REV. 29 (1999).

6. For accounts, see GEORGE LEWIS, MASSIVE RESISTANCE: THE WHITE RESPONSE TO THE CIVIL RIGHTS MOVEMENT 27–122 (2006); MICHAEL J. KLARMAN, FROM JIM CROW TO CIVIL RIGHTS: THE SUPREME COURT AND THE STRUGGLE FOR RACIAL EQUALITY 330–34, 350–55 (2004).

7. See, e.g., MARK TUSHNET, THE NAACP's LEGAL STRATEGY AGAINST SEGREGATED EDUCATION, 1925–1950 (1988); RICHARD KRUGER, SIMPLE JUSTICE: THE HISTORY OF BROWN V. BOARD OF EDUCATION AND BLACK AMERICA's STRUGGLE FOR EQUALITY (2004).

8. See MARK TUSHNET, MAKING CIVIL RIGHTS LAW: THURGOOD MARSHALL AND THE SUPREME COURT, 1936–1961 at 305 (1994) ("[Marshall] was . . . reported to have called King a 'first-rate rabble-rouser,' and complained about always 'saving King's bacon'").

9. *See* id. at 302–4 (1994); DAVID J. GARRY, BEARING THE CROSS: MARTIN LU-
THER KING JR. AND THE SOUTHERN CHRISTIAN LEADERSHIP CONFERENCE 11–82
(1986).

10. *See, e.g.*, MARK TUSHNET, MAKING CIVIL RIGHTS LAW: THURGOOD MAR-
SHALL AND THE SUPREME COURT, 1936–1961, at 189, 191 (for Justice Robert
Jackson, segregation cases posed question of politics rather than law); id. at 211
(quoting Jackson as saying that "this is a political question," that the problem
for segregation's opponents was "to make a judicial basis for a congenial political conclusion," and that "as a political decision, I can go along with it"). MI-
CHAEL J. KLARMAN, FROM JIM CROW TO CIVIL RIGHTS: THE SUPREME COURT
AND THE STRUGGLE FOR RACIAL EQUALITY 296 (2004) (quoting Jackson as saying
that "[there is] [n]othing in the text that says this is unconstitutional. [There is]
nothing in the opinions of the courts that says it's unconstitutional. Nothing in
the history of the 14th amendment [says it's unconstitutional]. On [the] basis
of precedent [I] would have to say segregation is ok"); id. at 295 (concluding
that "[w]hat [Justice Felix] Frankfurter found compelling was the moral, not the
legal, argument against segregation in the nation's capital"); id. at 298 (concluding that "if [Justice Hugo Black] is to be taken at his word about his method of
constitutional interpretation [his] personal views about segregation, not his legal
interpretation, must explain his vote").

11. At the time the Fourteenth Amendment was adopted, five northern states
excluded African Americans from public schools and eight additional northern
states had segregated schools. There is no indication that those ratifying the Fourteenth Amendment thought that these practices would have to change because
of the amendment. RICHARD KLUGER, SIMPLE JUSTICE 633–34 (1976). The same
Congress that enacted the Fourteenth Amendment passed legislation permitting
segregation in District of Columbia schools. Drafters of the 1866 Civil Rights Act,
which the Fourteenth Amendment was designed to constitutionalize, specifically
stated that the act did not interfere with segregated education. *See* Statement of
James Wilson, Cong. Globe, 39th Cong., 1st Sess. 1117–18 (1866). *But see* Michael McConnell, *Originalism and the Desegregation Decisions*, 81 VA. L. REV.
947 (1955) (arguing that the Framers intended to outlaw school segregation).

12. The Court concluded that the Fourteenth Amendment's history was "inconclusive" and stated that "we cannot turn the clock back to 1868 when the
Amendment was adopted." Brown v. Board of Education, 347 U.S. 483, 491–92
(1954).

13. *See* id., 494 n. 11 (1954) (citing social science studies for the proposition
that segregation had a detrimental psychological effect on African American children). On the dubious nature of the evidence, see Mark Yudof, *School Desegregation: Legal Realism, Reasoned Elaboration and Social Science in the Supreme
Court*, 42 LAW CONTEMP. PROBLS. 57, 70 (1978) (concluding that "[v]irtually
everyone who has examined the question now agrees that the Court erred [in
relying on the social science data]").

14. *See* Brown v. Board of Education, 349 U.S. 294 (1955).

15. Bolling v. Sharpe, 347 U.S. 497 (1954). For doubts about the legal, as
opposed to political, underpinnings of *Bolling*, see MICHAEL KLARMAN, FROM

JIM CROW TO CIVIL RIGHTS: THE SUPREME COURT AND THE STRUGGLE FOR RA-
CIAL EQUALITY 341(2004). *See also* Michael McConnell, *Michael McConnell
(Concurring in the Judgment)*, in WHAT BROWN V. BOARD OF EDUCATION SHOULD
HAVE SAID 158, 166 (Jack M. Balkin ed., 2001) (*Bolling* is "without foundation");
JOHN HART ELY, DEMOCRACY AND DISTRUST 21 (1980) (*Bolling* is "gibberish both
syntactically and historically"); Sanford Levinson, *Constitutional Rhetoric and
the Ninth Amendment*, 64 CHI.-KENT L. REV. 131, 147 (1988) ("no satisfactory
theory" justifies *Bolling). But see* David E. Bernstein, *Bolling, Equal Protection,
Due Process, and Lochnerphobia*, 93 GEO. L. J. 1253 (2005) (defending *Bolling);
Peter J. Rubin, *Taking Its Proper Place in the Constitutional Canon: Bolling v.
Sharpe, Korematsu, and the Equal Protection Component of the Fifth Amendment
Due Process Clause*, 92 U. VA. L. REV. 1879 (2006) (same).

16. *See* Brown v. Board of Education, 347 U.S. 483, 493 (1954) (supporting
Court's holding on the ground that "it is doubtful that any child may reasonably
be expected to succeed in life if he is denied the opportunity of an education").

17. *See* Gayle v. Browder, 352 U.S. 903 (1956) (buses); Homes v. City of At-
lanta, 350 U.S. 879 (1955) (municipal golf course); Mayor of Baltimore v. Dawson, 350 U.S. 877 (1955) (public beaches and bathhouses).

18. *See* Naim v. Naim, 350 U.S. 985 (1956) (finding without explanation that
the case was devoid of a properly presented federal question). For the leading
example of criticism by commentators, see Gerald Gunther, *The Subtle Vices of
the "Passive Virtue": A Comment on Principle and Expediency in Judicial Review*,
64 COLUM. L. REV. I, 11–12 (1964).

19. *See, e.g.*, Gideon v. Wainwright, 372 U.S. 335 (1963); Mapp v. Ohio, 367
U.S. 643 (1961); Miranda v. Arizona, 384 U.S. 436 (1966).

20. *See, e.g.*, New York Times v. Sullivan, 376 U.S. 2534 (1964); Brandenburg
v. Ohio, 395 U.S. 444 (1969).

21. *See, e.g.*, Reynolds v. Sims, 377 U.S. 533 (1964); Harper v. Virginia State
Board of Elections, 383 U.S. 663 (1966).

22. *See, e.g.*, Griffin v. Illinois, 351 U.S. 12 (1956); Shapiro v. Thompson, 394
U.S. 618 (1969); Goldberg v. Kelly, 397 U.S. 254 (1970).

23. *See* ALEXANDER M. BICKEL, THE SUPREME COURT AND THE IDEA OF
PROGRESS (1970).

24. *See, e.g.*, Illinois v. Gates, 462 U.S. 213 (1983) *overruling* Spinelli v.
United States, 393 U.S. 410; Coleman v. Thompson, 501 U.S. 722 (1991) *overruling* Fay v. Noia 372 U.S. 391 (1963).

25. *See, e.g.*, CHRISTOPHER KNAUSS, STILL SEGREGATED, STILL UNEQUAL:
ANALYZING THE IMPACT OF NO CHILD LEFT BEHIND ON AFRICAN AMERICAN STU-
DENTS (2007) (by 2003, 73 percent of African American students attended pre-
dominantly minority schools, and 38 percent of such students attended schools
that were over 90 percent minority).

26. From 1970 to 2009, the number of people incarcerated in the United
States grew from 196,429 to 2.25 million, an increase of more than 1,000 percent. *Compare* Margaret Werner Cahalan, Historical Correction Statistics in
the United States 1850–1984, at 35, 76 (1986), https://www.ncjrs.gov/pdffiles1
/pr/102529.pdf (196,429 incarcerated persons in U.S. in 1970) *with* Heather C.

West, Prison Inmates at Midyear 2009—Statistical Tables, Table 2 (2010), http://bjs.ojp.usdoj.gov/content/pub/pdf/pim09st.pdf (2,297,400 incarcerated persons in U.S. in 2009).

27. Black men are more than six times more likely to be imprisoned than white men. See id. at 2. Twenty percent of African American men born between 1965 and 1969 have been imprisoned by the time they reach their early thirties. See Becky Pettit & Bruce Western, Mass Imprisonment and the Life Course: Race and Class Inequality in U.S. Incarceration, 69 AM. SOC. REV. 151, 151 (2004). See generally MICHELLE ALEXANDER, THE NEW JIM CROW: MASS INCARCERATION IN THE AGE OF COLOR BLINDNESS (2010).

28. See, e.g., WILLIAM J. STUNTZ, THE COLLAPSE OF AMERICAN CRIMINAL JUSTICE 220–43 (2011).

29. See, e.g., Sam Wang, "The Great Gerrymander of 2012," N.Y. TIMES, Feb. 2, 2013 (in 2012 House elections, Democrats received 1.4 million more votes than Republicans, but because of gerrymander, Republicans controlled the House by a margin of 234–201).

30. See, e.g., San Antonio Independent School Dist. v. Rodriguez, 411 U.S. 1 (1973); Dandridge v. Williams, 397 U.S. 471 (1970).

31. See, e.g., STEPHEN L. CARTER, THE CONFIRMATION MESS (1994). Cf. Geoffrey R. Stone, Understanding Supreme Court Confirmations, 2010 SUP. CT. REV. 381.

32. According to a poll conducted by CBS News in 2012, three-quarters of all Americans believe that Supreme Court justices do not decide cases solely based on legal analysis, but rather "sometimes let their personal or political views influence their decisions." See Supreme Court/Judiciary, http://www.pollingreport.com/court.htm. In another poll, conducted by the Public Religion Research Institute in 2013, 55 percent of those surveyed thought that Supreme Court justices were influenced "a lot" by their own political views in making decisions, and another 32 percent thought that they were influenced "a little." Only 8 percent thought that the justices were influenced "not at all."

33. 554 U.S. 570 (2008).

34. Compare, e.g., id. at 584 (relying on eighteenth-century meaning of "bear arms" to conclude that the amendment was violated) with id. at 646 (relying on eighteenth-century meaning of "bear arms" to conclude that the amendment was not violated).

35. 135 S. Ct. 2071 (2015).

36. Lawrence v. Texas, 539 U.S. 558, 602 (2003) (Scalia, J., dissenting).

37. I have found no case where justices opposing affirmative action have discussed the original public meaning of the Fourteenth Amendment. For examples of these justices relying instead on their moral and political views, see, e.g., League of Latin Am. Citizens v. Perry, 548 U.S. 399, 511 (2006) (Roberts, C.J., concurring in part and dissenting in part) ("It is a sordid business, this divvying us up by race"); Gratz v. Bollinger, 539 U.S. 244, 349 (2003) (Thomas, J.) (voting to invalidate university racial admissions preference in part because "I believe blacks can achieve in every avenue of American life without the meddling of university administrators").

38. *See* Supreme Court/Judiciary, http://www.pollingreport.com/court.htm.

39. The AP-National Constitution Center Poll, August, 2012, http://constitutioncenter.org/media/files/data_GfK_AP-NCC_Poll_August_GfK_2012_Topline_FINAL_1st_release.pdf.

40. *See* Douglas H. Ginsburg, *Delegation Running Riot*, 1 REGULATION 89 (1995). *See generally Symposium: The Constitution in Exile*, 51 DUKE L. J. 1 (2001).

41. *See* Ruth Bader Ginsburg, *Sexual Equality Under the Fourteenth and Equal Rights Amendments*, 1979 WASH. U. L. Q. 161, 161–63 ("Boldly dynamic interpretation, departing radically from the original understanding is required to tie the fourteenth amendment's equal protection clause to a command that government treat men and women as individuals equal in rights, responsibilities, and opportunities"). *But see* Steven G. Calabresi & Julia Rickert, *Originalism and Sex Discrimination*, 90 TEX. L. REV. 1 (2011).

42. *See, e.g.,* Ronald Turner, *Were Separate-But-Equal and Antimiscegenation Laws Constitutional? Applying Scalian Traditionalism to Brown and Loving*, 40 SAN DIEGO L. REV. 285 (2003).

43. *See* Adrian Vermeule, *Beyond Originalism*, THE ATLANTIC, Mar. 31, 2020.

44. *See, e.g.,* Richard A. Posner, *Foreword: A Political Court*, 119 HARV. L. REV. 31 (2005).

45. *See* J. HARVIE WILKINSON, COSMIC CONSTITUTIONAL THEORY: WHY AMERICANS ARE LOSING THEIR INALIENABLE RIGHT TO SELF-GOVERNANCE (2012).

46. Mark V. Tushnet, *An Essay on Rights*, 62 TEX. L. REV. 1363 (1984).

47. Duncan Kennedy, *The Critique of Rights in Critical Legal Studies*, in LEGALISM/LEFT CRITIQUE (Wendy Brown & Janet Halley eds., 2002).

48. Peter Gabel, *The Phenomenology of Rights Consciousness and the Pact of the Withdrawn Selves*, 62 TEX. L. REV. 1563 (1984).

49. MARK V. TUSHNET, TAKING THE CONSTITUTION AWAY FROM THE COURTS (1999).

50. LARRY D. KRAMER, THE PEOPLE THEMSELVES: POPULAR CONSTITUTIONALISM AND JUDICIAL REVIEW (2004).

51. *See, e.g.,* Jeremy Waldron, *The Core of the Case Against Judicial Review*, 115 YALE L. J. 1346 (2006); Jeremy Waldron, *Judicial Power and Popular Sovereignty*, in MARBURY VERSUS MADISON: DOCUMENTS AND COMMENTARY 181 (Mark A. Graber & Michael Perhac eds., 2002).

52. MARK V. TUSHNET, TAKING THE CONSTITUTION AWAY FROM THE COURTS 11 (1999).

53. *See* Saikrishna B. Prakash, *America's Aristocracy*, 109 YALE L. J. 541, 553 (1999).

54. *See* SANFORD LEVINSON, FRAMED: AMERICA'S 51 CONSTITUTIONS AND THE CRISIS OF GOVERNANCE (2012); SANFORD LEVINSON, OUR UNDEMOCRATIC CONSTITUTION: WHERE THE CONSTITUTION GOES WRONG (AND HOW WE THE PEOPLE CAN CORRECT IT) (2006).

55. BRUCE ACKERMAN, WE THE PEOPLE (1991).

56. Akhil R. Amar, *Philadelphia Revisited: Amending the Constitution Outside Article V*, 55 U. CHI. L. REV. 1043 (1988).

57. Mark A. Graber, Dred Scott and the Problem of Constitutional Evil (2006).

58. J.M. Balkin, *Agreements with Hell and Other Objects of Our Faith*, 65 Ford. L. Rev. 1703 (1997).

59. Girardeau A. Spann, Race Against the Court: Supreme Court and Minorities in Contemporary America (1993).

60. Gary Peller, Critical Race Consciousness: Reconsidering American Ideologies of Racial Justice (2011).

61. *See, e.g.*, Robin L. West, *Constitutional Scepticism*, 72 B.U. L. Rev. 765 (1992).

Twelve. Bending Toward Justice?

1. King and Obama loosely paraphrased what Parker actually said:

> I do not pretend to understand the moral universe, the arc is a long one, my eye reaches but little ways. I cannot calculate the curve and complete the figure by the experience of sight; I can divine it by conscience. But from what I see I am sure it bends towards justice. Things refuse to be mismanaged long. Jefferson trembled when he thought of slavery and remembered that God is just.

J. Mark Worth, "The Moral Arc of the Universe," www.uuharvard.org/services/moral-arc-of-the-universe/ (last visited 1/26/22).

2. Septennial Act, 1715, 1 Geo. 1 St. 2, c. 38 (Gr. Brit.), as amended by the Parliament Act, 1911, 1 & 2 Geo. 5, c. 13 (U.K.), provides that "all Parliaments that shall at any time hereafter be called, assembled, or held, shall and may respectively have continuance for [five] years." For a discussion, see Robert Blackburn, The Electoral System in Britain 18 (1995).

3. During the emergency surrounding World War I, the parliamentary term was extended from 1910 until 1918. Id. at 46. Because of World War II, there were no parliamentary elections from 1935 until 1945. Id. The election of 1964 came seven days after the five-year period, but because Parliament had not been in session for a portion of the period, the statutory limit on the length of parliamentary sessions was satisfied. Id. at 22.

4. *See* Joseph Fishkin & David E. Pozen, *Asymmetric Constitutional Hardball*, 118 Colum. L. Rev. 915 (2018); Mark V. Tushnet, *Constitutional Hardball*, 37 J. Marshall L. Rev. 523 (2004).

INDEX

About the Author

Louis Michael Seidman is the Carmack Waterhouse Professor of Constitutional Law at Georgetown University, a former clerk for Thurgood Marshall, and a major proponent of the critical legal studies movement. He is the co-author of a casebook on constitutional law and the author of several academic books on the Constitution. He lives in Washington, DC.

Publishing in the Public Interest

Thank you for reading this book published by The New Press. The New Press is a nonprofit, public interest publisher. New Press books and authors play a crucial role in sparking conversations about the key political and social issues of our day.

We hope you enjoyed this book and that you will stay in touch with The New Press. Here are a few ways to stay up to date with our books, events, and the issues we cover:

- Sign up at www.thenewpress.com/subscribe to receive updates on New Press authors and issues and to be notified about local events
- Like us on Facebook: www.facebook.com/newpressbooks
- Follow us on Twitter: www.twitter.com/thenewpress
- Follow us on Instagram: www.instagram.com/thenewpress

Please consider buying New Press books for yourself; for friends and family; or to donate to schools, libraries, community centers, prison libraries, and other organizations involved with the issues our authors write about.

The New Press is a 501(c)(3) nonprofit organization. You can also support our work with a tax-deductible gift by visiting www.thenewpress.com/support.